W9-BYP-319

National Identity in
Eastern Germany

NATIONAL IDENTITY IN EASTERN GERMANY

Inner Unification or Continued Separation?

ANDREAS STAAB

PRAEGER

Westport, Connecticut
London

Library of Congress Cataloging-in-Publication Data

Staab, Andreas, 1965–
   National identity in eastern Germany : inner unification or continued
separation? / Andreas Staab.
      p. cm.
   Includes bibliographical references and index.
   ISBN 0–275–96177–X (alk. paper)
   1. Political participation—Germany—History—20th century.
   2. Political culture—Germany.   3. Political culture—Germany (East)
   4. Germany (East)—Politics and government—1989–1990.   5. Right and
   left (Political science)—Germany—History—20th century.
   I. Title.
   DD290.29S73   1998
   943.087'9'019—dc21   97–35135

British Library Cataloguing in Publication Data is available.

Library of Congress Catalog Card Number: 97–35135
ISBN: 0–275–96177–X

First published in 1998

Praeger Publishers, 88 Post Road West, Westport, CT 06881
An imprint of Greenwood Publishing Group, Inc.

Printed in the United States of America

The paper used in this book complies with the
Permanent Paper Standard issued by the National
Information Standards Organization (Z39.48–1984).

10 9 8 7 6 5 4 3 2

Contents

Acknowledgments

I consider myself privileged to have as my academic home the European Institute at the London School of Economics and Political Science. I have greatly benefited from the support and knowledge of Gordon Smith, Brendan O'Leary, Jens Bastian, Howard Machin, Nelson Gonzalez, and Adam Steinhouse. In particular, I would like to express my thanks to George Schöpflin, whose professional advice has been of immense assistance. I am also grateful to Dieter Roth for granting me access to the data of the *Forschungsgruppe Wahlen*. Heidi Dorn at the *Zentralarchiv für Empirische Sozialforschung* in Cologne deserves special thanks for her ready cooperation and cracking sense of humor. I have also been very fortunate to have received advice from Colm O'Muircheartaigh from the LSE's Methodology Institute.

Without the support and generosity of my family I would not have been able to complete this project. I therefore owe them a deep debt of gratitude. I am however, mostly indebted to my wife, Michela. Her patience, moral support, and intellectual encouragement made all the difference. It is to her that I dedicate this book.

1

Introduction

Press Officer
One has to ask whether it's really right
that we've basically taken a different system
and forced it on these people.
I don't know how the "Wessis" would have reacted
whether they would have been able to show as much
let's call it endurance
as some of the "Ossis" have had to have.
It's as if the Japanese had invaded West Germany and announced
from tomorrow you are under Japanese law
everything you have been doing up until now is irrelevant
whether it's traffic regulations or tax law
even the constitution
forget it!
From tomorrow everything's Japanese
        —Klaus Pohl, *Waiting Room Germany* (1995)

Following a year of intense public debate and rapid political developments, the German Democratic Republic joined the Federal Republic of Germany, adopting its legal, political, economic, and social structures. On October 3, 1990, Germany was formally reunified, the culmination of a process which had lasted merely one year since the decisive public upheavals in the autumn of 1989. Never before in world history have two countries been merged in this way. The unification of two societies that had been separated for four decades and had symbolized the systemic antagonisms of the Cold War marked a historically unparalleled cultural and political experiment. In rapid succession, the totalitarian system of the GDR was abolished, absorbed into the democratic FRG and taken into the European Community.

The pace of political developments indeed had been breathtaking. On October 18, 1989, Egon Krenz succeeded Erich Honecker as General Secretary of the East German Communist party SED. On November 9, the Berlin Wall opened its gates to the West. Four days later, the Communist reformer Hans Modrow became Minister President. On March 18, 1990, free elections to the *Volkskammer* were held, followed by the monetary, economic, and social union with the Federal Republic on July 1. The political and state union on October 3 resulted in the first all-German federal elections to the *Bundestag* on December 2. Proposals for reforming the Socialist system of the GDR, a federalist union with the Western part, or a third alternative between Capitalism and Socialism along the Scandinavian model were not able to generate sufficient public support. Chancellor Kohl's promise of "blossoming landscapes in the East" combined with the prospect of repeating the Federal Republic's postwar success resulted in widespread approval for a swift *Anschluß*. Popular support, the Chancellor's energetic drive to seize the unique historic opportunity for unification, as well as Gorbachev's willingness to cooperate ended in the speedy integration of the former GDR into the Western federalist structure. As with the transition processes in Eastern Europe and the former Soviet Union, the collapse of Communism in the GDR and the integration into the stable democratic society of the Federal Republic attracted widespread scholarly attention. The diplomatic history of the demise of the SED regime, the subsequent negotiations between East and West German governmental officials, or the "Two-Plus-Four" consultations between the two Germanys and France, Great Britain, the United States, and the Soviet Union stood at the center of much political analysis, as did structural interrogations on expanding the West German political, economic, social, and legal systems onto the former GDR.

However, this study intends to shed a different light on German unification; the starting point being the obvious recognition that virtually every aspect of the lives of East Germans were affected by the transition processes. For the new democratic citizens of Eastern Germany, unification bore the challenge of a profound reorientation within a markedly different environment. They had to bid farewell to the former all-encompassing welfare state as new regulations, pension schemes, medical care and health coverage spread to the East. At work, old routines broke down. For many the former constitutional right of work turned into the fear, prospect, and experience of unemployment, while the new market economy introduced new notions of initiative, individuality, performance, and competitiveness. Administration and bureaucracy operated under western guidelines and principles. Features of the West German political system were rapidly implemented. Elections were held according to Western rules, the Western party system expanded onto the Eastern *Länder*, and federalism was reintroduced. The former monolithic power of the SED and its affiliated mass organizations and block parties gave way to a complex system of political plurality for interest representation and participation. New laws and regulations governed the lives of East Germans in their relationship to the state. Western mass-cultural phenomena conquered the East. Commercialization, communication, consumerism, leisure, and lifestyles spilled over to Eastern Germany, which stood in stark contrast to the former gray Socialist reality of suppressed demands. These new legal, political, economic, social, and mass-cultural standards and rules of a new society had to be grasped and internalized. Former values and standards that had developed under forty years of Communist rule were now subject to severe scrutiny and reconsideration.

The phenomenon of a gap between the organizational principles of a society and their feedback from the population was not unique to German history. Within a period of merely 120 years, Germany has had to face the problems of continuity and change of political structure and corresponding orientations of its citizens on a number of occasions. The country had experienced several fundamental ruptures of the political system that were hardly matched by any other nation in modern history. The first German unification of 1871 established Germany as a late-comer to the European league of major nation states. Hierarchical in principle, the Second Reich represented an absolutist monarchy which survived until the end of World War I. After 1918, the progressive *Weimar* Republic failed against economic, social, and political pressures, while alienating opposing factions of Nationalists, Monarchists, Communists, and Democrats which ultimately culminated in Hitler's rise to power. Out of the ruins of World War II, the emerging Cold War forced the division of the country into a stable and successful liberal democracy and a totalitarian Stalinist regime. Obviously, the structural changes during this period were radical. The relationship between the ruling elite and the population, between standards and demands of the political structure and the individual's perceptions of them, between the structural requisites and political orientations of the citizens changed drastically each time a new political system appeared on the agenda of German history.

APPROACHING SUBJECTIVITY:
POLITICAL CULTURE AND GERMAN UNIFICATION

All these structural transformations—from Monarchy to Democracy to Fascism and to Democracy/Communism—were rapid and abrupt. Cognitive reorientations to structural changes, however, require time. A structural revolution was always followed by the individual's evolutionary adaptation to new political rules and standards. It therefore came as little surprise that the first investigation on orientations of a population toward their political system included the West German case. Almond and Verba's *Civic Culture* (1963) advanced conventional institutional considerations with the postulate that a congruence between the structure and the culture of a political system was elementary in guaranteeing system stability.[1]

The concept of political culture employed orientations of a population toward their political system as an analytical tool, suggesting that subjectivity gives meaning to, as well as influences the political system. As noted by Glenda Patrick (1984: 279), political culture represents "the set of fundamental beliefs, values and attitudes that characterize the nature of the political system and regulate the political interactions among its members." Political culture forms a reservoir of collective experiences of individuals within a functioning political system and develops into a collective memory which alters according to new experiences.[2] It is therefore fluid, since new experiences contribute and old experiences vanish from the collective reservoir. Because of the differing experiences of political individuals within the political system, political culture is expressed in varying facets that consist of various subcultures along social, economic, cultural, or generational lines.[3]

Without any doubt the East German transformation after 1989 represented a formidable case for the application of the concept of political culture and the prospect of democratic stability. The political system of the GDR was radically transformed from a Communist dictatorship to a liberal democracy. Former beliefs, values, and attitudes that developed under four decades of totalitarian rule clashed with a fundamentally different set of thought and behavior that were introduced through the unification with the Federal Republic. While the extension of the Western political, economic, and social structures onto the Eastern *Länder* certainly provided a stabilizing impact, the same cannot be said about the citizens' subjective orientations. Democratic stability could only be achieved if East Germans were capable of mustering a profound cognitive, affective, and behavioral reorientation that approved of the new political structures.

EXPANDING SUBJECTIVITY:
IDENTITY AND POLITICAL CULTURE

However, this study does not intend to produce a reinterpretation of Almond and Verba's *Civic Culture* (1989) after their last "visit" to Germany in 1980. On the contrary, the extent and depth of unification and its impact on the population renders a classical political culture approach difficult. As argued above, unification in East Germany affected virtually every aspect of an individual's life. East Germans experienced a radical break and discontinuity from their former life in the Communist GDR. In contrast to other Eastern European post-Communist states, East Germans joined an already well-established society and adopted its rules and regulations. The transition was not internal but external—designed to follow rather than to create.

For such sudden and colossal changes, the concept of political culture does not seem suited. For East Germans, the subjective reorientations caused by unification go far beyond beliefs, attitudes, and values toward the characteristics of the political system. Against the backdrop of these massive systemic transformations, questions such as "who am I?," "where do I belong?," and "where am I going?" automatically arise. Hence, for many the establishment of a democratic civic culture among East Germans was superseded by the necessity of finding and developing a new identity in a new and largely unfamiliar environment. While the state is a political, rational, and objective construct, the nation is a political-cultural phenomenon—emotional and an "attitude rather than a fact" (Connor 1978: 381). The establishment of a civic culture merely reflects on the development of formal participation patterns and cognitive support toward the new political realities.

On its own, however, democracy is not capable of forging emotional ties to the new environment. It only addresses a particular aspect of the individual's new experiences—that of the political individual within a new political system. The full depth and extent of present economic, social, or cultural experiences, as well as of past experiences under Communist rule, however, are left largely untouched. An investigation into the subjective dimension of German unification therefore has to broaden its scope. While a civic culture sustains the political stability of a state and addresses orientations toward political institutions, the task of establishing new identities in Eastern Germany corresponds to the unity of the nation and to a new-found sense of identity with formerly separated compatriots.

CONCEPTUALIZING NATIONAL IDENTITY

Identity reflects the state of mind of an individual toward his or her social community. It represents a process of discovering and generating a consciousness toward one's environment, a social assertion of the self as being somebody in the world. Through such an identity the individual locates and defines him- or herself in the world, acquiring a collective personality based on shared values, experiences and orientations. As with political culture, subjective orientations of the population give meaning to the overarching structural setting. Images of nations, of one's own as well as of foreign nations, are common and widespread in society and politics. The national community has been described as the indispensable link between the general mass of human beings and familiar local and regional environments (Wuthe 1987: 203). The nation represents a prominent object for people's emotional attachment and provides the scope for the individual's search for definition and location within the world. National identity levels individuality and emphasizes communality, whereas the nation forges common loyalties and emotional attachments out of a heterogeneous mass of individuals. National identity rests on common values that are born out of a shared past and a shared vision of the future. As such, the nation blends two fundamentally different sets of principles (Smith 1991: 11). Ethnically, the nation corresponds to shared cultural and genealogical traits, such as customs, traditions, language, religion, or descent. On the civic level, the nation encompasses orientations toward a particular set of political ideas, toward legal rights and civic duties, toward a common mass culture, as well as toward the nation's historic territory. Hence, national identity reflects the emotional attachment and degree of loyalty of an individual toward these ethnic and civic characteristics.

Following Anthony Smith's taxonomy, the present book organizes national identity into several sub-categories that consist of orientations toward five distinct elements (see Table 1.1). They include the civic-political sphere, a common mass culture, economics, ethnicity, as well as the historical territory or the homeland (Smith 1991: 15). Within these elements, the study addresses those issues which gained particular importance for East Germans in the immediate period before and after the revolution of November 1989. The underlying rationale is cogent. For East Germans, unification represented the ultimate vehicle for the formation of a national identity. Unification had such a drastic and overwhelming impact on the individual's life that orientations toward the recently unified nation were dominated and fundamentally generated by the individual's experiences and perceptions of the transformation processes. The formation of a national identity was in reality a response to unification—a testimony of the process of self-definition within a new environment.

Chapter 2 on territory addresses the division of the nation after World War II which generated contrasting territorial orientations in East and West Germany toward the stretch of land to which people feel attached. The FRG found a new spiritual home within the community of Western states, while the Cold-War antagonism pushed the awareness of the loss of the eastern territory further and further out of the public psyche. In contrast, efforts by the SED to instill an artificial identity as a German Socialist nation state were not

Table 1.1
Conceptualizing National Identity in Eastern Germany

Chapter 2	Territory	the fact of the division the prospect of unification perceptions of the homeland
Chapter 3	Economics	economic structure work mentality material prosperity social structure
Chapter 4	Citizenship	participation legitimacy state-citizen relations constitutional consensus
Chapter 5	Mass Culture	consumerism leisure and lifestyle media
Chapter 6	Ethnicity	German ethnicity legacy of the Third Reich ethnocentrism

convincingly adopted by the population. The notion of the divided nation and the prospect of eventual unification continued to dominate the minds of East Germans. In the economic analysis of Chapter 3 the discussion centers on how Easterners had to adjust to fierce job competition and the prospect of unemployment. The market economy emphasized such formerly neglected principles as self-responsibility and initiative, while the sophisticated, all-encompassing welfare system of the GDR which provided social security from cradle to grave faded into a notion of the past. Chapter 4 focuses on the relation between state and citizen, between rights and responsibilities of ruler and ruled. With unification, East Germans had to depart from the GDR's streamlined and hierarchical form of political participation. The functions of new institutions and new forms of interest representation had to be internalized. The collective goal of establishing the Communist society under the unchallenged ideological and practical auspices of the SED was replaced by the Federal Republic's emphasis on individuality and plurality. On the mass-cultural agenda of Chapter 5, East Germans were thrown into the postmodern age without the gradual development that West Germany had experienced after World War II. Consumerism, advertising, choice of leisure activities, as well as a quantitative increase and qualitative change in media consumption, washed over the new *Länder* in a gigantic wave that tried to make up for four lost decades of Communist parsimony. Chapter 6 on ethnicity addresses the question of birth and common descent that was problematized by markedly diverging experiences in East and West. The gradual confrontation of the Federal Republic with the traumatic Nazi past left the country's identity virtually bare of ethnic elements. In contrast, the Communist elite conveniently regarded the Third Reich's genocide and moral barbarism as a Western problem and responsibility. Furthermore, the *Bonn* Republic had never officially recognized itself as a country of immigration but nonetheless carried out a policy of integration that incorporated vast numbers of "guest workers" and ethnic Germans from East European territories. Although foreigners were by no means fully assimilated, increasing exposure to foreign ethnicities allowed for growing multicultural experiences. In the GDR, the SED's official rhetoric promulgated internationalism and Communist solidarity. Multicultural experiences, however, were highly limited because of severe travel restrictions and the very low numbers of foreigners living in the GDR.

METHODOLOGY

How can political science analyze and measure the feelings, beliefs, and attitudes of a population? How can the "black box" be opened to screen the mindsets of numerous individuals and hence, is it possible to develop a coherent orientation for the united Germany in its quest for establishing a common national identity?

Identity and political structure form a two-way symbiosis. Individuals accommodate, absorb, and respond to structural requisites and shape them in the process. With unification, the political, social, and economic structures of the Federal Republic extended to the new *Länder*. Over forty years these had formed, as well as were being formed by, a distinctive West German national identity in a process of mutual interdependence of subjective orientations and objective structures. After 1989, the superimposed structures of West Germany generated emotional responses from East Germans toward the unified nation. These were juxtaposed against orientations toward the now defunct GDR. Past and present collided, while the individual tried to accommodate the new experiences of unification to former values, standards, and beliefs. As a response, a particular set of thought and behavior developed that ultimately affected—either changed or stabilized—the structural setting. The post-unification developments in Eastern Germany are therefore analyzed against the backdrop of both the West and East German identities as they evolved throughout the postwar era. Consequently, each chapter covers four distinct areas of investigation. Conceptualizing remarks about the individual sub-categories of national identity are followed by political-historical analyses of the identities of the GDR and FRG. Out of these conclusions are drawn which address the post-unification developments regarding the question of the contemporary identity in Eastern Germany and its status as a separated or unified identity with the Western part.

Since national identity consists of several layers, it is vital to realize that the categorized orientations toward territory, economics, citizenship, mass culture, and ethnicity do not and cannot exist or develop separately. As argued by Smith (1991: 14), national identity is "fundamentally multi-dimensional." Elements overlap, merge, and mutually reinforce each other. For instance, mass-cultural behavior and attitudes toward consumerism certainly depict an economic element, since a satisfactory participation in the new consumer society requires a certain level of material prosperity and financial stability. Given the presence of such soft borders, the study organizes such multiple facets under the category where they exert the most decisive impact. Nonetheless, cross-references to other categories hopefully avoid a rigid fragmentation of national identity into five subgroupings, while the final conclusion intends to place the analytical results of the preceding chapters into a summarizing perspective.

According to Fredrik Barth (1969), aggregates of people share a common culture which develops interconnected differences that distinguish the group from other cultures. Out of social interaction, cultural traits emerge that construct boundaries for a community and ascribe an individual as a member or a nonmember of the group. To maintain its integrity the community possesses two fundamental functions. On the one hand, internal boundaries are created which define the member of a group as "one of us," whereas the individual adopts particular patterns of behavior and thought and shares the group's values, symbols, and traditions. Based on this behavioral, affective, and cognitive reservoir, social bonds are established which guide the interaction and socialization of the group members. On the other hand, external boundaries establish and define the community against other communities. In light of Barth's typology, identity can be understood as "sameness" (Smith 1991:75), whereas members of a particular group define membership characteristics which mark them off from nonmembers. Within internal boundaries, individuals interact and socialize, while external boundaries serve as identity markers that distinguish and separate the group from other communities.

The problem of boundary creation and maintenance becomes more transparent in the context of German unification. During the postwar division, the two German states developed distinctly different sets of boundaries. Internally, the different economic, political, and social organization of the GDR and the FRG provided for different sets of thought and behavior. Externally, the antagonistic concepts of democracy and Communism, market economy and Socialism, liberty and dictatorship, as well as the territorial separation offered numerous mutually exclusive definitions that marked one Germany off from the other. With unification these boundaries had to be redefined. The West German political, economic, social, and legal structures were expanded onto the East accompanied by corresponding sets of thought and behavior. The former external boundaries of West Germany were now transformed into normative internal boundaries for East Germans. With the introduction of Western structures, Easterners were expected to adopt Western standards and values, while the former patterns that constituted and maintained the East German community were fundamentally disrupted. The East German "collective destiny" (Smith 1991: 25) was dispersed and swallowed by the Western part. Again, as with the radical system transformations of *Weimar*, National Socialism, as well as with the Federal and the Democratic Republic, national identities had to be reestablished in direct response to the vast structural changes of the political system.

For East Germans, three distinctly different choices were available. First, over time, Easterners had approved of the Western set of structure, thought, and behavior and had accommodated the internal boundaries set by the Western system that ultimately resulted in a common national identity. Secondly, Easterners partly accepted the Western set of thought and behavior. Despite the persistence of mutually exclusive boundaries, this scenario allowed for the coexistence of identity markers shared by both Easterners and Westerners. Thirdly, East Germans did not accept the Western set resulting in dual identities of East and West. Such an outcome had been prompted by two causes. On the one hand, Easterners had been denied access, whereas West Germans continued to maintain external boundaries that excluded their fellow countrymen and denied them recognition as members of their community. Out of rejection, the East subsequently disapproved of the Western set of behavior and thought. On the other hand, Easterners had chosen to reject them, since the prospect of crossing the internal boundaries by adopting

Western principles did not seem appealing. Both of these scenarios resulted in a split national identity. The vacuum left by the demise of the GDR could not have been filled by the West. Subsequently, East Germans reestablished external boundaries to mark themselves off from the West in a move that stressed Eastern elements.

The present book relies to a considerable extent on public opinion surveys. For West Germany and for post-1989 Eastern Germany, polls by the *Allensbacher Institut für Demoskopie, Emnid,* or the *"Politbarometer"* of the *Forschungsgruppe Wahlen* are consulted. Apart from contemporary ad hoc surveys, the study tries to incorporate survey questions which were continuously collected over longer periods of time to demonstrate changing orientations. In the absence of quantitative material or to analyze certain phenomena further, qualitative data, such as literature or media sources and impressionistic accounts are used that play a particular importance in the case of the GDR, where surveys were hardly conducted or published. In 1978, the SED closed down its sole research organization on public opinion, the *Institut für Meinungsforschung* (Förster and Roski 1990: 15). The gap between the official dogmatism and rhetoric of state and party and the actual attitudes of the population caused widespread irritation among the political elite who feared that the strictly confidential results could eventually trickle down to the public. Instead, the SED increasingly relied on the Ministry of State Security—the surveillance apparatus of spies and unofficial informants which was nicknamed the *Stasi*—to monitor its citizens. In addition, the state-controlled media occasionally held public surveys. However, politically sensitive issues were never allowed to be publicized. The *Zentralinstitut für Jugendforschung* (Institute for Youth Research) was confronted with similar problems of censorship and tutelage. Focusing on young adults aged 14 to 25, the institute's research depended on the permission of state or party officials. As usual, results were strictly confidential and were not disclosed to the public. By 1990, surveys by the *Institut für Meinungsforschung,* as well as the *Zentralinstitut für Jugendforschung* which were not destroyed by state and party agencies became accessible to scholars and were subsequently published (Niemann 1993, Förster and Roski 1990). Both institutes guaranteed anonymity to their respondents, while safeguarding such research imperatives as standardized questionnaires or representative samples. The data collection was therefore legitimate. However, data interpretation was occasionally complicated by the biased ideological nature of some survey questions. The study therefore excludes such overt distortion of public attitudes. Quite often, however, questions hardly possessed a political-ideological undertone. Although questions unfortunately were not asked continuously over longer time periods, these results undoubtedly offered valid contemporary assessments of public opinion in East Germany.

STRUCTURE VERSUS CULTURE: THE PREDICTIVE POWER OF NATIONAL IDENTITY

How then can the symbiosis of structure and culture, of objectivity and subjectivity, be analyzed—not only for explanatory and descriptive reasons but furthermore for predictive purposes? Anthony Smith (1991: 91) argues that "nationalism is a form of culture—an ideology, a language, mythology, symbolism and consciousness"—and "the nation is a type of identity whose meaning and priority is presupposed by this form of culture." In a similar vein, Benedict Anderson (1983: 15) defined the nation as "an imagined political community. . . . It is imagined because the members of even the smallest nation will never know most of their fellow members, meet them, or even hear of them, yet in the minds of each lives the image of their communion."

Both approaches suggest that culture plays a crucial role in the subjective orientation toward one's environment, toward one's *imagined* community. But while the importance of a coherent identity for a nation seems relatively undisputed, it remains problematic to evaluate and explain the causal relationship between identity and political action. How do national identities trigger change or sustain stability within a particular political order, and how do national identities drive political action? All scholarly efforts so far have failed in establishing the "crucial link" that explains why and which elements of a national identity are conducive or respectively opposed to structural changes.[4] However, national identity offered a convincing explanation, for instance, for the tacit approval or even rejection of "Maastricht" by the peoples of various EU-member states. As George Schöpflin (1995: 44) correctly noted, postwar European integration represented an economic, technological, and administrative process. The political elite simply assumed that once those structures were in place, the importance of national-cultural differences, of nationhood, and of nationalism would lose their relevance. Close-call referenda and considerable public discontent showed that this "attempt to divorce the political community from its cultural-affective elements" was not met by adequate public enthusiasm. Commentators pointed toward a feeling of colonization by Brussels, anticipated cultural streamlining, perceived loss of political authority, or economic insecurity. In short, the identity of a common Europe based on integration and cooperation had not yet replaced the nation as the object for one's primary loyalties.

In this respect, national identity provided a deeper understanding of those processes and determinants which brought continuity or change to a political system. Since national identity is able to give early warning signs of potential dissatisfaction with policies, politics, and polities, political life becomes more transparent by integrating analytic results other than those offered by structural or institutional considerations. Nonetheless, national identity is neither able to determine the precise moment in time nor the precise scope and direction of political action. National identity does not offer the definite trigger that prompts individuals to seek political change. Instead, national identity has to be mobilized to generate political action. Agents who are capable of initiating such processes are wide-ranging—from political leaders to journalists or to international sport events, such as the Olympic Games or international football championships—as long as they touch on emotions that catalyze an understanding of belonging to the national commune. National identity clearly offers well-defined tracks along which political decisions will be received in a supportive or rejecting manner. National identity therefore does not offer the universal remedy for the explanation of complex political phenomena. It is, however, indispensable for enhancing the explanatory power and predictive capacity of political analyses since it broadens our understanding and enriches our political sensitivity. Nothing more, but certainly nothing less.

NOTES

1. Apart from Almond and Verba, a psychological account which stressed individual orientations to political objects had been offered by Parsons and Shils (1951). Sociological definitions, which included individual orientations as well as behavior, that carry orientations were given by Fagen (1965), Tucker (1973), and Geertz (1983). Emile Durkheim (1933) regarded culture as an objective composite of values and norms that are prevalent in society. Ideal-type constructs were applied by Weber (1968), Bell (1964), and Lipset (1958). Ronald Inglehart's "Silent Revolution" (1977) analyzed societies in light of fundamental changes in values, political behavior, and support for political parties toward the development of post-material attitudes, such as new political movements, lifestyle, and consumerism.

2. The relationship between structure and culture, between cause and effect is argued in more detail in Barry (1970), Lijphart (1989), or Pateman (1989).

3. For a more thorough discussion of methodology, theoretical shortcomings, and failures of political culture see, for example, Street (1993), Almond (1989), Gibbins (1989), or Iwand (1985).

4. Sidney Verba (1965: 529) noted that identity with the nation legitimizes the activities of political elites, which in return makes it possible for them to mobilize the commitment and support of their followers. Such a commitment would enable a political system to survive in times of crises. Stephen Welch (1993: 131, 135) argued that national identity not only emerged as "a response to social conditions" but also changes those circumstances, while John Street (1993: 113) concluded that culture is something that both shapes and is shaped by political interests. David Easton's "Systems Analysis of Political Life" (1965) differentiates among three distinct recipients of political support: the regime or the political order with its three components of values (goals and principles), norms, and the structure of authority, followed by the authorities (the occupants of authority roles), and finally the political community, defined as "a group of persons who share a division of labor for the settlement of political problems." Easton argues that dissatisfaction with the authorities can be neutralized by an identification with the regime and the political community which could provide for a buffer of support in times of a declining cohesion of the common political framework.

2

Territory

Territorial identities represent emotional orientations to "a definite social, a fairly well demarcated and bounded territory, with which the members identify to which they feel they belong" (Smith 1991: 9). The homeland—or to use the German term, the *Heimat*—constitutes the space where members of a community live and work, where generations respond to the changes and challenges of history, and where people have their formative experiences that bind them to the nation. Thoughts and behavior toward the nation that are generated by citizenship, ethnicity, mass culture, and economics are complemented by a territorial or spatial repository to a clearly defined stretch of land.

How then can territorial identities in unified Germany be operationalized? An analysis of German territorial identities which encompass the "lost" prewar territories of East Prussia, Pomerania, Silesia, and the *Sudetenland* represents a complex study in its own right. It could further include orientations toward Austria, German-speaking Switzerland, Alsace, Eupen-Malmedy, or the *Schleswig* province in Denmark. However, the unification treaty of 1990, as well as parallel provisions in the "Two-Plus-Four" treaty among the FRG, the GDR, the United States, the Soviet Union, France, and Great Britain acknowledged the Oder-Neisse line (the postwar demarcation between Poland and East Germany) as the permanent western Polish border (Kommers 1995: 190). The issue subsequently lost its remaining political edge. Also, for the purpose of this study considerations regarding the lost German territories hardly bore any significance. As argued in Chapter 1, the establishment of new identities in the aftermath of 1989 were triggered by vast transformation processes. As such, orientations toward the prewar territories outside the FRG and the GDR hardly possessed an impact on the establishment of new identities toward the unified nation. Although these territories might have remained in the public consciousness of both East and West, there was no significant political movement to call for their reintegration into Germany. They were pushed aside against the backdrop of establishing territorial orientations that now had to incorporate the respective "other" Germany across the former Iron Curtain.

Orientations toward the prewar territories were a phenomenon that did not affect the establishment of identities in their response to the structural changes brought about by unification. They are therefore left untouched.

A further approach is to ask respondents about the territorial unit to which they feel most loyal and attached. Bettina Westle (1994: 471) subdivided territorial identities in unified Germany into three categories: only the old or the new *Länder* respectively, the unified Germany, as well as double identities toward unified Germany and toward the old/new *Länder*. However, such identity markers hardly led to significant conclusions. Such loyal attachments were influenced by other identity markers which made it hard to detect the substance of territorial orientations. For instance, someone who possessed strong emotional attachments to the old *Länder* might have wanted the two Germanys to stay separate because of the significant tax burden that was imposed on West Germans to finance the massive transfer payments to the East. Likewise, loyal orientations toward Eastern Germany might have been prompted by perceptions of a political takeover of Western parties or an economic colonization of the new *Länder* by Western businesses that had resulted in a sense of defiance and exaggerated regional pride against the superimposed Western structures. Additionally, Germans were confronted with unification issues on a daily basis through massive media coverage. Although emotional attachments to the "other" German part might have been weak or even nonexistent, the fact that Germany and, hence, the German territory was now united was an obvious political reality. This could have prompted positive responses toward feeling loyal to the German territory of both East and West. Thus, by merely asking about loyalties to particular territories the explanatory power is limited because of implicit economic, political, cultural, or social connotations.

A closer look at the fundamental historical prerogative of German territorial identities in East and West, however, offered more rewarding analytical results. The postwar division of Germany resulted in two antagonistic political systems that stood at the front line of two opposing ideological camps. Market economics versus Socialism, Democracy versus Communism, civic liberty versus totalitarianism separated East from West. The most obvious signs of the division, however, were the tightly secured border, barbed wires, patrol guards, and since 1961 the Berlin Wall. For East Germans, regular contacts between East and West were complicated by severe travel restrictions.[1] When applying for a visa to visit the FRG, East Germans were confronted with intimidating interrogations by the Communist authorities within a lengthy bureaucratic procedure that could last several months. An almost impenetrable border, tight security, and limited travel opportunities to the West resulted in the effective territorial division into two separate entities.

How did Germans in East and West accommodate the fact of the division? How did they perceive the prospects of unification? One scenario would have implied that the political reality of a divided territory and the improbability of unification gradually trickled down to people's perceptions, resulting in orientations that regarded the "other Germany" as a territory to which one did not feel an emotional attachment; a territory that no longer represented part of one's spatial repository of emotions. Such attitudes would have profound implications on the establishment of national identities in the aftermath of 1989. Such emotional blockades, which perceived the other Germany as an alien territory outside of one's loyalties, would have severely hindered the unification of Easterners and Westerners as members of one national community. On the other hand, perceptions of a shared common territory of the German nation would have been able to persist despite the existence of two separated states with clearly marked borders. These would have acted as buffers of tolerance against the backdrop of significant economic, political, and social pressures caused by the transformation processes. An understanding would have emerged that, despite all the hardship, at least the divided people were finally reunited.

In short, this chapter addresses territorial identities in East and West by examining orientations toward the fact of the division and the prospect of unification which had developed prior to 1989. They will offer important insights into whether Westerners and Easterners perceived German unification as a welcome and long-awaited historic opportunity that reunites the German national community or whether unification was regarded as a gift from world politics to which one merely felt indifference.

THE FEDERAL REPUBLIC

In West Germany, over a period of 35 years people became accustomed to the division and largely began to accept the postwar status quo. Surveys by the *Allensbacher Institut für Demoskopie* demonstrated that the number of respondents who supported the proposition that West Germany should press for unification nearly halved between 1956 and 1983, from 65 to 33 percent. In return, the percentages who thought that unification should be left to the course of time more than doubled, from 25 to 55 percent. Although between 1979 and 1989, 75 to 79 percent were in favor of unification and only between 4.5 and 12 percent were against it (*Politbarometer*), the systemic antagonism of the Cold War left little hope for unification. Table 2.1 shows that the number of respondents who believed that it would surely or probably happen dropped from 27 percent in 1951 to a marginal 7 percent in 1983. Correspondingly, the share of pessimists who thought that the nation's division was an irreversible fact increased from 29 to 60 percent.

In addition, knowledge of and interest in the other Germany were limited. In 1979, a staggering 74.3 percent had never visited the GDR since the building of the Wall in 1961 (*Politbarometer*). By the beginning of 1989, 80 percent had not visited the other Germany in the last ten years (Noelle-Neumann and Köcher 1993: 411). Even for those with relatives on the other side of the Iron Curtain, where family ties provided for a particular interest, time took its natu-

Table 2.1
West Germans and the Likelihood of Unification (percentages)

Question: Do you think that the division of Germany will eventually disappear and a unified Germany will emerge?

	1951	1973	1983
Yes, surely	10	10	10
Yes, probably	17	7	5
Uncertain	36	32	33
No	29	53	60
No answer	9	6	-

Source: Emnid *Informationen* 8/9/1983: 15.

ral toll, since the number of respondents who had friends or relatives in the GDR decreased from 44 percent in 1953 to 32 percent in 1989. Thus, prior to unification in 1989, two-thirds of West German respondents did not have any close social relations to East Germans (Noelle-Neumann and Köcher 1993: 411). For those who still had relatives in the East, the severe obstacles to keeping in contact contributed to the gradual deterioration of family ties. Eventually, the descendants of the brothers and sisters of the immediate postwar generation mustered only a modest interest in their distant cousins.

It therefore came as little surprise that the political fact of the divided nation had only a subordinate importance in the minds of most West Germans. While in 1965 German unification was regarded by 69 percent and European integration by 24 percent as the more pressing political problem, attitudes had been reversed by 1983 with 36 percent and 60 percent, respectively (Emnid *Informationen* 5/6/1989: 13). When asked what Germany actually implied, 57.2 percent in 1979 named the Federal Republic and only 27.4 percent referred to the FRG and the GDR (*Politbarometer*). In addition, the willingness to permanently accept the Oder-Neisse line which had marked the border between Poland and East Germany since the end of World War II increased from a mere 8 percent in 1951 to 61 percent in 1972 (*Institut für Demoskopie* 1974: 525). The territorial identity of West Germans could therefore be labeled as minimalist. The prewar territories east of the GDR gradually disappeared from the public's perceptions as belonging to the German nation. More importantly, however, even the separated GDR did not represent a marker for the West German territorial identity. The *Heimat* was simply the Federal Republic as the clearly defined stretch of land for one's emotional orientations.

THE GERMAN DEMOCRATIC REPUBLIC

In correspondence to the Federal Republic, the Cold War antagonism could not erase the East Germans' will for unity. The Western-based *Infratest*[2] reported that support for unification was even stronger than the already high numbers of the FRG. In 1984, 89 percent of respondents were in favor of unification (Köhler 1992: 77). Despite decades of separate political, economic, social, and cultural experiences, the idea prevailed in East and West that the divided nation should eventually reunite. However, attitude toward the territorial division of the German nation were fundamentally different in the GDR. A survey by the East German *Institut für Meinungsforschung* in 1968 revealed that only 55 percent regarded the GDR as their "fatherland," while 42 percent attributed this notion to the whole of Germany (Niemann 1993: 310). Immediately after the fall of the Wall, a survey held in late November 1989 (Förster and Roski 1990: 94) showed that 76 percent had strong feelings toward being German, while the exact same percentage also felt strongly about being a citizen of the GDR. Clearly, loyalties that encompassed both the GDR and the divided German nation continued to exist side by side. Furthermore, *Infratest* showed that although 85 percent of responses perceived the FRG and the GDR as two separate states and 31 percent regarded the respective other Germany as a foreign country, a strikingly high 80 percent continued to uphold the notion of one common people (Köhler 1992: 76).

With gradually increasing material prosperity, political stability, and a firm anchoring in the West which was guaranteed by NATO and the Common Market, West Germans could live quite satisfactorily without the separated Eastern part. Life was more prosperous, stable, free, and secure than ever before in German history. Against such pleasing conditions, the situation of the compatriots across the Iron Curtain fell more and more into oblivion. This was clearly not the case in the GDR. A simple look at the data on migration to the FRG served as telling indicators of East Germans' dissatisfaction with the SED regime.[3] Between 1949 and 1988, 3.3 million people left the GDR and escaped, moved, or were expelled to the Federal Republic, which represented an annual average of 82,500.

The people of the GDR remained "fixated" (H. Weber 1993: 108) on the more prosperous, more democratic, and freer Federal Republic. Without anticipating analytical results of the subsequent chapters, the staggering migration statistics alone revealed that Easterners persistently perceived West Germany as the land of dreams which was far superior to one's own state. Fostered by gradually growing cross-border traffic[4] and foremost by Western television which was widely received in the East,[5] images of a better life across the Iron Curtain permeated the Eastern public psyche. Despite the considerable danger that was involved when attempting to cross the border illegally, and despite political harassment when applying for emigration, the possibility of improving one's situation by moving or escaping to the FRG[6] kept the Western *Länder* as territorial identity markers in the minds of East Germans.

The attractiveness of the Federal Republic was further helped by common cultural attributes, such as language and history, that eased the identification with West Germany as a part of one's territorial repository of emotional attachments. Also, the *Grundgesetz* (Basic Law or constitution) of the Federal Republic automatically gave East Germans citizenship in the FRG. As such, Easterners were entitled to the social services and welfare benefits of West Germany. Hence, the real emigration of friends and family members, the continuing hope for emigration, sporadic visits by Westerners, as well as Western television pictures kept the Federal Republic in the public psyche of East Germany. The experienced deficiencies of the SED state, including the provision of consumer goods, civic liberties, or inadequate material standards, further manifested perceptions of West Germany as a normative proposal of freedom and prosperity. In contrast to the Federal Republic, territorial identities in East Germany were not clear cut. Instead, they were double-sided. On the one hand stood the real experiences of the GDR, where one grew up and had his or her formative life experiences. On the other hand, however, the illusory Federal Republic stood as a reminder of the potential of one's existence which all too often was in sharp contrast to reality.

AFTER UNIFICATION

With the fall of the Wall and the opening of several border crossings in the autumn of 1989, the collective fixation on the West, accumulated interest, and curiosity resulted in a rush across the border. By November 1992, only 7 percent of Easterners had not paid a visit to the Western *Länder* (*Politbarometer*). This high level of interest, however, was not met by Western compatriots. In 1990, the share of main holidays of West Germans (usually in the summer) which had the new *Länder* as their destination totaled only 2.5 percent. In contrast, 32 percent of all East German holidays were spent in the old Federal Republic. By 1991, the Western figures had increased only marginally to 2.7 percent, while the old *Länder* continued to be equally attractive to Easterners, with a share of 33 percent of all main holidays (Deutscher Reisebüro-Verband 1996). Although the data did not include any short-term visits, the figures nonetheless indicated the remarkably low level of interest among West Germans in the new *Länder*. When visiting the former GDR in the aftermath of 1989, the limited numbers of Western cars and Western visitors, even in regions bordering the old *Länder*, were a surprising—yet obvious—feature. Although the tourist infrastructure was still rudimentary at the outset of unification, Westerners nonetheless disregarded the attractiveness of Eastern towns and countryside and did not consider the opportunity to experience first-hand and without travel restrictions the state of political, economic, and social affairs across the former border. The strikingly low ratio of holidays spent in the East pointed toward a lack of curiosity and interest among West Germans. The East German pent-up curiosity and eagerness to see the West had no emotional equivalent in the old *Länder*.

It is against this imperative that one has to judge the transformation processes in the aftermath of 1989. East Germans perceived the West as the promised land and regarded the unified nation as an eventual political goal that would give them political freedom, human rights, and material prosperity. A look at the changing momentum of the October and November demonstrations of 1989 served as a telling indicator. Calls for reforming Socialism within the GDR gradually gave way to an overwhelming support for joining the political, economic, and social structures of the Federal Republic (Zwahr 1993), and choruses proclaiming "we are the people" were gradually superseded by "we are one people." Attitudes toward unification were fundamentally positive in both East and West. For West Germans, however, the historic chance to unite the nation did not represent the unfulfilled and desperately pursued political dream that finally came true. While West Germans had conveniently accommodated the fact of the division, East Germans had lamented over it. From the beginning, therefore, unification started on an uneven footing, perfectly exemplified by the satirical joke on a prominent slogan of the Eastern revolution. The Easterners' call for "*Wir sind ein Volk*" (we are one people) was merely answered by Westerners with a cynical "so are we."

One has to ask what made West Germans pass off their territorial identity of the divided nation and what elements compensated for the lacking loyalty to the German territory consisting of both Eastern and Western *Länder*. In return, why were East Germans so eager to maintain and develop loyalties toward the Federal Republic? It is against this ambivalence that the study turns to the analyses of economics, citizenship, mass culture, and ethnicity within the transformation processes of unification.

NOTES

1. In 1964, the SED allowed its pensioners to cross the border to West Germany. By 1984, and in return for substantial hard-currency loans from the FRG, the party eased travel restrictions, and in 1986, some 570,000 people (excluding pensioners) visited the Federal Republic (H. Weber 1993: 97). Further exceptions included occasional tourist visits by Westerners which significantly increased as a result of Chancellor Brandt's détente policy with the Communist bloc.

2. Since 1968, *Infratest* had conducted surveys by combining participant observations and indirect questioning of Western visitors to the GDR. Respondents were asked to answer questionnaires in representation of a person "X" whom they had just visited (Köhler 1992: 60).

3. The number of total emigrants (refugees and authorized emigration) averaged around 200,000 per year between 1949 and 1961, with a high point of 330,000 in 1953, the year of the workers' uprising. In the first five years following the building of the Wall, some 32,000 per year left the GDR. Thereafter, total emigration dropped gradually to some 15,000 in the 1970s. In 1984, the flow increased significantly to

40,000, since large numbers of long-time applicants were granted permission to leave. Between 1985 and 1988 emigration averaged 27,000 (Ammer 1989: 1207).

4. Prior to 1986, only 2 percent of Easterners aged 14 to 29 had visited the FRG. For people aged 30 to 49, figures totaled 18 percent, and 80 percent of East Germans over the age of fifty had had the opportunity to visit the other Germany. In 1988, however, percentages had changed significantly: 14 percent for people aged 14 to 29, 33 percent for the middle generation, and 54 percent for the over-fifty-year-olds (Köhler 1992: 75).

5. A notable exception was represented by the low-lying area around Dresden, which East Germans therefore referred to as the "valley of those who do not know."

6. On the concepts of exit and voice in the GDR, see Hirschmann 1995: 9–44.

3

Economics

A decisive cause for the peaceful revolution of 1989 was the aspiration to buy material goods, to enjoy consumer choice, and to achieve better living standards. In the early autumn of 1989, banners and chants of the mass demonstrations called for freedom, democracy, and reformed Socialism (Zwahr 1993). Such slogans were gradually superseded and eventually replaced by material matters. A survey taken in March 1990 asked East Germans about their expectations from unification. Forty percent were looking forward to better living standards and 25 percent to economic recovery. Only 3 percent, however, mentioned democracy (Roth 1991: 115–138).

People followed the call of the *Deutschmark* hoping for levels of affluence that would match those of their Western neighbors. For years, East Germans watched enviously the standard of prosperity that was displayed on West German television and in East German so-called "intershops" that sold Western products for hard currency. In return, these experiences drastically revealed the economic and material shortcomings of the Communist system. They were further highlighted by rare trips across the Iron Curtain or by Western friends, family members, or tourists who visited the GDR. They heightened public discontent since the Federal Republic progressed from one economic boom to another which persistently widened the gap between the two Germanys. Although the GDR generated the highest living standards among all Communist countries, the permanent orientation toward the affluent Western part proved to be a powerful cognitive standard for East Germans which eventually contributed to the growing skepticism of the population toward their own system.

Unification offered the unique opportunity to make up for decades of lost chances and material deprivation. In the eyes of Easterners, the market economy was the land of dreams. For many, the economic miracle that transformed the Federal Republic after 1949 was just waiting to repeat itself in the Eastern *Länder*. In the run-up to the first federal elections of unified Germany, high expectations were further fueled by Chancellor Kohl's promise of "blossoming landscapes" in the near future.

In order to establish an affirmative national identity, these hopes generated by the arrival of capitalism had to be fulfilled. The improvement of one's economic situation was one of the decisive raisons d'être that sparked the revolution. After unification, Easterners eventually had to come to the conclusion that the risky and brave effort of bringing down the totalitarian SED regime—quite literally—had paid off. The market economy had to offer equal chances and opportunities for both Westerners and Easterners regarding financial security and social status. For those who did not benefit from the economic transformation, lower levels of affluence and fewer opportunities for material success could not have developed into coherent points of orientation for one's loyalty and emotional attachment. Of course, inequalities that resulted from the significant gaps in the provision of material standards between the FRG and the GDR could not disappear overnight. But they could only be tolerated if Easterners were given at least the prospect of improving their economic and social status. Otherwise, frustration and disappointment would have arisen that severely hampered people's emotional commitment and attachment to a unified Germany.

The economic identity of unified Germany addressed those characteristics of the market economy that generated material security. Hence, the sphere of work as the basic means of securing financial competence and participation in the consumer society possessed a central position. In general, work represents a potential realm for individual self-realization and social recognition. Work, its ethic, value, and status, however, are determined by structural characteristics of the respective economic system. Here, the GDR possessed fundamentally different features from those of the Federal Republic. In East Germany, state and party organized the individual's life. The East German worker was given a job, and he or she had to fulfill targets that were set by a centralized apparatus. The nationalization of most of the economic production, as well as the ideologically streamlined education system oppressed initiative, self-responsibility, and independence. The collective goal of establishing the Communist society was paramount to individual ambitions regarding professional, social, or material status. In contrast, the market economy of the Federal Republic emphasized individuality. Affirmative orientations toward the market economy developed out of career opportunities and material possessions and the mere prospect of achieving higher levels of financial, social, and professional status generated supportive economic identities. To benefit from the economic transition in the aftermath of 1989, Easterners were asked to change completely their former Communist mentality. Market economics depends on innovative individuals. Innovation and individualism, however, has been neglected for forty years.

In addition, provision and cost of social services affect the individual's material existence. Here, East Germans got used to a tight social net with progressive services that were supplied by the state and offered comprehensive coverage. Although still a sophisticated welfare state, this level of security was not provided in unified Germany. Certain social services were dismantled and costs for housing, living, and medical care increased. Quite logically, people had severe problems in adjusting to these abrupt changes. In particular, the reorientation regarding employment represented a crucial issue. In the GDR, work constituted the nucleus of one's social existence. Contacts with colleagues extended into private spheres. The collective was responsible for social services, such as day care centers for children, leisure, or holidays. In the aftermath of unification, the constitutional right to work of the GDR turned into fierce competition for a limited number of jobs. Suddenly, and for the first time in their lives, East Germans were confronted with unemployment that affected not only the individual's financial security but above all his or her self-esteem. A lifetime guarantee turned into the need for personal effort.

In short, this chapter intends to explain the economic identity of post-unification Eastern Germany by analyzing the historical currents and fundamental structural characteristics of the economic system of the GDR and the FRG. From this point of departure, it investigates the individual's work ethic, the value of work and employment, as well as standards toward the provision of social services.

THE GERMAN DEMOCRATIC REPUBLIC

After the collapse of the Third Reich, the industrialization of the GDR was rendered difficult by the consequences of war destruction and Soviet occupation. Industrial plants and the transport system lay in ruins. Substantial reparations to the USSR further hampered postwar economic development. Until 1946 over a thousand industrial plants were dismantled, as were the second tracks of the rail network. Additionally, the Soviet Union took reparations from the current production as mounting to 25 percent of the overall industrial output and transformed them into two hundred USSR-owned "Soviet Limited Companies" (H. Weber 1993: 11). Most notably, a Communist "Marshall plan" did not exist. The GDR had to develop its industrial base and production entirely by itself without any foreign assistance.

From early on, the GDR followed the Soviet conception of a Socialist economy. Despite lacking mineral resources and industrial plants, the SED authorities created an industrial structure that relied on heavy industry, in particular coal and steel, while neglecting consumer products and services. Industrial policies, therefore, did not pay attention to the particular skills of the work force and the existing industrial infrastructure. The opportunity to build up competitive structures in the realm of chemistry, fine mechanics, and optics with the prospect of the development of an advanced, high-tech oriented industry was lost, reduced to a reliance on aging industrial concepts and policies and a "simple imitation of the Soviet track" (H. Weber 1993: 37). The SED pursued a rigid policy of nationalization that extensively covered all economic spheres (Glaeßner 1989: 245). Small private businesses could maintain only a subordinate position within the industrial sphere, most notably in craft. The overall ratio of self-employed persons remained persistently low. In 1955, the share still totaled 20 percent of the work force but subsequently fell to a mere 3.4 percent in 1970 and to 2.2 percent in 1989 (Statistical Yearbook 1990: 127).

The planning apparatus functioned under the principle of democratic centralism. Planning had a long-term perspective. "Long-term prognoses" covering the future twenty to thirty years were specified by "long-term plans" (10 to 15 years). These proposals were based on outlines by publicly-owned companies (the so-called "VEB," *volkseigener Betrieb*) and were subsequently drafted by various central planning institutions under the authority of the Council of Ministers which acted according to directives from the SED. Additionally, councils of districts, towns, and regions provided territorial concepts. Based on these long-term analyses, five-year plans were developed in accordance to the intervals between party congresses. Directives for five-year plans were passed by the party congress and subsequently served as binding legislation for the entire economy. Five-year plans were then narrowed down into one-year targets by the various VEBs and regional councils (Glaeβner 1989: 255–262).

By the mid-1960s the deficiencies in economic planning and coordination became all too obvious. Individual initiative and self-reliance ran counter to the centralized and hierarchical principles of the Communist dictatorship. They fundamentally questioned and challenged the political dogma of the Marxist-Leninist system. The hierarchical structure of state and society fostered a lack of imagination and flexibility. The strict top-down pattern of directives and orders made it extremely difficult for scientists, industrial executives, and workers to participate in the decision-making process. Innovation and progressive concepts, as well as practice-oriented analyses were lost within the strict hierarchy of the SED state. Economic policies were consequently trapped between the experts' demands for reform and the party prerogative of absolute dominance and control of internal matters. Given the complicated and complex nature of the planning system, it came as no surprise that the GDR economy had to confront severe disruptions. Adaptation to the changing world economic climate, to new innovation, and to technologies was limited. The correction of ill-perceived future trends and prognoses took a considerable amount of time, if it was possible at all. The principle of long-term planning was, therefore, in stark contradiction to economic success. While the latter demands long-term vision it always has to be complemented by the ability for short-term reaction, correction, and adaptation.

Lacking mineral resources made the GDR largely dependent on imports. Since foreign exchange reserves were constantly low, the regime tried to keep such imports as minimal as possible. Oil was largely substituted by brown coal. Although the GDR was able to provide the highest living standard of all Comecon countries, the economic decline became evident by the 1970s. The VIII. Party Congress of 1971 confidently pronounced an economic expansion, as well as an envisaged growth in living standards. The strategy was to invest heavily during the next five years in technology, predominantly through Western imports. The subsequent financial liability should be cleared during the second half of the decade with increased exports.

By 1980, it became clear that the strategy had utterly failed. The economic crisis of 1973 sent oil prices to unexpected heights which had to be compensated by increased exports. The second oil shock of 1979, the ambitious housing program, and imports western of consumer goods resulted in severe debts. By as early as 1978, further loans were necessary to finance the already existing interest payments. By 1981/1982, the GDR lost her credibility and international banks refused to give further loans (Haendcke-Hoppe-Arndt 1995: 591–592). Only two substantial loans from the Federal Republic of one billion Deutschmarks each in 1983 and 1984 prevented an early financial collapse. Nonetheless, the authorities were forced to rely on a policy of autarky that subsequently resulted in severe economic and ecological problems (Glaeβner 1989: 241). By 1980, fundamental mismanagement and lack of innovation and investment, as well as structural deficiencies, deteriorated and brought the GDR to the verge of bankruptcy.

Work Mentality

The official political culture of the SED envisaged the development of the Socialist and eventually Communist society, based on such values as optimism, solidarity, studiousness, freedom, equality, and social justice, and created by the "new Socialist man" who went through a lifelong process of ideologically conditioned and state-organized education. This anthropological view of the SED—the optimistic belief in the possibility of educating man toward a utopian goal—resulted in extremely high demands and expectations in the economic sphere. They included the acceptance of the competence and responsibility of the state which was limited only by the acceptance of the normative leadership function of the SED. The citizen was expected to commit him- or herself to economic growth and the enhancement of individual technical skills. These demands were complemented by the unanimous acceptance of the priority of collective and social matters over private and individual interests (Rytlewski 1989: 22, Krisch 1988: 58). Theoretically, therefore, economic development was dependent on the active and voluntary cooperation and engagement of self-sacrificing individuals. Not surprisingly, the regime gave this participatory role a strong legal status. The constitution of 1968 proposed a commanding moral commitment to every citizen by stating the necessity to "contribute to working, planning and governing." The SED demanded not only an active but furthermore an affirmative participation in the development of the Communist society. The new Socialist citizen, educated and guided by ideologically sound agents, should willingly contribute. His or her efforts should not be based on coercion but instead on reason and understanding of one's individual responsibility for the general development of society.

The East German work mentality was conditioned by a variety of structural prerogatives that slackened individual work performances. Although the GDR offered full employment, it could only do so by splitting jobs and spreading the work load onto more individuals. This significantly reduced the amount of work that one had to fulfill. Deficiencies in planning and a chronic shortage of parts and goods further affected the industrial process. The economy was characterized by a permanent go-slow (Scherer 1991: 309) that contributed to reduced demands to the individual employee who simply did not and could not work to his or her full potential. Furthermore, incentives for the individual to improve his or her work performance were limited. Material stimulation hardly existed because of streamlined wage levels and a restricted choice of consumer products (Belwe 1989: 101). Sanctions which could have encouraged better work performances were hardly enforced. With a guaranteed job there was no fear of unemployment and no existentialist coercion to perform. Working under one's potential, laziness, dawdling, and slackness did not result in significant material or professional disadvantages. The outdated reliance on heavy industries prompted a lack of innovation and modernization. The centralized nature of the economy had a severe impact on the individual. Interdiction and control, the permanent task of fulfilling hierarchically-designed, often unrealistic plans conditioned a lack of imagination, flexibility, and suppressed participation. Individualism and private initiative were oppressed. Self-responsibility was missing, since it was all too easy to blame an abstract party apparatus for productivity failures. The chronic weakness and shortage in innovation demonstrated the system's lack of creativity and problem-solving capacity. The GDR faced the prototypical Communist dilemma: the political-ideological indoctrination generated a monocausal, uniform view of life that was in sharp contrast to the necessary requirements of autonomy and individuality, as well as independent and responsible decision-making, in order to modernize an economy.

The economic identities of East Germans were highly ambivalent. Regarding economic achievements, Easterners undoubtedly showed a certain and well-justified pride. It was an obvious fact to every traveler to Eastern Europe that East Germany had achieved the most prosperous living standards and even produced goods that were competitive on the Western markets, for instance in optics. Easterners were proud of their economic productivity and material living standards as compared to other Comecon countries. This achievement gained an additional importance since the GDR was forced to rebuild its industrial structure without any foreign support, as had been available to the Federal Republic. Pride and a sense of togetherness among the population were, therefore, quite justified. Nonetheless, in comparison to the West, the deficiencies in the provision of consumer goods and the standards of living were all too obvious. By the 1980s, the widening gap to the West and the persistent organizational and structural deficiencies, which hardly showed any signs of improvement, caused increasing irritation. Progress was slow, and there was little hope that performance and productivity would result in better standards of living. Economics increasingly had a disillusioning and depressing connotation, and the fixation on the more prosperous Western counterpart became a predominant feature of the GDR psyche.

The Social System

The welfare state of the GDR represented one of the most complex and extensive social systems of the world. For minimal contributions, East Germans enjoyed health care, child care facilities, training and education, as well as pensions. Employment was guaranteed. Rents and energy costs, as well as certain food products and clothing, were heavily subsidized. To some extent, the subsidy system had bizarre consequences, as exemplified by some LPGs (*Landwirtschaftliche Produktionsgenossenschaften*; agricultural cooperatives) who fed pigs with bread, for it was considerably cheaper than the usual hog diet. The social system was characterized by a high degree of paternalism. From cradle to grave, the state inhabited the position of the sole provider in all spheres of life. Income, consumption, social and physical security, leisure, health, and education were organized by a complex bureaucratic apparatus which determined the social and economic wants of the population. Ambitions, needs, and desires were streamlined and categorized by apparatschiks. Life followed a beaten centrally-planned track designed and presented by the top-down hierarchy of party and state. The citizen was placed in the position of a permanent and eternal beneficiary. This protection, however, created dependence and complacency while hampering self-responsibility. The individual was solely dependent on the bureaucracy and on state measures. Self-reliance was absent. According to the poet Irene Böhme the state infantilized the citizen (Meyer 1989: 45). Social security acquired a given, obvious, and natural standard. With no space for individual initiative and independence, the citizen developed into a dependent and obedient recipient.

Nevertheless, the social system acquired a high-ranking status among the population. In the autumn of 1990, respondents had been asked to evaluate the particular strengths of the FRG and the GDR (Köhler 1992: 78). In the social realm, East Germany was given a considerably better vote. Of the respondents, 91 percent regarded child care in the GDR as superior to that of the FRG. Similarly, 72 percent praised the GDR's social security (26 percent FRG), and 43 percent the public welfare work for the individual (22 percent FRG). The school system was judged by 46 percent as an advantage of the GDR (39 percent FRG), while provision of housing (30 percent GDR, 34 percent FRG), as well as social justice (35 percent GDR, 33 percent FRG) had roughly equal support for both East and West.

Nonetheless, particular programs of the GDR's welfare conception were subject to criticism. In a survey taken in February 1990, only 12 percent perceived the care for elder people as an advantage of the GDR, while the overwhelming majority (64 percent) mentioned the FRG (Förster and Roski 1990: 125). The same applied to the quality of medical care (15 percent GDR, 62 percent FRG) and to decent housing conditions (18 percent GDR, 48 percent FRG). It seemed that East Germans generally appreciated the comprehensive nature of the social system. Social services provided a secure life that safeguarded against illness and age and offered educational and professional opportunities to every member of society, albeit within established ideological tracks. Despite its care from cradle to grave, however, certain services, such as medical care or housing were seen as more efficient and sophisticated in the FRG. The comprehensive design was highly welcomed, while practical operation displayed deficiencies. Quantity was appreciated but quality criticized.

Educational policies subscribed to the ideal that the Socialist society should offer every individual equal chances to acquire training and qualifications. From early childhood, East Germans passed through a complex web of educational agencies. They included kindergartens, the ten-grade general polytechnic secondary school, vocational training, the extended secondary school leading to university entry qualifications, engineering and other specialized schools, universities, continuous education (Glaeβner 1989: 284), as well as the East German army NVA (*Nationale Volksarmee*). The system was entirely in state hands. Private agencies were nonexistent. Ideological prerogatives accompanied students throughout education. The regime not only raised the expert but furthermore disciplined the loyal Socialist citizen. Education was understood as the acquisition of Marxist-Leninist principles that should guide the individual through his or her professional life and provide the ideological base for one's place in society. Educational standards presented the individual with a uniform view of life through Communist spectacles. Such monocausality, however, stood in sharp contrast to the complex nature of reality (Lemke 1989: 87). Reductionism and simplicity left the student ill-prepared for modern requirements of change and adaptability. Additionally, through the selective granting of apprenticeships, student admission, and jobs, the SED was able to actively control career patterns. Compliance with and adaptation to the political and ideological norms were rewarded by enhanced career opportunities. Hence, the regime determined the socio-structural development of the society. Social and professional status were ultimately dependent on party directives, while the urge to conform and accommodate within the general totalitarian system ran counter to the development of individuality and motivation to change (Lemke 1989: 87).

THE FEDERAL REPUBLIC

The development of the West German economy after the collapse of the Third Reich has been described widely as an economic miracle. Already by the 1950s the *Wirtschaftswunder* was well under way. Growth rates of percent were no exception, while the generated wealth benefited broad segments of society. Gradually, the degree of financial stability, social security, industrial harmony, high living standards, and material prosperity became the envy of Europe. The strong economic performance contributed immensely to the stabilization of the young republic. Amid the Cold War antagonism, the division of the nation, and the shameful legacy of the Third Reich, the economic realm provided a formative focus and a source for self-esteem and pride. The economic slogan of the 1950s, *"Es geht wieder aufwärts"* (things are looking up), became a general motto for West Germans, who trusted their new system to generate constant and unsurpassed levels of prosperity. Until the mid 1960s full employment, low inflation, export surpluses, increasing incomes, expanding social services, and growing public investment in schools, universities, hospitals, and the highway system became a given standard (G. Schmid 1990: 228). Surveys by the Allensbacher *Institut für Demoskopie* demonstrated the ever-growing satisfaction with the market economy. While in 1951 a planning system was favored by nearly half of respondents and only one-third supported a free market, the figures had already reversed by 1953. In 1974, the approval rate for market economics had reached an impressive 70 percent (Noelle-Neumann 1981: 300).

The concentration on the economic recovery served as a strong integrative factor. The general striving for material success was a cognitive point of orientation for the millions of refugees who tried to establish themselves in a new environment. The same applied to the masses of Nazi followers who managed to slip through the loose nets of denazification measures (see Chapter 4). Because of the economic success, formerly anti-democratic forces saw no reason for political opposition to democracy (Fulbrook 1994: 217). The widespread and consistent satisfaction with the economy prompted the philosopher Jürgen Habermas to refer to this new-found pride as *"Deutschmarknationalismus"* (Habermas 1990).

The positive orientation toward the economy had its roots in the progressive concept of Ludwig Erhard's *Soziale Marktwirtschaft* (social market economy). Adenauer's Minister for Economic Affairs argued that market capitalism had to benefit both business and employees, while economic profits should partly be used to craft and finance an extensive social net. *Soziale Marktwirtschaft* meant the reconciliation and parallel importance of a competitive economy, accompanied by social justice, shorter working hours and wage increases. Despite these labor-friendly features,[1] the *Soziale Marktwirtschaft* nevertheless displayed the typical characteristics of a market economy. Competition and competitiveness represented the bases for innovation and the striving for technological perfectionism accompanied by increasing prosperity. Higher salaries and promotion constituted the incentives for the individual's work performance. Social status was largely determined by one's professional status, income, and prestigious job. Work was regarded as a sphere for self-realization. Table 3.1 shows that such active attitudes to work as fun, commitment, challenge, and ambition were more widespread than the passive notions

Table 3.1
Attitudes Toward Work in West Germany, 1990 (percentages)

Response Category	Absolutely True	More Or Less True
Work has to be fun and should interest me	70	25
I am committed to my work	59	33
I like new challenges	48	38
I have ambitious goals in my career	26	37
Work is primarily duty	27	35
Work is routine	16	34
I like being told exactly what I have to do	10	23
N: 5518		

Source: Gruner und Jahr 1990: 282.

of duty, routine, or delegation. The sphere of work was regarded as a source for self-esteem, fueled by a craving for recognition and a striving for material and social prestige. A further incentive for improved work performance was represented by the prospect of dismissal, although it was significantly softened by a complex labor legislation that offered the employee protection against unfair and disproportionate removal.

The Social System

The proportion of GDP allocated to social expenditure was persistently high in the Federal Republic. Between 1960 and 1981 the share rose from 20.5 percent to 31.5 percent, which established the FRG in the top group of Western nations. In 1981 it was surpassed only by Sweden, Denmark, the Netherlands, and Belgium, but it was ahead of the United States, Japan, Switzerland, and significantly ahead of the Socialist countries (OECD 1985: 21, 81). West Germany followed the model of a conservative-reformist welfare state, holding a position between the social democratic concept of, for instance, Sweden, and the liberal selective version of Japan and the United States (Schmidt 1990: 126). The social system of the Federal Republic offered security against such standard risks as age, invalidity, accident, sickness, unemployment, and other loss of income, as well as further support schemes, such as children's allowance or rent subsidies. The booming economy, absence of recessions, low inflation, and full employment (since the end of the 1950s) constituted the bases for increasing prosperity that safeguarded the development and further advancement of the social state. The expanding number of employees and growing wages increased tax revenues as well as the income of social insurance.

However, the FRG did not offer total public assistance. Social policies paid heed to the utmost principle of the Federal Republic—currency stability—on which social security was ultimately based (Schmidt 1990: 130). Also, the extent of social reforms was tied to the increase of productivity and competitiveness (Mertes 1994: 11). A further threshold for the state's social intervention was based on the Catholic social doctrine that responsibility rested with the smallest social circle that is capable of solving arising problems (Rudzio 1991: 133). Hence, public social measures came into effect only in those cases where social security could not be safeguarded by private, non-state measures, such as gainful employment or family support. The state, therefore, functioned as a final source and not as the automatic guarantor of security.

Although the welfare state was gradually taken for granted, it was not a right "per se." The Basic Law gave only limited attention to social justice, while social rights, such as the right to work, to education, to housing, and so on were missing. Instead, the constitutional principle of the *Sozialstaat* (social state) only referred to the legislative obligation to foster social balance, as well as to guarantee a minimum of social security. The prerogative of the *Sozialstaat* merely constituted a normative focus for the state. However, it was not a social guarantee or a factual claim for the individual (Degenhardt 1988: 303–315). In contrast to the GDR, a constitutional right to work did not exist. The state provided the social boundary which offered security against standard risks. Within these, however, the individual had a high degree of self-responsibility for his or her financial and social security.

However vague the constitutional formulations were, they nevertheless generated a standard among the West German population regarding the social responsibilities of the state. The *Sozialstaat* was in reality a coercing principle for political parties, as well as for trade and business unions. West Germans could only enjoy these progressive social reforms in return for high tax burdens and significant health care contributions. The public expectation of a continuous provision of welfare measures was, therefore, expected out of considerable individual contributions. People paid a high price for their welfare state and, thus, sensed that the state was obliged to give social programs in return. This notion was market-oriented in the sense of "service-for-money." With the country's increasing prosperity, people sensed that the state was even more obliged to offer comprehensive and extensive social measures in return. Nonetheless, the *Sozialstaat* was not an automatic prerogative.

During the 1960s and with the exception of 1966/1967, the Federal Republic enjoyed full employment. At the end of the 1960s and during the early 1970s there was even a shortage of workers which was compensated by inviting 2.5 million foreign *Gastarbeiter* (guest workers). The first recession of 1966/1967 came as a sudden shock and temporarily brought the economic miracle to an end. For the first time, the Federal Republic was facing severe unemployment problems, with numbers growing to over one million. The two subsequent economic crises of 1974/1975 and 1980/1981 further manifested unemployment on the political agenda. Although in the aftermath of the crises, inflation, productivity, and balance of payments were kept under control, unemployment remained a staggering problem. The average rate of unemployment rose from 1 percent between 1963 and 1973 to 3.2 percent between 1974 and 1979 and to 6 percent between 1980 and 1985 (G. Schmid 1990: 230). A further stress on the job market was prevented by sending around one million *Gastarbeiter* back to their countries of origin. For West German employees between 60 and 64, social policies offered early retirement, which subsequently reduced their employment rate from 75 percent in 1970 to 33 percent in 1985. Between 1974 and 1983 one-third of the work force had at one stage experienced unemployment. For a significant number of West Germans the experience—or at least the prospect—of unemployment became a familiar feature of life. The number of long-term cases with little employment prospects grew steadily. In 1970 only 10 percent of the unemployed could not find a job for more than one year. By 1985 the number increased to one-third (G. Schmid 1990: 233).

The Federal Republic never followed a policy of full employment, as, for instance, Sweden or Austria had done. By the end of the 1980s *Bonn* had to confront severe stress on the labor market because of growing automation and technological advancement. Government, industry, and unions discussed proposals of job-sharing, time-sharing, or a four-day working week. The aim was to reduce the working hours of broad segments of the work force which could compensate for the total loss of employment of a few. Various institutional measures[2] tried to counter the malaise. Unemployment insurance was financed through equal contributions by employer and employee, wherein both parties paid 2 percent each of the latter's gross income.

In the end, unemployment had established itself as a social phenomenon. Broad segments of society had to familiarize themselves with the experience or prospect of being laid off. Various measures by the state prevented the overwhelming majority from facing existentialist crises. Unemployment benefits provided for a certain financial back-up. Publicly funded projects and employment mediation fostered a reintegration into the labor force. The results of these measures were largely positive, although a considerable number could not find a job on a long-term basis, which caused bitterness, disillusionment, and social and financial hardship. For the large majority, however, unemployment represented a problematic but manageable and temporary phase in their lives. Aided by public institutions and programs, one's own initiative and eagerness to regain his former social and material status provided for a certain flexibility and adaptability in pursuing higher qualification levels or seeking different jobs in different economic sectors. Most significantly, and in contrast to other western nations, adulthood did not start on a sour note, since the FRG managed to integrate most of her young work force (G. Schmid 1990: 234). An affirmative experience toward the country's economic system was, therefore, granted from the beginning of an individual's working phase in life.

THE NEW LÄNDER

The currency reform of July 1990 integrated Eastern Germany within the economic structure of the Federal Republic. The legal framework, the Deutschmark, and the free market were abruptly introduced to the Eastern *Länder*. The decision by *Bonn* to pursue shock therapy did not fail to produce an immediate impact. When revisiting the former GDR after the first years of transition, one is struck by the vast changes in the economic sphere. Between 1991 and 1995 the net transfer of public funds from West to East rose from an annual 110 to over 150 billion Deutschmark. Roads, rail tracks, airports, highways, and the telephone system have been modernized or newly built. Western consumer outlets are offering their goods and services throughout the region. Entire economic sectors, such as banking, insurance, and retail had to be established from scratch. Until the end of 1993, the overall investment of private industries totaled 340 billion Deutschmark (Asche 1994: 233). New businesses opened and former state-owned firms were reorganized under new ownership. Small enterprises sprang up, creating a *Mittelstand*, a formerly missing class of small and medium-sized independent businesses. Between 1991 and 1994, some 870,000 new businesses were registered.

Privatization proceeded much faster in comparison to other former Communist countries. The *Treuhandanstalt*, the public but highly independent trustee agency, was responsible for privatizing the former state-owned enterprises of the GDR, aiming to restructure, rationalize, and refinance them in order to compete within a market environment. At the time of unification, the *Treuhand* administered around 14,000 companies. Only small businesses, such as bars, restaurants, and pharmacies were excluded. With the agency, *Bonn* had established overnight the world's biggest industrial conglomerate. At the end of 1994, the *Treuhand* had fulfilled its core task of privatization and all but 60 firms had been sold (Eisenhammer 1995: 7).[3] Wages increased continuously. Between 1991 and 1994, basic wages in the East rose by 53 percent. Although Western levels have yet to be equaled, trade unions equipped with experienced Western staff were able to negotiate highly advantageous contracts. The financial situation for East German employees improved significantly. The choice of goods quickly approached Western standards, and people had the money surplus to purchase them. In mid-1994 the purchasing power had already reached between 70 and 80 percent of the West, which more than outweighed the 35 percent rise in living costs (Asche 1994: 234). Prior to unification, the *Ostmark* had a market exchange rate of approximately 4.50 to 1 to the Deutschmark. Chancellor Kohl's decision to introduce an average 1.8 conversion rate turned the sizable East German savings into a respectable financial surplus. In 1993, the sum of private financial capital doubled in comparison to 1992 and reached DM 35 billion (Asche 1994: 235). In this respect, the market economy provided for exciting prospects of prosperity and participation in the consumer society.

However, these clear indicators of a successful and rapid economic transformation were overshadowed by the state of the Eastern economy. During the initial unification euphoria, unrealistic parallels were drawn to the successful postwar transformation of the West German economy after World War II which led to a fundamental misjudgment of the extent of the structural deficiencies. In 1991, Detlev Rohwedder, the first head of the *Treuhand*, who was later assassinated by Red Army Faction terrorists, estimated that the sell-off of the GDR's state-owned enterprises would result in revenues of DM 600 billion. In the end, the *Treuhand* recorded losses of DM 265 billion. Productivity fell by more than half, down to 35 percent of the Western standard. Production costs were 20 percent above the already high levels of the old *Länder*. Industrial production rapidly declined. By 1991 it had reached a mere one-third of that of 1989. Many enterprises without any hope of reaching profitable standards in the future closed down. Between 1991 and 1994 their number totaled some 450,000 (Statistical Yearbook 1995: 129).

Analysts were quick to offer cogent explanations. Although the GDR claimed to be the tenth industrial power in the world, economic deficiencies were revealed drastically in open competition. Infrastructure had been neglected for years. Capital stock was worthless. State-owned firms of the GDR were highly overstaffed. The constitutional right to work resulted in astonishingly high labor forces which had no relation to the degree of productivity. With the introduction of the free market, managers did not hesitate to reduce labor capacities. The 1.8 conversion of the *Ostmark* was regarded as economically unwise. Political necessities, however, superseded economical rationality. Against a growing tide of emigration from the East, the government was forced to provide a generous financial package that was able to convince Easterners not to move to the prosperous West. It also served as a welcoming gesture, expressing the spirit of uniting the nation, not only in territorial but also in social and financial terms.

The issue of ownership represented a severe damper to economic activity. In the days of the GDR, people acquired land and property according to the contemporary status of law. This right was now questioned by former owners whose property had been expropriated in the aftermath of World War II. Conflicting claims on confiscated property were the consequence. It made the *Treuhand*'s ambition of selling and breaking up the vast state conglomerates a task of utmost difficulty. The government's decision to favor restitution over compensation meant that every property claim had to be processed. Legal battles over ownership stretched over years. Consequently, notions of distrust, anger, and hatred toward the new authorities and the new legal system emerged quickly. Legal controversies formed psychological barriers between East and

West, between defendants and plaintiffs, between winners and losers in the post-unification battle of property. The *Treuhand* attracted opportunistic Western business people, eager to take advantage of the agency's requirement to proceed rapidly with selling and restructuring. According to one official of the *Treuhand*, "the jackals were everywhere, people looking to snap up companies and flog them for the real estate. . . . In those first two years there was never time to check out investors properly. It was a mass business and everything had to go" (Eisenhammer 1995: 7). This gold-digging mentality caused further resentment amongst Easterners. The massive take over of Eastern firms by Western managers and the accompanying lack of commitment to local matters, job losses, and cases of bribery, brought harsh feelings of anger and disgust—of a colonization of the East by the prosperous and unscrupulous West. Gold-digging was further encouraged by *Treuhand* policies. The agency was hard-pressed to sell off unattractive units. Quite often, it attracted only one bidder. It therefore came as no surprise that governmental inducements regularly totaled 40 percent of the costs (Eisenhammer 1995: 7).

Until 1992, the government pursued a policy of moderate tax increases (tobacco, insurance, petrol, telephone). A solidarity token of 3.75 percent of one's income tax had to be paid by all employees in 1991 and 1992. By 1992 it became clear that these revenues amounted to only 23 percent of the required transfer payments to the East (*Der Spiegel*, April 27, 1992: 20). Subsequently, the political rhetoric evolved around mutual accusations of responsibility between the respective economic actors. Employers argued for cuts in wages, and trade unions for increased taxes on business profits, while federal, state, and local authorities blamed each other for excessive spending. It became obvious that the unforeseeable costs of unification and of the reorganization of the Eastern economy caught political and economic elites by surprise. By 1995, the government had reintroduced the solidarity token with a rate of 7.5 percent, with an envisaged reduction to 5.5 percent by 1998.

In contrast to governmental authorities and economic analysts, East Germans initially were more realistic as to the amount of time it would require to approximate living conditions between East and West. In the spring of 1990, Easterners sensed that it would take an average of seven years in order to reach the Western level of affluence (Förster and Roski 1990: 67).[4] Hence, only a small proportion of East Germans had the illusion that prosperity would come within a short period of time. From early on in the unification process people had already realized that the economic gap between East and West was far too wide to allow for a rapid approximation of living standard.

However, in the early days of unification the political rhetoric gave the impression of historic and challenging but nevertheless manageable task. In the run-up to the federal elections in December 1990, Chancellor Kohl's promise of blossoming landscapes earned him considerable support in the new *Länder* and was taken as a promise. The political rhetoric that the market economy could single-handedly finance the colossal transformation processes fostered a mixture of naïveté and optimism. Decisions were determined by political pressure to seize the historic opportunity of unification. Thus, decisive measures, such as the approximation of wages and the conversion of the *Ostmark* were made hastily, regardless of their economic consequences. This initial positive outlook on the manageability of unification left the public in both East and West ill-prepared for the enormous task of unification, including economic restructuring, unemployment, and financial burdens.

At first glance, the East presented a functioning economy. This, however, was achieved only through massive transfer payments. The new *Länder* were the most subsidized region in the world. In 1993 alone, Eastern Germany received between DM 150 and 180 billion (Gensicke 1994: 806). The discrepancy was further documented by the striking difference between productivity of the Eastern economy and personal spending. In 1994 domestic consumption exceeded production by DM 150 billion (Eisenhammer 1995: 7). With the approximation of wages and the advantageous *Ostmark* conversion, Easterners benefited directly from unification.

Nonetheless, expectations regarding the speed and practicability of unification were increasingly out of proportion. Impatience in the East was accompanied by ignorance in the West. The aversion against unification grew steadily. In 1991, two-thirds of all Westerners sensed that the limit of acceptable financial burdens had been reached (*Der Spiegel*, January 18, 1993: 53). Although West Germans regarded the collapse of Communism as a unique chance in history, they were not willing to confront the upcoming and foreseeable financial and economic burden. In the East, 72 percent of respondents in 1992 were dissatisfied with the approximation of living conditions (*Politbarometer*). By the end of 1994, the figure was still considerably high at 64 percent. Supporters for the neo-Communist PDS, as well as the middle generation between 25 and 40 years old were particularly critical.[5]

This widespread dissatisfaction can be explained by the prevalent practice of comparing the current economic situation with the much higher level of prosperity in Western Germany, but not with the status quo of the old GDR or of other ex-Communist countries. This seemed rather logical behavior, since the FRG represented a blueprint of life for the people in the former GDR. For decades, East Germans watched enviously the increasing material wealth as expressed on Western TV and as displayed by Western visitors. By the 1980s, the growing number of tourist visas issued by the state provided for an additional hands-on experience of life in the West. West German standards and images of prosperity had already penetrated East Germany prior to the revolution and served as a normative focal point. Since the orientation toward Western levels of affluence was one of the contributing factors that brought down the SED regime, the continuous comparison and evaluation in the aftermath of 1989 seemed only logical, in particular since the political and economic principles that created the Western material wealth were now introduced to the East. Thus, the salary gap between East and West caused widespread bewilderment and dissatisfaction. Over a period of 31 months, the figures of disapproval hardly changed. In February 1991, 85 percent and still 79 percent in November 1993 considered the wage difference unjust (*Politbarometer*). Easterners, however, realized that their personal situation had improved. In 1992 47 percent evaluated their economic standard as better in comparison to the days of the GDR (*Politbarometer*). By 1994, the figures had increased to a solid 54 percent, and only 19 percent claimed that they fared worse.

The blame for the economic malaise was directed against the economic and political elites who orchestrated the change. In 1993 78 percent and still 75 percent in 1994, thought that *Bonn* was not doing enough for the equalization of living conditions between East and West (*Politbarometer*).[6] The same applied to West German managers, where 88 percent agreed that measures by Western industries were not sufficient (*Politbarometer*). The work of the *Treuhand* was perceived even more critically. In 1992, 92 percent held the opinion that the *Treuhand* did not fulfill its task properly (*Politbarometer*). A year later, the figure rose to 94 percent. In the East, the *Treuhand* became the symbol of merciless Western capitalism, Western arrogance and colonization. Rohwedder's successor Birgit Breuel acknowledged the scapegoat function of the agency and stated that "for four years we protected the backs of the politicians by taking unpopular decisions" (Eisenhammer 1995: 7). Furthermore, Easterners developed the notion that they alone had to carry the burden of unification while the rich Western neighbor showed a rather indifferent attitude. In January 1993, 68 percent of the Eastern population agreed that West Germans, despite their material wealth, had not learned to share. Only 16 percent acknowledged that unification represented a great burden to Westerners, while 33 percent sensed that the financial load for the West was minimal (*Der Spiegel*, January 18, 1993: 58).

Work Mentality

After decades of centralized, planned economics that fostered obedience and conditioned a lack of initiative, imagination, and flexibility, the new arrival of the market economy demanded a radical reorientation for East German employees. Self-reliance, risk-taking, and individual decisionmaking often came as novel concepts. How did the individual adapt to these new requirements in the sphere of work? In his play *Waiting Room Germany* author Klaus Pohl interviewed a Western insurance manager who was sent east to set up a new office. The manager complained bitterly about a traditional working ethos that persisted as a legacy of Communism. His colleagues went to the hairdresser during working hours, showed severe deficiencies in the polite handling of customer relations, and were in general overwhelmed by the new demands of taking responsibility and showing independence.

By the same token, the "Federal Association of Independent Businesses" (*Bundesverband mittelständischer Wirtschaft*) referred to a deficit in managerial qualities. In 1995, according to its bureau in Potsdam, entrepreneurial shortcomings lay in the realms of sales and internal organization, as well as hortatory and contract proceedings. The development of an entrepreneur culture still lagged drastically behind Western standards. People were hesitant to take economic risks and to invest. The ability to "think big" regarding horizontal and vertical expansion was pushed aside by a traditional, minimalist, and safeguarding approach, perfectly exemplified in the old German proverb of "*Schuster bleib bei Deinen Leisten*" (stick to your last).

A study for the employment ministry of the state of Saxony-Anhalt by the Eastern-based *Institut für sozialwissenschaftliche Informationen und Studien* ("Isis") largely substantiated such perceptions. Held in 1995, the study asked Eastern business executives of 2,000 small and medium-sized businesses to rank entrepreneurial skills. The study revealed substantial managerial deficiencies.[7] "Isis" showed the prevalence of such traditional values as diligence, sense of duty, honesty, and reliability. Crucial entrepreneurial skills, such as creativity, flexibility, compromise, and willingness to take risks, however, were lacking. Proper market analyses were missing in two-thirds of the queried enterprises, as were innovation and emphasis on the development of future products. Only 20 percent employed trainees, which pointed toward a lack of commitment to vital investment in personnel and training. Cooperation with other businesses was hardly established. Instead of having recourse to former Socialist contacts in order to enhance regional economic structures, 60 percent of the respondents simply had no intention to do so. Instead, the Eastern manager was characterized by a high degree of social competence, who valued amiable social relations.

However, the Eastern work mentality was by no means as bleak as suggested by these accounts. Over the short period of merely five years since the currency reform, Easterners showed a remarkable potential to adapt to market economic standards. The high number of new businesses furthermore indicated a strong dynamic to face the challenges of the transition, in particular the prospect of unemployment. "Isis" itself pointed toward the high degree of motivation of young entrepreneurs who were supported by a strong desire for self-responsibility and self-realization. Moreover, the Eastern manager was characterized by a preparedness to accept personal hardship, such as long working hours and low income, in order to uphold their businesses. In an East-West comparison, the Eastern employee possessed a higher working morale than his or her Western counterpart. A study by Emnid in 1994 (*Informationen 7/8*: 72–76) demonstrated that the sense of duty and commitment of Easterners within their working environment not only met but more often exceeded Western standards. Longer breaks, calling in sick, illicit work, and arriving late were particular attitudes that were more discredited by East Germans. Even if lack of initiative, self-reliance, and flexibility—as criticized by "Isis" and the *Bundesverband mittelständischer Wirtschaft*—undermined the East Germans' performance at work, commitment and a sense of duty certainly represented valuable attitudes that no enterprise could do without (see Table 3.2).

Unemployment

Economic restructuring carried the heavy burden of a dramatic decrease in overall employment. Since the GDR had a job guarantee for every citizen, uni-

Table 3.2
Ranking of Entrepreneurial Skills Among East German Managers (1995)

Skill	Male	Female
reliability	1	1
responsibility	1	2
diligence	3	5
sense of duty	4	3
honesty	5	4
determination	6	6
decision making	7	9
optimism	8	12
self-confidence	9	11
thoroughness	10	7
establishing social contacts	11	8
ability to prevail	12	15
rigidity	13	15
vision	14	18
thriftiness	15	17
creativity	16	15
intuition	17	10
willingness to compromise	18	20
flexibility	19	19
willingness to take risks	20	21
orderliness	21	14

Source: Press Office, Ministry for Employment, Social Affairs and Health, Saxony-Anhalt, August 1995.

fication revealed formerly hidden unemployment of overstaffed enterprises. With unification, excessive manpower was drastically reduced. By sector, manufacturing was affected most, with a decrease of 60 percent. Mining and energy (39 percent) and services (22 percent) also had severe reductions. Only in construction did the number of jobs increase by 10 percent (Kocka 1994: 181). High profile investments by Elf, Siemens, or Opel (the German subsidiary of General Motors), which were all supported by heavy government inducements, could by no means compensate for such heavy reductions.

Between 1991 and 1994 the number of employees dropped from 9.3 to 6.6 million. The degree of unemployment occasionally reached higher levels than the depression years of the late 1920s and early 1930s. The disproportion of unemployment between East and West was striking. In 1994, figures reached 17 percent in the new *Länder* and 9 percent in the old Federal Republic. A year later the gap had not disappeared, with 16 percent in the East and 9 percent in the West. Moreover, between 40 and 50 percent of all Eastern employees had experienced unemployment at one stage since unification. These figures did not include migrants and commuters to the West, those who registered for public work schemes or retraining courses, and early pensioners who in 1993 alone totaled some 600,000 (Sakowsky 1994: 118).

At the outset of unification, Easterners were largely positive about their material and social future. In April 1990 respondents were queried about their personal perspective for the next two to three years and were asked to place them into four categories from highly optimistic to highly pessimistic. Regarding employment, the two categories for optimism totaled 67 percent. In addition, the responses for material situation (63 percent) and social security (61 percent) were also largely positive (Förster and Roski 1990: 84). In contrast, unequivocal pessimism was expressed by only 7 percent (employment) and 6 percent (material situation and social security). Over the course of the year, discomfort, in particular about the security of employment, grew. In December 1990, 59 percent sensed that their job was in danger. Only 40 percent were sure about keeping their employment (*Politbarometer*). Two years later, however, the proportion had reversed. Now 55 percent perceived their job as secure and only 44 percent feared unemployment. Between 1992 and 1994, figures did not improve. The percentage of East German respondents who were uncertain about their employment future remained at around 40 percent.[8] Hence, a considerable proportion of the Eastern work force perceived their employment prospects as worrying and as a leap into the dark. Not surprisingly, Easterners, confronted with the loss of jobs and with a sudden reorientation toward more demanding and skilled work performance, as well as often toward an entirely different working environment, became increasingly critical of "Capitalism." Whereas support for "Socialism" remained at constant levels,[9] the approval of the market economy among East Germans dropped drastically, from 77 percent in the spring of 1990 to only 44 percent in the summer of 1992 (Eisel 1994: 160).

For East Germans, still used to the tight social net of Socialism that provided for jobs and a steady income, the sudden confrontation with unemployment and financial insecurity was harsh and devastating. For those without jobs, a feeling of betrayal and exclusion from the material benefits and the increasing prosperity around them became prevalent. The sudden changes in the sphere of work, fear of unemployment, and increasing competitiveness for jobs had drastic implications on the individual's life and found their expression in a general perception that one's social relations to friends or family were worse than in the days of the GDR. In 1992, only 5 percent of Eastern respondents sensed that the relations within their social environment had improved since unification. On the contrary, 44 percent held the opinion that things got worse (*Politbarometer*). Moreover, between 1992 and 1994 around two-thirds regarded their social security as being worse as compared to the days of the GDR (*Politbarometer*).

The former stable and foreseeable circles of work, family, and friends were now under pressure. Demographic statistics undermined the perceptions of change and uncertainty. Between 1989 and 1993 the birth rate of Eastern Germany had fallen by 60 percent, the marriage rate by 62 percent, and the divorce rate by 63 percent (Statistical Yearbook 1995: 69–70, 79). These drops can to some extent be explained by the reduction in certain social services, such as affordable child care facilities and day nurseries or the abolition of the "baby year" (maternity leave granted to first-time mothers at full pay). In addition, unemployment had a disproportionate effect on women. In 1990, 54 percent of the unemployed in the East were female. By 1994, the figure had risen to 63 percent (Statistical Yearbook 1994: 130), with the effect that family and marriage plans were often postponed. Still, such vast changes are extremely rare and find no comparable expression in Western Germany or in any other western society. Instead, they represented strong indicators for the transitory, unstable, and imbalanced life in the East.

CONCLUDING REMARKS

Economics had an ambivalent connotation in the GDR. On the one hand, the country's status as the champion of the Comecon represented a significant source of pride among East Germans. On close scrutiny, however, economics was a source of continuous frustration. In comparison with the West, people all but ignored the fundamental deficiencies of their own system and the increasing wealth that prospered outside the Iron Curtain. Economic stagnation, mismanagement, the outdated reliance on heavy industry, and growing ecological problems prompted resignation and embitterment. Internal comparisons to other Communist societies merely functioned as temporary remedies for the battered collective self-esteem that tried to restrain the thought that years of struggle and hard labor had resulted only in minor economic and material accomplishments.

In contrast, economics had a very positive connotation in the Federal Republic. The economic miracle brought widespread prosperity. West Germany was united under the principle of material reconstruction that safeguarded the integration of millions of refugees and silenced potential anti-democratic opponents. The necessity to establish a formative focus after the catastrophe of the Third Reich resulted in a highly consensual economic system. Inevitably, it generated a good deal of conformism to the principles of economic success and general prosperity.

With unification, economics continued to possess a negative undertone for Easterners. The deadbeat state of the Eastern economy rubbed further salt into the wounds that, in retrospect, decades of hard work constituted only a period of failure and underachievement. The Eastern economy did not represent a contribution but a mere burden to the unified Germany. The introduction of market principles destroyed any remaining sources of pride. Production and productivity dropped, overstaffed enterprises were restructured, and unemployment spread. The necessary investments in roads, railways, communication, or housing further documented the discrepancy between Western standards and Eastern shortcomings. East Germans had to confront the bitter reality that one's past working life did not pass the Western test of time. Instead, it was an utter failure. There remained a solution, however, in looking ahead and leaving the past behind. Here, unification provided for exciting and optimistic prospects. The choice and variety of goods grew dramatically and people increasingly had the money to purchase them. For those with jobs, the financial situation improved and was evaluated in a positive manner. Only five years after unification, East Germans had already reached a level of considerable contentment with their material situation.

This new-found affluence, however, was an automatic and subsidized given from the political elites. East Germans were lulled into prosperity. The so-called *Aufschwung Ost* (Progress East) changed the economic landscape of the new *Länder*. Public funds were allocated for governmental projects and investment. As with the former Communist regime, Easterners were passive recipients. The economy of the GDR with the principles of centralism, nationalization, and planning suppressed self-responsibility and independence. The individual was a streamlined underling, excluded from participation and responsibility in the economic process. Just as the Communist system was imposed on East Germany, so was the market. In each case, East Germans were the passive "victims" without choice. This was bound to create a rather inactive economic identity. Prior to unification, the blame for general economic deficiencies was directed against an abstract and inefficient centralized apparatus. Now, political elites, Western industries and business people, and foremost the *Treuhand*, had to bear the brunt of public discontent. The mechanism remained the same: blaming distant authorities. As with the old days, the individual did not attribute responsibility to him- or herself but to the apparatus, to the elites who organized and determined one's working life.

Back in the GDR, work performance did not necessarily determine social and material status. Ideological compliance played as much a role. The absence of efficient incentives to work more and harder accounted for a lack of cognitive commitment to work. Work was not a sphere for self-realization but a financial necessity and a duty to the state. Initiative came from above and not out of personal ambition. The worker was a mere tool and means of production within the economic process, utilized by the totalitarian system. These perceptions of the mechanisms of one's working life lingered on in the new *Länder*. Again, economics was regarded as a utilization of the individual by elites and authorities: opportunistic business people from the West bought Eastern companies in search for the quick money while disregarding local needs, in particular employment. The post-unification battles over property further manifested people's impression of a colonization of the East by merciless Western capitalism. Easterners were overwhelmed by market principles, their firms degraded to investment opportunities, their jobs made redundant, their social safety being threatened.

Such attitudes were in sharp contrast to those generated during the successful economic miracle of the FRG. Work represented a formative focus and an affirmative experience for the individual who was thriving for financial success and craving for social recognition. Responsibility lay with the individual, capable of determining his or her own life. In the new *Länder*, such inbred notions of democracy and capitalism as activity and self-realization clashed with the conditioned passive and recipient mentality of the Communist years. The active compelling urge to perform collided with the passive notion of provision. Subsequently, the frustration and anger caused by the post-unification economic malaise was channeled into expressions of defiance and lamentation, such as perceptions of a colonization and exploitation by the West, as well as the discomfort with the persisting gaps in wages and living standards. In addition, the nature of Socialist economics generated cognitive and behavioral patterns, which left East Germans ill-equipped for the upcoming transformation to a market economy. The strict hierarchy of the GDR's economic structure with rigid top-down patterns of planning and target fulfillment severely hampered the individual's capacity regarding imagination and flexibility. It nurtured apathy, lethargy, and self-complacency, as well as tutelage and the readiness to obey and oblige. Furthermore, the streamlined educational apparatus fostered an urge to conformity, compliance, and accommodation within the totalitarian system and suppressed individuality and motivation to change. Upon unification, such skills were badly missed in a market environment that thrived on competition and competitiveness and where initiative, individuality, independence, and constant readjustment were paramount principles. The underdeveloped entrepreneur culture as well as the general difficulties of the labor force in adapting to new working environments and demands served as telling examples.

Nonetheless, East Germans also showed remarkable signs of adaptation. The presence of an attitude to succeed within the free market—whether out of personal ambition or of financial necessity caused by the prospect of unemployment—was documented by the committed and conscientious work ethic and the readiness to commute or move to the West for better employment opportunities.[10] Departing from a life on the beaten track of the Communist society, people left well-established social circles and readjusted to an unfamiliar environment. These were promising signs which indicated that Easterners would eventually muster the mental transition to market-economic standards. Skills are learned over time. They, however, have to be preceded by the individual's willingness to acquire them.

With unification, the value of work underwent a drastic reorientation. In the GDR, employment represented a constitutional right and a natural given that was automatically organized by the state. Under Communism, work had no particular value. Every citizen was entitled to it. Identities that were constructed around employment, such as self-realization in the private sphere or social contacts with colleagues, were not seen as arising out of any individual achievements at work. West Germany, however, was the reverse. Individual work performance had an indisputable impact on one's social and material status. The severe job cuts in Eastern Germany, therefore, came as a shock. Unemployment was an entirely new experience that now affected up to half of the labor force. Thus, it came as little wonder that approximately two-thirds of the Eastern population regarded unemployment as the most important issue in their lives (Gensicke 1994: 802). A lifetime guarantee turned into a never before experienced feeling of existentialist uncertainty. Self-contentment and complacency about work were now replaced by demands to show initiative in finding new jobs, in acquiring new qualifications, and in improving work performances. Disorientation and loss of self-esteem were the consequences.

In the realm of social services, the GDR citizen internalized an extensive system of comprehensive care at minimal costs. The welfare state that provided security from cradle to grave achieved a high standard among Easterners and was gradually taken for granted. As with work, people developed a recipient mentality. In contrast, the Federal Republic did not offer an automatic guarantee against social misfortunes. The *Sozialstaat* constituted more of a normative focus for the state than a prerogative for people's demands. It therefore came as no surprise that Easterners perceived general living circumstances as harder now than in the days of the GDR. Progressive social services were abolished and old routines broke down. Vast demographic pressures indicated the feeling of uncertainty. They showed that the collapse of the GDR was not merely the demise of a system but, moreover, the collapse of a particular form of life. Against the backdrop of such dramatic changes, the growing criticism of Capitalism and the persistent support for Socialism was inevitable. The transformation from secure and infantilized recipient to self-responsible individual was too harsh and too rapid. Faced with social and financial risks and uncertainties, the retrospective attachment to a safe and secure past represented a logical emotional escape.

Nonetheless, several positive developments allowed for cautious optimism. Satisfaction with one's personal financial situation represented a vital systemic stabilizer. People realized that they benefited from the introduction of the market economy and that they fared far better in comparison to the days of the GDR. Despite some depressing economic facts, in particular unemployment, there was no major social unrest. The hardship caused by the decline in social services and unemployment, as well as new working requirements and environments, seemed to have been outweighed by material gains for those who were able to secure jobs. Furthermore, despite the euphoria at the outset of unification, Easterners initially showed a great deal of realism regarding their employment prospects and the approximation of living standards. Individual prognoses about one's future were far more accurate than contemporary statements of political and economic experts (Wagner 1992: 85). Such realism prevented overambitious material demands from unification and provided a cognitive buffer of acceptance of the persistent gap in the approximation of living standards between East and West. Also despite the shock of encountering a hitherto unknown phenomenon, the early familiarization with the possibility of unemployment psychologically prepared East Germans for the actual experience of it.

Still, the economic identity in unified Germany stood on shaky ground. The transition from Socialist to market structures significantly contributed to the growing antagonism between East and West. The two-class society continued to exist and manifested itself. Despite some impressive advances, wages, living standard and employment opportunities, the East had not reached Western levels. Such economic inequalities bore the dangerous potential to heighten psychological discontent (Stern 1993: 121). Anti-Western sentiments emerged and did not fade, such as the perceived colonization and exploitation, merciless capitalism, and Western indifference to Eastern problems. Positive evaluations of East Germans were largely attributable to the increase in the material well-being of the population, in comparison to the Communist period. This, however, was only made possible through massive governmental subsidies. Before unification, Easterners followed the call of the *Deutschmark*. After unification, they were kept on life support by billions in transfer money. This approval of the Western-imposed market economy could only be maintained through the continuous improvement of the individual's material basis. Thus, the expectations of East Germans regarding material standards have to be met by increases in job opportunities and levels of affluence. Hence, the Eastern economy has to progress from a subsidized case of illness to an economically sound region. People at least have to be given the prospect of advancing material standards to complete unification in economic terms. Only then are Easterners capable of developing a positive orientation toward economics that would equal that of the Western part. Only then can recipient mentalities, passivity, frustration, and embitterment turn into affirmative experiences in the sphere of work, including the development of notions of initiative, self-realization, and self-fulfillment. East Germans had already shown supportive attitudes toward market economics. The persistence of defiant notions, however, indicated the fragility of the collective psyche.

NOTES

1. Labor relations were characterized by a progressive system of collective bargaining with the mediation of a third and neutral party, as well as by *Mitbestimmung* (co-determination of the work force), whereas trade-union representatives were granted seats on company boards.

2. The Federal Office for Employment (*Bundesanstalt für Arbeit;* BfA) offered training and vocational rehabilitation and possessed a monopoly on mediating vacant positions. Publicly funded projects (*Arbeitsbeschaffungsmaßnahmen;* ABM) created further jobs, while advancing the qualification levels of the participants.

3. The agency is still in operation, albeit on a much smaller scale. One of its successor organizations, the *Bundesanstalt für vereinigungsbedingte Sonderaufgaben,* is responsible for supervising contractual obligations made by purchasers of sold businesses. As a second successor, the *Beteiliungs-Management Gesellschaft* supervises the remaining enterprises that have not been privatized (Eckart 1995: 585).

4. The responses differed only slightly according to age or party allegiances, with the margin of answers lying between 6.5 and 8 years.

5. In October 1994, for instance, dissatisfaction amongst PDS supporters amounted to 82 percent. For those between 25 and 40, disapproval rates rose to 70 percent (age 25 to 29) and 68 percent (age 30 to 39).

6. PDS supporters and respondents between ages 25 and 50 were particularly critical. In October 1994, for instance, dissatisfaction amongst PDS supporters totaled 91 percent. For those between ages 25 and 50, disapproval rates amounted to 82 percent (age 25 to 29) and 81 percent (age 40 to 49).

7. Information according to Saxony-Anhalt's Ministry of Employment, Social Affairs and Health, Press Office, August 1995.

8. According to age cohorts differences were marginal. Those 50 to 59 years old were slightly less and people over 60 years slightly more secure.

9. The cumulated data of the *Politbarometer* for 1990 showed that 28 percent of respondents thought "much" or "very much" of Socialism. By 1994, the figure had increased slightly to 30 percent.

10. In 1990, some 200,000 commuted to work from East to West. By 1993, the number had risen to 600,000, only to drop slightly to 550,000 a year later (*Source:* Press Office, *Bundesanstalt für Arbeit*).

4

Citizenship

Citizenship can be understood as the relationship between the individual and the political community he or she lives in. The citizen is entitled to a variety of rights and privileges in return for a set of duties and responsibilities. The state offers its citizens political, legal, civil, and social rights, while the individual is expected to obey laws, pay taxes, or fulfill military duties. This interdependence forms a vital anchor for the establishment of loyalties and emotions. What are the citizen's attitudes and emotions to his or her political community? Can the individual form an identity toward the state out of willingly accepted responsibilities and confidently claimed rights?

Rights and responsibilities within state-citizen relations were fundamentally different in the two Germanys. The official political culture of the GDR (Rytlewski 1989: 22, Krisch 1988: 158) was derived from the principles of Marxism-Leninism that transcended and penetrated all spheres of life and society. At the core of this *Zielkultur* stood the development of a Socialist and eventually Communist society, based on such values as optimism, solidarity, studiousness, freedom, equality, and social justice, and created by the "new Socialist man," who went through a lifelong process of ideologically conditioned and state organized education (Sontheimer 1990: 61).

This philanthropic view of the SED—the optimistic belief in the possibility of educating man toward a utopian goal—resulted in extremely high demands and expectations from the citizens of the GDR. East Germans were forced to accept the state doctrine of Marxism-Leninism as the ideological basis of their political, social, and economic lives. They were obliged to accept the leading role of the SED including its normative interpretations of all aspects of society. They had to accept the competence and responsibility of the state in all political, social, and economic matters that were limited only by the leadership function of the SED. The citizen was expected to show interest and engage in political and social organizations under the dogmatic and practical guidance of the party. Demands also included a personal commitment to economic growth and the improvement of individual technical skills, as well as military duties.

Collective matters possessed priority over private and individual interests. The supreme goal of the GDR was represented in the creation of a new and better society. The envisaged development of the Socialist toward the Communist society depended on the active and voluntary cooperation and engagement of self-sacrificing individuals which required a firm, rational, and emotional commitment to the Communist cause.

Hence, state-citizen relations in the GDR followed rigid top-down patterns. The individual was expected, even coerced, to participate. The Communist party's monopoly on the interpretation and implementation of Marxist principles was justified by Lenin out of its "avant-garde" position within society as the leader of the revolution. Only the party possessed the political conscience and scientific knowledge to lead society toward the logical end-point of historical development—the Communist society. In contrast, democracy, and hence the Federal Republic, possessed fundamentally different values of citizenship. While the Communist society emphasized collectivity, democracy stresses individuality.

Greek philosophers paid particular attention to direct participation of the individual in the political process. Within the liberal tradition of Montesquieu, James Madison, Adam Smith, or John Locke sovereignty lies within the people, circumscribing the power of the state. Rousseau argued for an enlightened citizenry, individual liberty, and accountable governments. Even the elitist philosopher Schumpeter (1992: 269), who viewed democracy as an "institutional arrangement where individuals acquire decision-making power in a competitive struggle for the people's vote," cannot but emphasize the individual within the political process. Today, while neo-conservative thinkers point toward deferential and orderly behavior, and liberal theorists stress active participation in public and community affairs, democracy in either conception offers the individual the opportunity for active engagement in political affairs.

Thus, citizenship in unified Germany required the individual to pursue an active, informed and conscious interest in public affairs. As a normative standard, the ideal citizen had to be knowledgeable, concerned, supportive, and participative to his or her social community.[1] In reality, however, the common citizen represents only an unsatisfactory approximation to this ideal. Societies have to accept that various circumstances remove the individual from such normative virtues. This perfect model is simply not a part of any political reality. Obstacles may include access to information, knowledge, time pressure, or differing intellectual capacities. Also, the demands of liberal democracy for the individual's initiative and self-responsibility can be counteractive to the citizenship ideal in regard to the well-being of the whole society and the sublimation of selfishness.

But how do these deviations affect the stability of the political system? An answer can be given by analyzing the causes that made a citizen pass off citizenship attributes. Someone who cheats on income-tax declarations does not necessarily want to abolish democracy. Danger occurs, however, when the principles of citizenship are surrendered to anti-democratic ideological objectives and political party advantages, or when loyalty and allegiance to a democratic community turn into destructive disobedience or antipathy. Here the question of legitimacy of the political system enters the agenda. In the GDR, Marxism-Leninism offered legitimacy to the SED regime, since the party in its vanguard position possessed the Communist conscience and scientific knowledge to lead in the revolutionary process of establishing the Communist society. For the young *Bonn* Republic growing support for democratic institutions and parlamentarism, as well as high turnouts at elections, represented strong processes of legitimation for the recently established democracy. In both societies, however, the quest for a stable political community became one of acceptance of the political system by the individual. As the SED had to realize in 1989, form of government and political organization of society were only well-established as long as the political system enjoyed a certain degree of legitimacy among the citizens. Max Weber viewed legitimacy as equivalent to a belief in legitimacy. Legitimate power is simply the power that is regarded as legitimate by the people (1958: 493). Seymour Martin Lipset (1958: 88) defined legitimacy as the "capacity of the system to engender and maintain the belief that the existing political institutions are the most appropriate one's for society."

Weber and Lipset emphasized the ability of states or governments to persuade citizens of the legitimate nature of the political system in a top-down process. In contrast, David Beetham (1991: 100) stressed the importance of a society's values and rules. A government can only be successful if it represents a rightful source of authority, while its action meets consent within society and is based on established legal rules. Here the pattern is one of interaction between top and down, between ruler and ruled. In either case the emphasis is on the positive and meaningful identification of the citizen with the rules and principles of the political community. This implies that the individual's thought and behavior should be guided by a constitutional consensus that, in unified Germany, included agreement on parlamentarism, acceptance of political institutions, and respect for human rights and civic liberties (dignity, equality, freedom of expression and belief). Additionally, in a democratic system a proper mediation between ruler and ruled holds center stage. The citizen is entitled to an adequate aggregation and representation of interest. The governing elite ought to maintain reasonable contact with its subjects, which provides for a mutual exchange of information, ideas, and demands. Regarding the legitimacy of the system, it remains vital that the citizen possess the capacity, or at least is given the prospect of influencing the decision-making process.

In short, in the understanding of this chapter, participation and legitimacy represent the cornerstones of citizenship. In the context of unified Germany the public's general knowledge of and interest in the political process are analyzed, as are participation patterns in East and West, including turnouts at elections and membership in political parties, interest groups, or citizen initiatives. The question of legitimacy of the new democratic system is examined with the help of public attitudes toward the state, while asking whether East Germans had accepted the institutional setting of democracy and whether their thought and behavior complied with the implicit values and rules of democracy. The chapter therefore addresses attitudes toward the bureaucracy, political actors, and institutions. Mediation of power between ruler and ruled is analyzed by looking at attitudes toward the system of interest representation, while trying to examine the extent to which East Germans felt at all represented.

THE GERMAN DEMOCRATIC REPUBLIC

Marxism-Leninism understands politics as the relationship between various classes of society and the political power of the state. Generally speaking, the state serves the ruling class: the capital-owning bourgeoisie in the Capitalist and the working class in the Socialist society. In a Marxist-Leninist state the individual has to submit all private ambitions to the paramount interest of society which is formulated through the avant-garde role of a Communist party. To define and redefine the proper needs and interests of a Socialist society, a constant and reverse exchange of ideas between party and citizens is necessary. Marxism-Leninism therefore requires the "new Socialist man"—an active participant in the political process with a permanent interest and eagerness in creating the Communist utopia.

The SED regime gave this participatory role of citizens strong legal status. The constitution of 1968 proposed a hefty moral commitment to every citizen by stating the principle of "contribution to working, planning and governing." The SED demanded not only an active but furthermore an affirmative participation in the development of the Communist society. The new Socialist man, educated and guided by ideologically sound agents, should willingly contribute. His or her efforts should not be based on coercion but on reason and understanding of the individual's responsibility in the general development of society. But how did the theoretical and normative concept of the participative, informed, and affirmative citizen correspond to the political reality of the GDR? What were the opportunities and chances of each individual to exert an influence on the political process?

Participation

The SED had a strong base within society. In 1981, 17 percent of all people over age 25 and even 42.5 percent over age 40 owned a party membership card. As of 1986, the SED had 2.3 million members which equaled around one-sixth of the total population. The membership base was broad and covered all segments of society. A political career within the SED hugely depended on an ideologically sound performance. A move toward influential political positions was manipulated and controlled by the hierarchical structures of the Communist party or its political and societal mass organizations and appointments were made after a certain period of SED membership. The demands of the party upon its members were striking. They had to be moral and professional role models, both at work and in the private sphere. The comrade was asked to represent the SED in all aspects of life, to forego private and uphold party interests. The SED did not accept members, but instead recruited them. It required two sponsors and a one-year probation period in which the candidate was instructed in his or her duties and responsibilities. The judgment of the party apparatus was final. The way in which the party member performed within the SED structures affected his or her life, not only on the political level but also professionally and socially (Zimmermann 1988: 237).

From its beginning the SED followed the example of the Soviet KP. In 1949, the *Politbüro* was installed, which crafted all political guidelines and basic principles and decided upon their implementation. It constituted the true government of the GDR. Resolutions made by its members had the character of laws (H. Weber 1993: 73). The centralized power of the *Politbüro* was complemented by the Secretariat of the Central Committee, which represented the SED's central organ to control both party and party members and secure their conformity with the guidelines set forth by the *Politbüro*. By eliminating any form of inner-party democracy and interest aggregation, social, political, and economic decisions were exclusively undertaken by the SED elite. With the help of the hierarchical party apparatus they were able to govern the GDR in a totalitarian, oligarchic fashion. The SED did not allow any form of power sharing. Instead, it oppressed pluralism and reached a position of comprehensive, all-embracing, dictatorial, and uncontrolled rule (H. Weber 1993: 98). The GDR gave a classic example of democratic centralism, with a strict party discipline and a rigid hierarchy of all party organs. Control commissions safeguarded the ideological purity of all organizations which had to be in line with the principles set forth by the party. The vanguard role of the SED implied that the party and only the party had the right and knowledge to transfer and interpret Marxism-Leninism into practice. The SED derived its legitimation from an ideology that was deemed to be perfect. Inputs from below were therefore unnecessary and even damaging, because the party was the sole guardian of the ideology. Thus, politics and policies were grounded in the scientific knowledge and application of Marxism-Leninism which led the SED to the conclusion that "the party is always right."

Such "monolithic unity" (H. Weber 1993: 32) was a fiercely safeguarded principle of the SED. Because of its central position in the political process, the party theoretically had to fulfill two opposing functions. On the one hand, it reflected the political spectrum of society. On the other, it brought together various strains and antagonisms within society. The SED escaped this functional ambivalence by denying open discourse and inter-party pluralism, while pursuing a path of purges and internal political cleanups. The demise of Stalin in 1953 sparked a reconsideration of Communist policies throughout the Eastern Bloc. In the GDR, prominent intellectuals, such as Ernst Bloch and

Robert Havemann, advocated a "third way" that criticized both Stalinism and Capitalism. The political establishment around Ulbricht, however, was keen to undermine any open discourse. Subsequently, the judiciary and the Ministry for State Security—nicknamed the *Stasi*—were engaged in purges and trials. By 1958 the opposition movement lost momentum, and the reactionary course manifested its superiority. In the end the Stalinist faction managed to eliminate any form of opposition. Opponents from within the party chose internal exile, were expelled to the FRG, or were imprisoned. Until 1989, the hegemony of the SED and its Stalinist principles remained unchallenged.

Apart from membership in the SED, the citizen was able to join various so called "block parties" (see Table 4.1). Closely watched by the Communist authorities, these parties had to submit themselves to the avant-garde role of the SED and its program as a compulsory guideline for their activities. The totalitarian regime established a new version of Communist rule in the form of a Socialist plural-party system, where block parties possessed an "alibi function" (H. Weber 1993: 33) by disguising the one-party rule of the SED. They represented valuable transmitting vehicles with the task of integrating "bourgeois" and religious groups, as well as "capitalist" classes into the Socialist society.

However, formulating and advocating political alternatives were absent from the block parties' political agenda. Again the SED did not allow any op-

Table 4.1
Membership in Block Parties (in thousands)

	1977	1982	1987
CDU (Christian Democratic Union)	115	125	137
LDPD (Liberal Democratic Party)	75	82	104
NDPD (National Democratic Party)	85	91	110
DBD (Democratic Farmer Party)	92	103	115

Source: H. Weber 1993: 93.

posing interests or policies. In the end, the role of the block parties was more social than political. They functioned as a structural part of the totalitarian regime, with hardly any intellectual or practical independence (Zimmermann 1988: 275).

As further means of mediating Communist concepts and programs to individual members, mass organizations were utilized to educate ideologically and control the citizens (see Table 4.2). Theoretically, they were designed to represent the interests of their members and to form a consultative, informative and critical source of information. In practice, however, interest articulation and

Table 4.2
Membership in Mass Organizations 1988

Organization	Membership
FDBG	9.6 million
FDJ	2.3 million (1986)
DFD	1.5 million
Kulturbund	277,000
Verein der gegenseitigen Bauernhilfe	646,000
Pionierorganisation Ernst Thälmann	1.5 million
Gesellschaft für deutsch-sowjetische Freundschaft	6.4 million
Volkssouveränität	2.1 million

Source: Statistical Yearbook 1989: 410, 412, 414.

aggregation again were dominated by top-down patterns, hierarchical structures and dogmatic biases.

Since 1949, the SED determined the organizations' political agenda as well as the recruitment to key positions. As with the block parties, all mass organizations were forced to accept the vanguard position of the SED unanimously (H. Weber 1993: 33). Mass organizations were vital components of the political system and were allocated seats in parliament. Their mediating and controlling function in society completed the totalitarian hegemony of the SED. The FDGB (*Freier Deutscher Gewerkschaftsbund*) represented the uniformed and all-encompassing organization for blue- and white-collar workers. The FDJ (*Freie Deutsche Jugend*) and its subsidiary, the pioneer organization *Ernst Thälmann*, were the only legal groups for younger people in the GDR. The DFD (*Demokratischer Frauenbund Deutschlands*) was founded to foster women's Socialist conscience and encourage active political participation. The *Kulturbund* was designed to support the development of a Socialist national culture, as well as to broaden the cultural horizon of its members in such fields as history of the *Heimat*, preservation of monuments, or nature and environment. The VdgB (*Verein der gegenseitigen Bauernhilfe*) was the Socialist mass organization for the collectivized farmer and gardener and promoted agricultural policies of the SED (Glaeßner 1989: 187–188).

Mass organizations were caught between the interest of the party and the interest of their members. Influential positions were staffed with high-level functionaries from the SED. The SED, however, expected ultimate obedience from its members. The interests of mass organizations were subordinated to those of the paramount party. Their functionaries therefore struggled between party discipline and pressure from the organization's base. Although participation in mass organizations was voluntary, it nevertheless represented an elementary condition to advance politically and professionally, as well as to gain social status (Zimmermann 1988: 267). For instance, for school children and university students membership in the FDJ was almost a prerequisite for later professional success and university placements. The complete structuring of all aspects of life through the help of mass institutions imposed the totalitarian principle on every individual in every aspect of his or her existence and assured the unchallenged supremacy of the SED.

The election process in the GDR resembled a general mobilization of the whole society rather than a conscious decision between political alternatives. The results were mostly predetermined. Political contents and procedures were controlled through directives of the Central Committee and the *Politbüro*. Elections represented mere agitational propaganda to show consent to a centrally-designed program and unity among the population. The electorate had to cast its vote openly. Pressures not to abstain or invalidate the ballot were immense. Not surprisingly, the turnout reached absurdly high figures. Approval votes for the unity list amounted to little below 100 percent. By simply looking at the vast number of refugees (see Chapter 2), the people's dissatisfaction with the political reality became evident and cast doubts on the legitimacy of elected representatives (H. Weber 1993: 31). Hence, elections in the GDR were symbolic actions. They did not guarantee but merely reflected participation. The "chosen" candidates possessed a mediating function. In Western democracies members of parliament and other elected officals are supposed to represent the interests of their constituents. In the GDR, however, the SED expected the elected representatives to encourge active participation and the fulfillment of party directives as well as to inform the state apparatus on public opinion in their constituencies. The representatives tried to stay actively involved in their communities and generally kept their jobs to provide closer social contact. However, suspicion against the party "big shot" who had a newer car and bigger house remained. Again, a reverse flow of information and interest was absent since top-down directives ruled over a discourse between base and elite.

With the establishment of the GDR in 1949, Christians had to confront severe pressure from the state. From the outset the SED attacked religion as a cultural trait and faith, as well as its institutions. Classic Marxism regarded the church as a representative of the ruling class with religion being the "opium of the people." As such, religion was erased from school curricula. With oppressive measures and indoctrination, in particular of the young, the SED believed it was able to systematically push back the influence of the churches. These tactics were the logical extension of the party's ambition for total control of society and the elimination of independent organizations. With the introduction of the *Jugendweihe* in 1954, the state further tried to undermine the churches' position in society. This secular confirmation service for 14-year-olds sought to supplant religious loyalties by an oath to Socialism, the GDR, and the Soviet Union (Cordell 1990: 49). Although not compulsory, refusal to participate in the *Jugendweihe* hampered educational and professional opportunities. Until the demise of the GDR up to 97 percent of the children participated in the *Jugendweihe* (Cordell 1990: 49).[2]

Eventually, the churches began to acknowledge the leading role of the SED and did not engage in ideological competition with state and party. In 1957, Evangelical churches in the GDR issued a statement of loyalty to the regime. In return the state guaranteed religious toleration (Cordell 1990: 50). Furthermore, in 1969 the Eastern Evangelical churches departed from the all-German umbrella organization EKD (*Evangelische Kirche Deutschlands*; Evangelical Church of Germany) and founded their own organizational unit, the BEK (*Bund der evangelischen Kirchen in der DDR*; Association of Evangelical Churches in the GDR). This move was welcomed by the SED since the BEK acknowledged the political reality of two separate German states. As the SED gradually withdrew from a policy of aggressive atheism, churches in East Germany were gradually able to establish themselves as the only legal autonomous organization that was independent from state and party. Throughout the existence of the GDR they remained the sole institutions that were disentangled from the principles of democratic centralism, while their principles and programs represented the only alternative to the SED-dominated political and cultural institutions.

Prior to the revolution, the Evangelical church provided the protection necessary to establish the civic movement. *Demokratie Jetzt* (Democracy Now) was established during a meeting of the BEK synod in Eisenach in September 1989. *Demokratischer Aufbruch* (Democratic Awakening) was co-founded by Pastor Rainer Eppelmann, who after the demise of the SED state became Disarmament Minister of the GDR. The Evangelical church offered a "sanctuary" (Cordell 1990: 55) for political and individual expression in an otherwise streamlined and stifled society. Leading clerics publicly addressed political problems and shortcomings (H. Weber 1993: 94), such as authoritative state-citizen relations, military training at school (*Wehrkunde*), propaganda, or censorship. From this perspective, the Evangelical church provided the basis for a political potential that was capable of initiating a peaceful revolution.

Although the significant contributions by the Evangelical church in sparking the revolution should not be underestimated, the BEK remained an institution that was pulled into politics as a surrogate for absent interest representation for which it ultimately was not suited. Increasingly the Evangelical church had to confront enormous difficulties in incorporating the various political groups, such as peace movements, feminists, and human rights activists, as well as maintaining its mediating function between state and society. Not only were these particular interest groups dependent on the protection of the church against authoritative seizures, but the church also found it extremely difficult to maintain a *modus vivendi* with the regime that would guarantee its autonomy. Hence, the BEK was forced to walk along a tightrope between appeasement of state and party, as well as the incorporation of an opposition movement which was directed precisely against the same authorities. In the end, the churches were able to survive only by avoiding a direct challenge to the regime. The BEK neither issued a single official stance against the regime nor did it help formulate opposition (Lease 1992: 269). Instead, the churches were institutionalized within the political system. Their autonomy was safeguarded by state and party since both recognized the vital importance of the churches as a release for tension and frustration. Thus, the churches did not constitute institutional outsiders of the system but were in fact an integral part of it.

Most importantly, churches were crippled by a massive loss in membership. Judging from the rate of secularization the SED had clearly won the battle between religion and Socialism. In 1946, around 80 percent of the population in the Eastern *Länder* were still Evangelical. By 1970, only 40 percent of East Germans retained membership. In 1986, the number of Evangelical followers had dropped to 30 percent of the populace. All religious denominations together, including around one million Catholics, totaled only 38 percent (Statistical Yearbook 1990: 451). The revolutionary upheavals of 1989 undoubtedly originated within the environment of the Evangelical church, and clerics such as Eppelmann and Stolpe personally shaped the unification process. However, the role of the Evangelical church was limited to the—quite literally—provision of space, as a site for "pluralistic thought" (Lease 1992: 269). It functioned as a meeting place for political opponents of the regime who had nowhere else to convene but within the sphere of the only autonomous organization of the GDR. Nonetheless, the BEK did not call for the downfall of the regime. It merely provided a hollow protective shell whose contents were ultimately filled by programs and demands that did not have their cognitive origins within the church.

State-Citizen Relations

The political process in the GDR was characterized by a strong distrust of the political maturity of the population. The failure and fatal experiences of other Eastern European countries in reforming their societies—the upheavals in Hungary and Poland in 1956, the end of the Prague spring in 1968, strikes and unraveling tendencies of the political system in Poland in the 1980s—as well as the paramount strategic position of the GDR and a vast presence of Soviet military forces, further manifested the suspicion of the totalitarian elite toward a more participatory involvement of its citizens. Throughout its forty-year-long hegemony, the SED vigorously defended its position of monopoly. The Ministry for State Security (*Stasi*) was established as early as 1950. An independent body, it was responsible only to the *Politbüro* (H. Weber 1993: 30). A far reaching web of informants and agents guaranteed an almost total observation of the entire society. The opening of the *Stasi* archives in the aftermath of 1989 revealed that the apparatus employed a full-time staff of 97,000 people, with perhaps as many as 170,000 unofficial informants (Golz 1994a: 344). From this source of sheer manpower, the *Stasi* was able to trace and eventually destroy any signs of opposition.

Further repression was exerted through direct intervention of the SED in the judicial process. Relying on the cadre principle, the party recruited judges and lawyers according to their ideological conformity. By the 1970s hardly any jurists came from outside the party ranks. Judicial independence was a myth. The *Politbüro* and Central Committee were directly involved in the crafting of bills in an evident attempt to adjust the law and the constitution to political circumstances. Party officials, including Honecker or Mielke, actively intervened in the jurisdiction by submitting their opinion on a particular case to the Director of Public Prosecutions. Additionally, criminal prosecution was mostly handled outside the realm of publicity to avoid repercussions on the growing international reputation of the GDR (Meyer-Seitz 1995: 32–33). Apart form these direct interventions, a variety of indirect measures restricted any notions of individuality. The strictly hierarchical organization and bureaucratization of society, the cycle of regulations, applications, and permissions, as well as the cadre principle guaranteed that any activity within the GDR—whether official or not—was controlled and supervised by the regime. Educational agencies, mass organizations, work brigades, and political parties safeguarded the principle of paternalism, as well as the conditioning and utilization of conforming followers, subjects, and obedient individuals. The party's monopoly on information resulted in a selective view of life. Not only was the citizen brainwashed with one-dimensional, ideologically-filtered information, but he or she was also excluded from certain information and ways to absorb it (see Chapter 5). Books and news were censored, travel permission granted only to ideologically sound citizens. Economic activity required the permission of state and party. Choice of employment and profession were limited. In the GDR there was no public arena for discussion or discourse. Opportunities to express individual demands were absent. The individual could only comply or be silent. The party's monopoly was total in qualitative and quantitative ways.

Against the powerful and centralized state and party apparatus, the individual possessed limited options for protest. However, complaints against bureaucratic procedures and petitions addressed to any institution of state or party were handled internally and no outside party was involved (Zimmermann 1988: 276). The SED state justified the oligarchic nature of the administrative process in an ideological manner. The Socialist state existed as a state for all people. It did not cater to special interests but realized the paramount interest of the whole Socialist society. Individual complaints could only be regarded as exceptions, which justified an internal handling of the matter. Individualism and the individual right to justice were superseded by the general interest of the Socialist society. Therefore, the classic Marxist-Leninist system that was preserved in the GDR excluded the idea of neutral arbitration as inherently impossible.

For more than 35 years the upheavals of June 1953 represented the last occasion when East Germans took their frustration and disillusionment with the regime to the streets. On June 17, strikes and demonstrations were held in more than 300 towns and villages. In Halle-Merseburg and in Magdeburg, strike committees seized power and set prisoners free. Increasingly, economic demands over reduced planning targets and the provision of consumer goods were complemented by political calls for freedom and free general elections. For a short while, the SED elites lost control over their state until Soviet tanks crushed the uprising and restored order. The events of 1953 fundamentally eroded the legitimacy of the worker-and-peasant state. It became obvious that the SED state had to rely on oppression and military strength, while Socialist idealism and the Communist utopia were revealed as myths. People realized that a transformation of the Stalinist system ultimately depended on Soviet policies and directives. The idea, however, of actively participating in improving and designing one's society was given a decisive blow.

The GDR did not have a prominent public figure of the stature of Vaclav Havel or Lech Walesa around whom a dissident movement could have developed. Oppression and surveillance in the GDR achieved near-perfection. Dissidents and intellectuals were "interviewed" by the *Stasi*, indicted, imprisoned, or more vigorously expelled to the FRG. A critical opposition therefore could never get off the ground. The coercive conformism deprived the SED of much needed feedback and information. Imprisonment and expulsion to the West caused a "brain-drain," while others chose or were forced to adopt internal exile. Moreover, the vast numbers of refugees who fled the GDR contributed to an ever-decreasing potential for opposition. In the end, accommodation to and within the system, retreat into the private sphere, and political indifference were the remaining solutions. The SED regime succeeded in silencing any form of dissent. The Orwellian web of surveillance and oppression had the country under firm control. However, by 1989 the discrepancy between the ideological notion of the Socialist society and the dictatorial reality became unbearable for the population. The dramatic series of events which led to the downfall of the Democratic Republic were sparked by public discontent over local elections in May 1989. Although the authorities had persistently forged election results over the past decades, East Germans were no longer willing to accept the distortion of their public will. Hundreds of citizens laid criminal charges against officials, accompanied by protests, most notably in Leipzig. For the regime, the downward spiral into defeat had begun. In June further protests emerged after the SED's strong denunciation of the democracy movement in China and the party's approval of the Tiananmen Square massacre. The easing of border restrictions between Hungary and Austria led to a mass emigration wave. Over the summer thousands of East Germans traveled south to escape through the first hole in the Iron Curtain since the building of the

Berlin Wall in 1961. On its own territory the regime had to confront a growing number of protest groups, who decided against emigration but instead demanded reform. In August the Social Democratic Party of the GDR (SDP) was founded. In September the civic movements *Neues Forum* and *Demokratie Jetzt* emerged on the scene. The *Neues Forum* demanded a democratic dialogue with the authorities. *Demokratie Jetzt* issued a proposal for the democratic reform of the GDR (H. Weber 1993: 104).

The regime did not see the writing on the wall both at home and in other countries of the Communist bloc that followed Gorbachev in his pursuit of change. In an arrogant fashion the party denounced any reform tendencies as counterrevolutionary. "The party is always right" still determined its dogmatic attitude. Consequently, the state responded with force. Mass arrests and imprisonment followed. These further heightened public discontent and aggravated even politically neutral citizens. The indignation over the Stalinist dictatorship, its misinterpretation of the sweeping changes within the communist bloc and the all too obvious out-of-touch state of their elites finally prompted East Germans to challenge the regime and—after 36 years—take their anger to the streets. But not only civic deficiencies were addressed. Growing confidence now resulted in the expression of resentment at the systemic shortcomings in the realm of consumer provision and economic production.[3] In Leipzig the weekly "Monday demonstrations" became the barometer for the dawning of the revolution. On October 2, 20,000 marched through the streets. Two weeks later, the numbers had increased to 120,000, followed by 300,000 on October 23. The civic movements enjoyed growing support. By mid-October, *Neues Forum* already had 25,000 members (H. Weber 1993: 105). On November 4, around one million people demonstrated in East Berlin for freedom of speech and press, for the easing of travel restrictions—but foremost for free elections. With the fall of the Wall the peaceful revolution reached its climax. On December 8, Honecker's successor Egon Krenz resigned, and the SED dictatorship finally collapsed.

The implications of forty years of totalitarianism for the civic standards of the population were extraordinary. The ambition of the SED to infiltrate all aspects of political life resulted in political apathy and passiveness. The propagated ideology of Marxism-Leninism, of the "new Socialist man" and the "Communist utopia" remained shallow dogmatism; their contents did not infiltrate the political conscience of the general population. The citizens fulfilled their participative duties, often as in the case of elections in a ritualized, dispassionate manner. The people gave the state what the state required, but nothing more, and hardly anything voluntarily. Life in the GDR was characterized by a peculiar arrangement between the political elites and the population. Over the course of forty years a consensus developed that guaranteed the former a certain degree of respect and obedience, and the latter social protection and general material benefits (Grunenberg 1988: 98). The relationship between the totalitarian apparatus and the masses can be described as toleration for security.

As long as the regime was able to pass on guarantees, the people were willing to sustain public order and to accept the political power structures (Rytlewski 1989: 19). Hence, by the late 1960s economic consolidation and an increased provision of consumer goods accounted for a modest contentment with the regime.

However, the emotional commitment remained shallow. Official duties and private identification with the political system stayed on separate grounds. The people accommodated themselves to the state. The fulfillment of duties lacked any idealistic notions. They were performed out of material concerns. Ideological conviction was missing. Conformity to the principles of society was honored by the authorities with the provision of education, pensions, and general social security in a Socialist welfare state. Generally speaking, identification with the political principles of a society generates a buffer of support that is able to overcome periods of crises. This buffer of ideological commitment was absent in the GDR. By the mid-1970s the gap between official promises and reality grew wider. Worldwide recession, oil shocks, and the influence of Euro-Communism ended the short spell of system satisfaction. Criticism against the inadequate provision of consumer goods, stagnating living standards, and the persistent repression of opposition and individuality (H. Weber 1993: 87) demonstrated that attitudes toward the political system were strictly output-oriented. Clearly, ideological commitment was severely lacking in the GDR. To achieve political, professional, or societal status, the citizens were required to accommodate themselves within the totalitarian system. People had to function, had to follow orders. Individualism, creativity, and plurality were suppressed, which resulted in a generalized and streamlined society. The SED and its satellite parties and mass organizations, its socialization and education agencies, formed a network that had the GDR society under firm control. Interest aggregation was subject to party domination, articulated through state or party institutions, while the consideration of particular interests rested upon the exclusive approval of the party. The state withdrew any individual political responsibilities from its citizens. It interfered in private affairs and laid down the tracks for every individual's life. The people were in fact politically and socially incapacitated.

THE FEDERAL REPUBLIC

After the collapse of the Third Reich a general disillusionment with politics was widespread in the newly established *Bonn* Republic. The catastrophic experiences of *Weimar* and the Nazi dictatorship left a deep and traumatic mark on the population. Over a period of less than thirty years three political systems—the Wilhelmian Empire, the *Weimar* Republic, and the Third Reich—had failed. Political supporters of the previous regimes were often subject to harsh punishment after a new political order had been established. The treatment of the political opposition after the rise of Hitler and the denazification programs in the aftermath of World War II convinced many people that politics was a dangerous, unrewarding business. The tasks of organizing the new state, of crafting the new constitution and of designing new policies were undertaken with hardly any public participation. Participation during the Adenauer era was characterized by a strong representative principle. The *Grundgesetz* (Basic Law) showed little trust in the political individual. Based on the experiences of *Weimar*, plebiscitary elements were regarded as a potential danger to democracy. For the founding fathers of the Basic Law and for the allied authorities the enthusiastic mass support for Hitler represented the critical point of departure for the installation of democracy in Germany. A consensus emerged that sought to safeguard the newly democratized citizens from the danger of populist and demagogic appeals. Consequently, the active participatory rights of the *Weimar* constitution, such as the direct election of the president or provisions for the initiative of referenda, were carefully avoided in the Basic Law. Mass political participation was "simply not encouraged" (Conradt 1989: 238).

Turnouts at federal and *Länder* elections already reached high standards by 1953. Although, generally speaking, participation in elections has the tendency to turn into a dutiful habit, the high numbers were particularly impressive in light of the absence of a compulsory obligation to cast one's vote. Moreover, in international comparison, turnouts were already higher than in the United States or in Great Britain (Dalton 1993: 179) and constituted a "permanently renewed legitimacy for the political system and the political parties" (Hesse and Ellwein 1992: 208) (see Table 4.3). Nevertheless, beyond the civic duty of voting, participation remained reluctant and by no means active. The total membership figures of all political parties during the 1950s hardly exceeded one million (Rudzio 1991: 465). Although the formal legislative, executive, and judicative institutions of democracy, as well as political parties and interest groups, were well established, passivity prevailed. The individual kept a suspicious distance from politics. It seemed that the intense and often forced political commitment and involvement of the Nazi era was followed by a retreat from politics, resulting in a "detached, practical and almost cynical attitude towards politics" (Almond and Verba 1963: 429).

The early years of the *Bonn* Republic were characterized by a succession of political and economic successes. The young republic provided the framework for a miraculous economic recovery, and for growing material wealth, as well as for international security during the emerging Cold War. Indeed, the proverb "*Es geht wieder aufwärts*" (things are looking up again) accurately described the Adenauer era. The public's participation in politics until the 1960s, however, was characterized by passivity. Formal participatory acts such as voting required little commitment. Almond and Verba (1963) described the civic attitude of the populace as a "passive subject orientation" which had yet to be balanced by a "participant orientation." For most West Germans, there was no

Table 4.3
Participation in West German Elections (percentages)

Legislative Period	Federal Level	Länder Level
1949–53	78.5	73.8
1953–57	86.0	77.5
1957–61	87.8	75.9
1961–65	87.8	74.8
1965–69	86.8	76.9
1969–72	86.7	78.1
1972–76	91.1	82.3
1976–80	90.7	79.2
1980–83	88.6	81.8
1983–87	89.1	75.7
1987–90	84.4	72.5

Source: Statistical Yearbooks.

apparent reason for dissent or dissatisfaction with the new system that would have forced him or her to seek more active participation and involvement.

Despite their discontinuities, the three political systems prior to the *Bonn* Republic had managed to subordinate the public under the power of the state. Their governments had always "conditioned" (Dalton 1993: 115) or forced the public into accepting authority. Democratic standards, such as majority rule, minority rights, individual liberties, and pluralism were alien concepts to most West Germans (Dalton 1993: 125). Stability and order were superior to individual freedom. Political power originated from the state and not from the people. This cultural trait fostered the establishment of the new political order after the demise of Hitler. As the public was used to subordinating individualism, political decisions and directives from the new authorities were accepted in an obedient fashion. Paradoxically, the legacy of the *Obrigkeitsstaat* helped to get the new democracy off the ground.

Participation after 1960

By the mid-1960s, the prevalent patterns of passivity, obedience, and subservience had been subject to an impressive transformation. Beginning in 1967, the student movement vehemently criticized the *modus vivendi* of political representation and participation. An anti-authoritarian protest swept across the Federal Republic. Fostered by leftist intellectuals from the "Frankfurt School," criticism was directed against the strictly representative and oligarchic nature of the political system. The limited chances of contributing to the political process were judged as an authoritarian relic of the past. The absence of a clear break from the Nazi era was criticized, arguing that the *Bonn* Republic had merely been built on economic and material wealth, while neglecting a moral resurgence and democratic commitment. The elitist, strictly representative phase of the early Federal Republic came to a gradual end. The symbol of postwar stability, Chancellor Konrad Adenauer, had already departed in 1963. The rise of Willy Brandt and the SPD to power signaled the dawn of a new era. *Politik wagen* (dare to do politics), the slogan of the Social Democrats, found a far reaching echo. Controversial policy innovations of the Brandt government of 1969 (in particular, *Ostpolitik*) fostered a widespread political discourse that was accompanied by the growing involvement of the population in election campaigns (Conradt 1989: 248).

These trends, combined, elevated West Germany toward a more politicized democracy. Although the student movement also brought elements of political radicalism, even culminating in terrorism, the cultural and generational clashes of the 1960s and 1970s did not fail to exert a permanent participative impact. The legacy of the student movement was represented in the political mobilization of a formerly passive and recipient society. Extra-parliamentary activism, peace initiatives and public interest groups were significant approximations to the normative citizenship virtues of active, concerned, and informed political individuals. The increase in and growing opportunities for political participation prompted a more positive evaluation of the degree of perceived freedom of expression and, in particular, to the more open character of that participation (Conradt 1989: 243). West German society was now regarded as freer and more inviting for political discourse and expression. According to the *Institut für Demoskopie*, the number of respondents who held the opinion that they can freely express themselves politically rose from 55 percent in 1953 to a peak in 1971 of 84 percent (Conradt 1989: 242). By the 1970s affirmative democratic experiences during the *Bonn* Republic outweighed obedient and subservient notions that were generated during the oppressive era of the Third Reich.

As shown in Table 4.4, the general interest in politics grew from humble beginnings to respectable figures. The increase from 27 percent in 1952 to 48 percent in 1980 allowed for the conclusion of a trend toward a politically more interested citizenry. Although this rather general trend should not be overestimated, other indicators also pointed in the general direction of improved participation. For instance the proportion of citizens who frequently held political conversations grew from 60 percent in 1952 to 79 percent in 1979, while the number of people who rarely held political conversations dropped from 40 to 21 percent (Conradt 1989: 248). Active political participation took a decisive step forward. Total party membership rose from 1.1 million (1960) to over 2

Table 4.4
Political Interest in West Germany (percentages)

Question: Are you interested in politics?

	June 1952	January 1960	September 1969	February 1973	January 1980
Yes	27	27	41	49	48
Not very much	41	40	44	38	43
Not at all	32	33	15	13	9

Source: Noelle-Neumann 1981: 150.

million (1980). In 1975 membership in unions and other interest groups amounted to 59 percent of the total adult population, as compared to 44 percent in 1959 (Rudzio 1991: 471). Suspicion toward politics and the political profession gradually decreased. Although in 1976, 43 percent of the population would still not have liked to see their son become a politician, the figures nevertheless improved significantly from their former count of 70 percent in 1955 (Noelle-Neumann 1981: 153). Furthermore, in 1975, 59 percent of a national survey stated that they were members of at least one organization—a political party, interest group or citizen initiative—which represented a considerable increase from the documented 44 percent of the Civic Culture study of Almond and Verba (1963). Moreover, within this time frame the number of active participants in these organizations rose from 7 to 17 percent (*Institut für Demoskopie* 1979: 21).

This trend toward more active political involvement coincided with the growing importance of citizen-initiative groups. By the mid-1960s such public interest groups addressed such issues as peace, environmental protection, women's emancipation, educational reforms, and the prohibition of nuclear plants. The development of these new political orientations were analyzed by Ronald Inglehart's theory of value change (1977). Within his typology of materialism and postmaterialism, Inglehart maintained that in times of depression or civil unrest, economic stability and security receive superior attention. After satisfying such needs, however, a society may shift toward other values, such as individual freedom, participation, or equality. This theoretical background bore great significance to the societal development of the Federal Republic. By the mid-1960s a growing generation gap emerged between those who experienced their formative years under the oppressive regime of the Third Reich (followed by years of severe economic hardship and material privation) and those who grew up under the influence of an ever-increasing prosperity, international stability, social security and an open society that fostered political involvement and broader cultural experiences. Material values of economic security and stability, of law and order, collided with postmaterialist notions of freedom of expression, participation, gender equality, or environmental protection. The postwar consensus of the Adenauer era ceased to exist and was replaced by a growing political polarization. By the mid-1970s there were about 3,000 such groups with a total membership of two million (Ellwein et al. 1975: 136–179). By the 1980s membership in public-interest groups had exceeded that of political parties, totaling 13 percent of the adult population in 1985. On the national level, the *Bundesverband Bürgerinitiativen Umweltschutz* (Federal Association of Citizen Initiatives for the Environment—BBU) gained central importance. At the high point of its influence, the BBU coordinated the activities of some 1,000 citizen initiative groups with nearly one million members (Dalton 1993: 193–194, 260). This development toward direct citizen participation was complemented by the rise of *die Grünen* (the Greens). The party conquered the political landscape of the Federal Republic with an ever-increasing, impressive level of support. Founded in March 1979, the Greens already had 10,000 registered voters by December—a figure that eventually reached its peak at the end of 1987 with 42,000 (Müller-Rommel and Poguntke 1992: 349). Initiatives worked mainly outside of the electoral setting and mostly lacked a party-political focus, with the exception of some environmental and peace issues. The majority of participants were drawn from younger, well-educated, middle-class segments of society. Still, during that period surveys indicated that over a third of the adult population—though not actively involved—at least considered membership in some public-interest group (Ellwein et al. 1975: 139). Citizen initiative groups represented an important advance toward a participative society. The scope of political issues broadened significantly. The numbers of politically interested people increased considerably. Most importantly, participation in public-interest groups demanded a higher level of commitment—intellectually as well as timewise—than the simple ritualistic notion of voting.

State-Citizen Relations after 1960

Increased political involvement paved the way for more critical attitudes towards political authorities. The notion of subservience gradually decreased and resulted in a growing civic confidence—in the belief that citizens can influence the course of political decisions. As shown in Table 4.5, an ever-growing number of people were willing to express their dissatisfaction with an administrative measure. Hence, the large majority of West Germans thought that their participation could influence the political process. Such a perception represented a fundamental prerogative of democracy: the individual's belief that his or her action has the potential to alter the course of politics.

The social upheavals caused by the student revolution and the more critical civic confidence, however, did not undermine the constitutional consensus. Parliamentarism gradually but firmly established itself as the favored principle

Table 4.5
Potential Protest against Unjust Action in West Germany (percentages)

Question: What would you do if an administrative agency acted unjustly in a matter that concerns you?

	January 1950	November 1958	December 1964	November 1978
Would protest	52	53	51	70
No point in protesting	37	33	32	22
Undecided	11	14	17	8

Source: Noelle-Neumann 1981: 190.

of political organization. A guarantor for the success of democracy in the Federal Republic was represented in the stability of the party system. While the first federal *Bundestag* consisted of ten parties, the number continuously decreased to six in 1953 and to four in 1957. The concentration along the political center was the consequence of a variety of postwar developments. With the introduction of the 5 percent threshold in 1953, smaller parties came increasingly under existential pressure. While some groupings joined the Christian Democratic Union (CDU), others failed to establish themselves as significant political forces and hardly achieved political mandates on both federal and land levels (Rudzio 1991: 119–120). In the end, smaller parties all but disappeared from the political scene, resulting in a parliamentary concentration on CDU, its Bavarian sister party CSU (Christian Social Union), the Social Democrats (SPD), and the Free Democrats (FDP). The political, social, and economic successes of the Federal Republic encountered a potential resurgence of extremist parties. The strikingly positive performance of democracy and the *Soziale Marktwirtschaft* managed to draw growing support from former anti-democratic sympathizers. Democratic parties, most importantly Christian and Social Democrats, were able to absorb political extremes to the Left and Right within their party agenda. The *Bonn* Republic therefore succeeded in avoiding the diversion and splintering of political groupings that characterized the *Weimar* Republic and eventually contributed to the collapse of the political center and the rise of the Nazi regime. By 1961, a three-party system had already emerged on the federal level, consisting of Christian, Social, and Free Democrats. In 1983 the Greens expanded this prevailing pattern with their election to the *Bundestag*.

The voters' orientation along a mainstream line can largely be attributed to the appeal of the two big parties. Both CDU and SPD established themselves as *Volksparteien* (catch-all parties). In the absence of a stark Left-Right dichotomy, CDU and SPD tried to win voters across traditional milieus, by avoiding affiliations along the lines of class, profession, religion, or material status. The social developments of postwar West Germany further fostered the establishment of the all-encompassing *Volksparteien*. The number of social groups that oriented themselves exclusively around one political force, such as farmers, workers, Christians, or self-employed people decreased. Subcultural cleavages lost in importance. Blue-collar workers enjoyed a wider social integration. The landed nobility, as well as the military, were not able to regain their prewar political influence, while the "successful integration of over 10 million refugees from the former Eastern territories reduced the importance of regional cleavages" (Conradt 1989: 260). In return, the number of people with only loose party affiliations grew, for whom Social and Christian Democrats represented equally viable political solutions. Over forty years, SPD and CDU alternately shared the governing responsibility. The third force, the Free Democrats (FDP), functioned as a regulating power. With the exception of the absolute majority of the CDU between 1957 and 1961 and the "Grand Coalition" between Social and Christian Democrats (1965 to 1969), neither SPD nor CDU was able to form a federal government without including the FDP as a coalition partner.

The established party system gave West Germany a remarkable continuity and stability. The political rhetoric was spared the ideological division between Left and Right. The splintered party politics of the *Weimar* Republic, traditional conservatism with its anti-democratic, nationalistic, and confessional cleavages, on the one hand, and anti-clerical, anti-bourgeois Socialism on the other, were replaced by centrist mass parties. Competition for political responsibilities was a "constant battle for the center" (Mertes 1994: 14). After decades of political turmoil and sweeping system changes, the West German voter perceived stability as the utmost desire. "No experiments," the slogan which brought Adenauer the absolute majority in 1957, represented the vital denominator in electoral preferences. The parties moved along a rather narrow choice of policies within the lines of economic stability, international security, and social welfare. Politics was characterized by a striving toward harmony and peace, both on the domestic as well as on the international level (Mertes 1994: 17). Drastic policy changes occurred only rarely in practice (as with Willy Brandt's *Ostpolitik* rapprochement with the GDR in 1969), or even in rhetoric (as with Helmut Kohl's propagated *Wende* in 1983). Major crises, such as the first economic recession in 1966–1967, the oil-price shock in 1973, the subsequent recession of 1974–1976, or political terrorism in the 1970s and 1980s did not arouse a reorientation but instead strengthened the already established policy principles. Even the emergence of the "Greens" as a leftist addition that incorporated alternative forces of the citizen-interest groups and the SPD did not constitute a threat to the prevailing system but instead followed along the established tracks of party politics through a number of coalition governments with the SPD on both local and *Länder* level.

Over the years, parlamentarism gained strong support among the population. While in 1950, 25 percent favored a one-party rule and 53 percent opted for a multi-party system, the figures subsequently improved. By 1978, 86 percent approved the multi-party system and only 5 percent still perceived the existence of one party as the best solution (*Institut für Demoskopie* 1979: 78). Positive attitudes toward the Federal parliament consolidated. In eighteen surveys taken between 1951 and 1983, respondents had been asked to place their opinions about the *Bundestag* into four categories, ranging from "exceptionally good," to "good," "mediocre" and "bad" (Emnid 4–1983: 11, 5/6–1983: 30). During this time percentages for the top two categories rose from 35 percent to 77 percent. The public's approval of the *Bundestag* is further documented in Table 4.6. In 1979, only 8 percent thought of the federal parliament in a negative fashion. Additionally, the trust in the competencies of other political institutions and in their abilities to solve problems was astonishing. Perceptions toward the federal president, the *Bundesrat* (the second chamber consisting of representatives from the *Länder*), as well as toward the federal and *Länder* governments, were overwhelmingly positive.

Approval for political institutions was complemented by a rise in the general support for democracy. In 1967, at the outset of the student protests, one-fourth of respondents questioned were dissatisfied or undecided as to whether democracy was the best form of government. By 1976 the ratio of support had improved to a solid 90 percent (Conradt 1989: 234). Moreover, responses showed few differences according to party affiliations and socioeconomic or age groups. This trend was particularly impressive against the backdrop of the politi-

Table 4.6
Attitudes Toward Political Institutions in West Germany (January 1979, percentages)

Question: Do you tend to think well of these institutions or are you inclined to think poorly of them?

	Very Good	Good	Good and Bad	Rather Poor	Very Poor	No Opinion
Federal President	43	39	12	2	1	3
Bundestag	12	38	37	7	1	5
Bundesrat	8	33	39	6	1	13
Federal Government	17	35	35	8	2	3
Government of Länder	8	29	49	5	1	8

Source: Noelle-Neumann 1981: 185.

cal and economic crises of the 1970s. The oil shock-related recession of 1974–1976, political terrorism, or criticism against *Ostpolitik* did not undermine the democratic commitment of the population. The decline in support for the "government of the day" had little effect on the overall support for liberal democracy (Conradt 1989: 263). Instead, by the mid-1970s the political system of the Federal Republic could rely on a broad and strong consensus regarding its basic character and structure.

THE NEW LÄNDER

In the immediate aftermath of the revolution, interest in politics in Eastern Germany was high. Sensitivity toward political matters continued throughout the summer. According to Table 4.7, in August 1990 50 percent had a strong or very strong interest in politics. By the end of the year, these figures had dropped to 45 percent. By 1994, "very strong" and "strong" were further reduced to 36 percent. A certain downward trend in political interest became evident. This, however, came as no surprise against the backdrop of the overwhelming importance of unification for the individual's life, as well as against the extensive media coverage of the first months after the upheavals of autumn 1989. Unification turned from revolutionary excitement into a daily, routine affair. After five years, the effects of novelty, of systemic-democratic changes, or of *Stasi* allegations began to show signs of wear.

Lessened interest in politics, however, should not be confused with a trend toward apathy. Instead, it represented a step towards normalization—a fact

Table 4.7
Political Interest in the New Länder (percentages)

Question: How strongly are you interested in politics?

	August 1990	December 1990	1990(*)	1993(*)	1994(*)
Very strong	16.3	10.3	13.0	11.1	9.4
Strong	34.3	35.4	34.9	29.0	27.1
A little	34.0	43.4	39.2	42.4	45.1
Hardly	9.6	7.9	8.7	12.3	14.1
Not at all	5.7	3.0	4.2	5.2	4.3
N	967	1182	2149	5197	6415

(*)Cumulated data.

Source: Politbarometer.

that was further supported by the comparison with the Western level of political interest. According to *Politbarometer*, East and West showed quite similar figures by 1993. The top two categories combined accounted for 44 percent in the West (East 40 percent), while the two negative answers amounted to 13.5 percent (East 17 percent). In contrast to the Federal Republic of the immediate postwar era, political interest was well developed in the Eastern *Länder*. Although three years after unification the Eastern levels were slightly lower than those of the West, they nonetheless were satisfactory. Furthermore, participation in elections initially reached astonishing figures in the East. In March 1990, 93.2 percent cast their votes for the *Volkskammer* (Förster and Roski 1990: 133) (see Table 4.8). Hence, the first free elections had a turnout that was almost as high as the forged results of the SED era. Clearly, the run for the ballot was prompted by a thirst for participation and for expression of free will after four decades of party tutelage.

As with political interest, the course of unification demonstrated that these high levels of participative euphoria were only shortlived. Elections for the *Landtage*—the parliaments of the *Länder*—in October 1990 already showed lower turnouts, although they nonetheless interested a satisfactory number of voters. The same can be said for the subsequent election for the federal *Bundestag* in December 1990, where participation in the East was only marginally lower than in the West. Four years onward, electoral participation in the East

Table 4.8
Participation of East Germans in Elections (percentages)

| | Bundestag | | Landtag | |
	1990	1994	1990	1994
Brandenburg	73.8	71.5	67.1	56.3
Mecklenburg-Westpomerania	70.9	72.8	64.7	72.9
Saxony	76.2	72.0	72.8	58.4
Saxony-Anhalt	72.2	70.4	65.1	54.8
Thuringia	76.4	74.9	71.7	74.8
total new Länder*	73.3	72.2	69.1	62.1
total old Länder**	78.5	80.5	---	---

*Excluding Berlin.

**Including Berlin.

Source: Statistical Yearbook 1994: 98, 100; 1995: 91, 94.

had yet to equal that of the West, although few differences remained. Comparing the elections for the *Bundestag* in 1990 and 1994, the margin between East and West rose from 5 to 8 percent. In addition, voter participation for the Eastern *Landtage* in 1994 dropped by 7 percent in comparison to 1990. Since *Länder* elections in the West regularly had lower turnouts than those for the *Bundestag*, the average participation of 62.1 percent in the East still was a satisfactory number, in particular against the backdrop of Western turnouts, such as 64 percent in Northrhine-Westphalia in 1995 or 67.8 percent in Bavaria in 1994. Hence, political interest and election turnouts in the East stabilized at acceptable levels. Judging from these basic and passive virtues of citizenship, Easterners adapted well to the introduction of democracy.

The respectable figures for passive participation, however, were not met by active participation in political parties. The downward trend was so striking that one could suggest a widespread rejection of the party system. Upon unification, the West German party system was to a large extent transformed to the East. The major political parties quickly sought for partners in the new *Länder*. Within one year following the mass demonstrations of 1989, the party system had consolidated along Western lines. The DSU (*Deutsche Soziale Union*, German Social Union) found a willing ally in the Bavarian CSU. In February 1990, the party joined forces with the former Eastern block party CDU and the civic group DA (*Demokratischer Aufbruch*, Democratic Awakening) to form the electoral *Allianz für Deutschland* (Alliance for Germany). With the *Volkskammer* elections in March looming, the Western CDU and in particular Chancellor Kohl pushed for a cooperation of center-of-right forces. Unification with the Western CDU followed in October 1990.

In February 1990, an equally streamlined process in the run-up to the *Volkskammer* elections occurred in the liberal democratic camp. The former block parties LDPD and NDPD joined forces with the civic group *Deutsche Forum Partei* (German Forum Party), which in itself was a splinter group from the *Neues Forum* (New Forum), as well as with the Eastern *Freie Demokratische Partei* (FDP, Free Democratic Party). Unification with the Western FDP followed in August 1990. The Eastern Social Democrats (SDP) established themselves as an independent party from its Western counterpart in October 1989. Unification with the Western branch occurred in September 1990. The SED successor organization of Honecker's Stalinist party changed its name to SED/PDS in December 1989 only to drop the first three letters two months later. The Eastern Greens were founded in November 1989. Here, the various *Länder* organizations joined the corresponding Western party throughout 1991. The three civic movements *Neues Forum, Demokratie Jetzt* (Democracy Now), and the *Initiative für Frieden und Menschenrechte* (Initiative for Peace and Human Rights) merged immediately before the Volkskammer elections in March 1990 under the name *Bündnis 90* (Alliance 90). The last merger, *Bündnis 90/Die Grünen*, had to wait until March 1993. While the PDS was able to fall back on an extensive infrastructure of local and regional offices, the Eastern branches of SPD, CDU, and FDP were guided by their Western allies in setting up a network of local and regional organizations that safeguarded participation in elections and the staffing of political posts (see Table 4.9). At first glance, the system seemed established. Soon however, cracks appeared on the surface.

Membership in political parties remained persistently low. In 1990, the Christian Democratic membership stood at over 130,000 since the party took over 100,000 members from the GDR Block-CDU. Four years later, the CDU had lost some 40,000 members in the East. The Social Democrats could not rely on a block party organization, and five years after unification, membership had consolidated at low levels. The FDP reached its high of 114,000 members in the East in 1990 by incorporating the block parties LDPD and NDPD. Two-thirds of the all-German membership came from the new *Länder*. Subsequently, the downward trend within the FDP represented the most radical of all parties. Within four years, the Free Democrats lost almost three-fourths of its Eastern members. Within *Bündnis 90/die Grünen* the extremely low levels

Table 4.9
The Transformation of the Eastern Party Landscape

Party (East)		Founded	Merged with (Western party)	Date
Block Parties	CDU	06–45	CDU	10–90
	DBD	06–48	CDU	10–90
	LDPD	07–45	FDP	08–90
	NDPD	05–48	FDP	08–90
New Parties	SDP	10–89	SPD	09–90
	Die Grünen	11–89	B'90/Die Grünen	11–93
	DSU		none; only regional importance	none
Civic Movement	Demokratischer Aufbruch (DA)	10–89	CDU	10–90
	Neues Forum	09–89	B'90/Die Grünen	11–93
	Demokratie Jetzt	09–89	B'90/Die Grüen	11–93
	Initiative Frieden und Menschenrechte	10–85	B'90/Die Grünen	11–93
PDS		02–90	None; sucessor party to SED	none

Source: Press offices of respective parties.

of membership could partially be explained by organizational turmoil within the civic movement and the existence of separate Eastern and Western Greens. With the party mergers of 1992, however, membership was not given a significant boost. In fact, by 1994 only 2,800 members joined their ranks. Even the impressive electoral successes of the PDS did not result in more party activists. Instead, numbers fell dramatically from 172,000 in 1991 to 122,000 in 1994. The ratio of party membership per capita further accentuated the striking differences between East and West. With the Eastern population constituting some 20 percent of unified Germany, the ratio in the CDU/CSU was 2 to 1 in favor of the West. Within the SPD, the figures were 7 to 1, within *Bündnis 90/die Grünen* 3.5 to 1. Of the established Western parties, only the FDP had more members per capita in the East, with a ratio of 2:1. In contrast, the PDS continued to maintain its almost exclusive Eastern orientation. Four years after unification, membership in the West remained insignificant (see Table 4.10).

For party officials, the search for candidates and activists to fill various political posts represented a frustrating task. For instance, in the communal elections of *Brandenburg* in December 1993, the mighty *Volksparteien* SPD and CDU failed to provide a complete list of candidates for all constituencies. The CDU managed to cover only half of the municipalities, while the SPD fared even worse and competed for only one-third of the seats (Schmid 1994: 797). Formal ties to the SED or allegations over the involvement in *Stasi* activities forced several leading Eastern politicians to resign. Within the CDU, the block

Table 4.10
Membership in Political Parties in East and West

	December 1991 (1000)		December 1992 (1000)		December 1994 (1000)	
	East	West	East	West	East	West
CDU	111.0([1])	650.0	94.3	619.6	92.5([2])	578.9([2])
SPD([3])	27.2	892.6	25.7	860.2	27.7	821.6
FDP([2])	73.9	63.6	41.2	62.0	29.1	58.5
PDS([4])	171.7	0.8	145.8	0.9	119.4	2.3
Bundis 90/ Grüne (3)	1.3	37.5	0.8	35.4	2.8	41.1

([1]): Estimates.

([2]): East: including Berlin. West: excluding Berlin.

([3]): East: excluding Eastern Berlin. West: only old *Länder*.

([4]): East: excluding Western Berlin. West: including Western Berlin.

Source: Press offices of respective parties.

party's long-time leader Gerald Götting had to step down in November 1989. Lothar de Maizière—the only freely elected Prime Minister of the GDR—resigned from his posts as deputy chairman and chairman of *Brandenburg* in 1991. By late 1992, three out of four CDU Minister Presidents had been forced to step down. Within the Social Democrats, the leader of the Eastern SDP, Ibraim Boehme, resigned in April 1990. In 1992, *Brandenburg*'s popular Minister President Manfred Stolpe had to face stiff media scrutiny over alleged conspiracies with the SED authorities during his time as an Evangelical pastor. The charismatic leader of the PDS, Gregor Gysi, had to confront rumors over his *Stasi* involvement as an unofficial informant.

Involvement in the SED state and *Stasi* allegations of the old leadership, as well as the lack of political expertise of younger recruits, forced the political parties to fill the void with Western staff. This import of politicians caused widespread resentment among Easterners. It severely hampered the process of establishing trust among the Eastern populace. Most "imports" were of modest or fading political reputation. Quite often it seemed that their Western careers were about to draw to a close, which made the new position in the East look like an extension of their political fortunes. Many refused to take up permanent residence in the East and continued their involvement in Western politics. The notion of imported political "secondhand goods" spread among the population. Also, East Germans were under-represented in the party's decision making bodies. In the FDP, only 260 out of 626 delegates for the unification congress in August 1990 came from the East. Of 13 members of the presidium, four were Easterners. Only the ratio of deputy chairmen gave the East a proper representation with two out of five (Ammer 1992: 469). In the CDU, three posts on the 14-member presidium and seven on the 26-person executive committee were reserved for Easterners. The position of deputy chair was created for de Maizière. In 1992, his successor Angela Merkel won reelection, although the post was expanded to five seats and opened to all contenders, which then included Saxony's Interior Minister Heinz Egger. The first "unified" cabinet of 1991 incorporated only two East Germans, who were both given minor portfolios—Transportation to Günther Krause and Family and Youth to Merkel (Clemens 1993: 215–217). Within the SPD, one out of five deputy chairmen came from the East (Wolfgang Thierse). The 39-member executive committee contained only six Easterners. In 1995, the committee was expanded to 49 seats. Still, Easterners accounted for only seven posts. Only the Greens managed to establish a representation according to the population ratio between East and West—150 out of a total of 750 party conference delegates, as well as four out of nine federal executives, came from the East. In the end, some 40 percent of all *Länder* ministers were from the West. They occupied central positions and were supported by top-ranking civil servants who also had been recruited from the old *Länder*.

The feeling of a political takeover by the West therefore came as no surprise. In a survey in 1993, a strikingly high 93 percent perceived that only those who have lived in the East have the right to talk about problems in the East (*Der Spiegel* 3/1993: 56). Clearly, the feeling of misrepresentation was widespread. Easterners wished for authentic political officials who, if not from the East, at least were familiar with the Eastern situation. However, this did not result in resentment *per se* of Western politicians. Asked whether top political posts should only be filled with Eastern politicians, a majority of respondents (69 percent) argued that it depended on the respective person. Of the remainder, 27 percent insisted on Eastern politicians, while 3.6 percent favored a Western official (*Politbarometer*). Although one-fourth still flatly rejected any Westerners at all, the large majority showed a readiness to accept representation by a Western official—as long as he or she was willing to further the Eastern cause. This notion became evident in Saxony. After the demise of Minister President Reichenbach (CDU) over alleged *Stasi* cooperation, the incoming Western Kurt Biedenkopf—the former CDU chairman for the state of Northrhine-Westphalia—managed to acquire the nickname *Sachsenkönig* (King of Saxony). With compassion, initiative, and eagerness, Biedenkopf overcame initial suspicious sentiments of "yet-another-Wessi" which subsequently culminated in the absolute majority in the land elections of 1994.

Given the prevalence of sentiments of a political takeover, political parties faced severe difficulties in establishing electoral loyalties. They were forced to aggregate the interests of a population that had just experienced abrupt and severe upheavals in their lives. The rapidity of the political, social, and economic changes of unification could not allow for the emergence and establishment of sound party affiliations. Instead, these remained persistently weak. The CDU stayed at 19 percent between November 1991 and November 1994. During the same time SPD dropped from 24 percent to 17 percent. A downward trend also affected *Bündnis 90/die Grünen* with a decline from 5.6 percent to 2.3 percent. The FDP dropped more drastically from 6.5 percent to 0.9 percent (*Politbarometer*). The number of people who did not have any kind of orientation toward a political party continued to stay at the exceptionally high level of 46 percent in 1994. While the identification with fringe parties, such as the right-extremist *Republikaner*, paled into insignificance, the established parties of SPD, CDU, FDP, and *Bündnis 90/die Grünen* were not able to generate sound voter orientations. In contrast, the number of people who leaned toward these parties decreased from 48 to 44 percent. Nearly half of Eastern respondents did not possess a party identification as compared to one-third in the West.[4] Party identification describes a long-term, stable orientation, a form of "psychological party membership" (Rattinger 1995: 232). One might argue that such affiliations were not able to develop, given the short time span since unification. However, prior to 1989, East Germans by no means lived in a political vacuum. Information about the political landscape in West Germany was transmitted through the media or visits from friends and relatives (Schmitt 1992a). In a survey taken in early 1993, 40 percent of respondents claimed to have had identifications toward a Western party before the *Wende* (Rattinger

1995: 233). Moreover, until 1993 the number of East Germans who before 1989 possessed an identification toward a Western party but now abandoned it, totaled 32 percent, while the amount who did not have a party identification but developed one after unification was only 28 percent (Rattinger 1995: 236). Thus, in total, the transformed party landscape of Eastern Germany was not able to generate stronger affiliations among the population. Identification with political parties persistently stayed at moderate levels, trailing significantly behind Western standards.

The programmatic base of some political parties and the orientation toward particular societal segments could not aggregate reliable support. The civic movement almost disappeared into oblivion. In the aftermath of unification, the agenda that developed in opposition against the SED regime, such as individual liberties and human rights, was sidelined against the overall importance of material issues. Parallel to this, the minor importance of environmental issues rendered campaigning problematic for the Greens. The Liberal Democrats traditionally supported free market mechanisms to support small or independent businesses, while stressing legal principles, such as democratic participatory rights or liberal protective rights against the state. As with the civic movement, liberal concerns of freedom and civil liberties had only minor significance against the paramount importance of materialist concerns. Also, independent and small businesses were still few in numbers, while the CDU established itself as a strong contender for this subgroup. The SPD still had to carry the baggage of its fatal *Bundestag* campaign of 1990. Arguing for a moderate pace of unification, the party was perceived as a traitor to German unity. The initial surplus of respect that Brandt's *Ostpolitik* generated in the 1970s melted away over Oskar Lafontaine's approach to German unification. Furthermore, the traditional orientation of the SPD toward workers and those with lower incomes was obsolete in the East. As a declared classless society, the differences in wages and status—excluding party apparatschiks—were minimal in the GDR. With unification, the party's traditional support among the less-well-off could therefore not materialize, since a societal rift along the lines of poor versus rich, of blue versus white collar, was virtually nonexistent.

Parteienverdrossenheit (weariness of political parties) aptly summed up the attitudes of East Germans toward the political system. Despite high interest in politics, despite satisfactory turnouts at elections, people failed to identify with political parties as their agents for interest representation. The political parties were left with the daunting task of establishing long-term loyalties. In this atmosphere of disorientation one party made a considerable exception. Growing out of the ashes of the Stalinist SED, the PDS (Party of Democratic Socialism) turned into an authentic body of interest representation for Eastern issues. In December 1989, after the ousting of Honecker's successor Egon Krenz, the party renamed itself as SED/PDS. Two months later, the neo-Communists dropped the SED from their name and argued for a democratic renewal around the reformists Gregor Gysi and Hans Modrow.

In the numerous elections of 1994, the PDS enjoyed surging successes and was able to significantly increase its share of votes, as compared to the first free elections in 1990. It drew support from all political directions, notably from the SPD but also to some extent from the CDU. In addition, young and first-time voters, as well as former non-voters, found the party particularly appealing (Bortfeld 1994: 1284). The five *Länder* elections of 1994 firmly established the party on the political agenda. In Saxony-Anhalt, cooperation with the neo-Communists safeguarded the minority coalition of Greens and Social Democrats which was subsequently termed the "Magdeburg model of tolerance" (*Der Spiegel* 44/1995: 24). In Thuringia and Mecklenburg-Westpomerania only grand coalitions between Social and Christian Democrats prevented the party from assuming governmental responsibility. Particularly on a local level, the PDS was able to achieve some remarkable success. In several counties—both urban and rural—the majority of votes went to the neo-Communists. As of early 1996, 180 towns and municipalities were governed by PDS mayors. The party had 129 seats in the various *Länder* parliaments and 6,000 parliamentarians in local governments (*Der Spiegel* 3/1996: 40). In the local elections in Berlin in November 1995, the neo-Communists emerged as the strongest political force, capturing 36.3 percent. Often only the cooperation between the remaining parties prevented the PDS from capturing further county and city halls (Golz 1994b: 676). On the federal level, the split between East and West was aptly documented by the share of votes for the neo-Communists. Table 4.11 shows the striking disparities between the respective percentages. In the East, the PDS further manifested its political position,

Table 4.11
Percentage of Votes for the PDS

		1994	1990
Bundestag	East	19.2	11.0
	West	0.9	2.0
	Total	4.4	2.4
Länder	Mecklenburg-Westpomerania	22.7	15.7
	Brandenburg	18.7	13.4
	Saxony	16.5	10.2
	Saxony-Anhalt	19.9	12.0
	Thuringia	16.6	9.7

Source: Statistical Yearbook 1995: 91, 94; 1994: 98, 100.

while in the West the party sank into insignificance. Still, both in 1990 and in 1994, the PDS entered the German parliament.[5]

Although the demise of the SED regime resulted in a dramatic drop in membership—from 1.8 million in December 1989 to 119,000 in 1994—the PDS still had by far the strongest membership base of all political parties in the new *Länder* which stood in sharp contrast to the West, where the neo-Communists largely failed in attracting new members. Nonetheless, as relics of the SED past, the PDS possessed an extensive network of local offices, solid financial resources, and experienced party activists. The party's electoral base increasingly transcended the broader segments of society, moving beyond the traditional support from the old, unemployed, and former SED functionaries. The programmatic base suffered from vague explorations of the GDR history. In the party programs of 1990 and 1993, the SED past was addressed only in general terms, while lacking a critical confrontation with economic and political shortcomings of the system. The party obviously tried to distance itself from the SED by simply rejecting the past without questioning the causes of the failure of the Socialist experience (Pfahl-Traughber 1995: 28).

The party program did not give the impression of a reformed Socialist party. However, although the PDS grew out of the Stalinist SED, whose totalitarian grip on society prompted East Germans to take their anger to the streets, the public seemed relaxed about the surging success of the neo-Communists. Gradually, the PDS managed to leave its image as the successor party to the SED behind. Gysi's *bunte Truppe* (colorful troops)—a mixture of former dissidents, intellectuals, and reformist SED apparatschiks—included Bismarck's great-grand-nephew Graf Einsiedel, the former GDR economics minister Christa Luft, and the writers Stefan Heym and Gerhard Zwerenz. The tactics of naming prominent people—even without party membership—as candidates proved to be a striking success. Despite the aging membership structure and the persistent internal quarrels between reformists, fundamentalists, and former SED apparatschiks, the party's image was unorthodox, young, uncomplicated, and bold.

The predominantly Eastern success of the PDS can partly be explained by its exclusively Eastern orientation. With the exception of *Bündnis 90* (the struggling successor party of the civic movement) and the DSU (which paled into insignificance and remained present only in the local area around Dresden), all other political groupings had their origin in the West. This feeling of mis- and under-representation opened the gates for the spectacular rise of the PDS. In July 1994, 62 percent of respondents in the East declared that the PDS was needed in the new *Länder* to assert East German interests. Consequently, 57 percent wanted to see the PDS in the federal *Bundestag* (*Politbarometer*). In addition, the PDS had the tactical advantage of voicing particularly Eastern issues and grievances, while being the only party in the East that possessed a strong social, locally-oriented network. Political activism included regular talks and discussions, communal activities, advice and information on such critical issues as rents or pensions. This network did not only operate during the build-up to major elections, but rather represented a permanent institution. The PDS established itself as a genuine *Volkspartei* in the Eastern *Länder*. Accusations over the *Stasi* activities of Gysi and the party chairman Lothar Bisky, as well as hostile political rhetoric from established parties and the media, could not undermine the PDS's growing success. The aversion of Western political elites, most notably Chancellor Kohl, who labeled the party as red-painted fascists, was not shared by the Eastern public. In 1994, 39 percent of respondents believed that the PDS had parted from its SED past. Relying on this considerable stock of trust, the party was taking advantage of the void of affiliation which the Christian, Social, and Free Democrats failed to fill. In contrast to the traditional Western parties, the PDS was the sole political agent capable of generating the spirit of solidarity and communality in a time of abrupt and sweeping changes in an individual's life.

In contrast, the former power and influence of the civic movement gradually decreased. As with the PDS, the civic movement found itself without a powerful ally in the West. The ideologically most suitable Western counterpart, the Greens, were the party which most resented unification (Poguntke and Schmitt-Beck 1994: 93). Additionally, whereas most political groupings supported quick unification and were consequently geared toward an organizational merger with Western parties, the civic movement held on to the notion of an independent East Germany, arguing for a Socialist alternative with a human face. From the start the civic movement was organizationally dispersed and ideologically fragmented (Poguntke and Schmitt-Beck 1994: 93). In the revolutionary days of autumn 1989, attitudinal differences were brushed aside only by the common goal of achieving political freedom. During the popular upheavals of 1989, several opposition movements emerged on the political scene. In addition to the *Initiative für Frieden und Menschenrechte* (founded as early as 1985), *Neues Forum* and *Demokratie Jetzt* were established in September 1989. In October they were joined by the *Demokratischer Aufbruch*. While the latter merged with the CDU in October 1990, the remaining three joined forces in March 1990 under the name of *Bündnis 90*. The Eastern Green Party which also grew out of the resistance movement against the old regime was founded in November 1989.

The first electoral results were depressing. Standing separately in the *Volkskammer* and *Länder* elections in March 1990, the Greens and the citizen movement trailed far behind those parties that had found Western allies. In the first all-German elections in December 1990 (with a separate 5 percent threshold for Western and Eastern Germany), the Western Greens failed to enter the federal *Bundestag*. The electoral alliance of Eastern Greens and *Bündnis 90* sent only two representatives of the Eastern Greens and six from the citizen movements to *Bonn*. The prospect of staying under the newly-introduced all-German threshold in the federal elections of 1994 undoubtedly boosted pragmatism toward a unification of the Greens and the citizen movement

(Poguntke and Schmitt-Beck 1994: 93)—a move that paid off by achieving 6.9 percent. On the *Länder* level, however, the impact of the party remained moderate. In 1994, only the parliament of Saxony-Anhalt had representatives from *Bündnis 90/die Grünen* which had received just 5.1 percent of the votes. Membership participation in the civic movement declined dramatically. In late 1989, some 200,000 signed the founding declaration of *Neues Forum*. This figure however, represented more of a protest and rejection vote against the regime than actual support for the movement. With Western parties appearing on the Eastern political scene, public interest in *Neues Forum* and other civic movements decreased. The prospect for rapid unification with the West was clearly more appealing to Easterners than the persistence of an Eastern Socialist alternative. By June 1991, *Neues Forum* had a membership base of 5,000, while *Demokratie Jetzt* consisted of six hundred and *Initiative Frieden* of two hundred active participants.

Although the formation of *Bündnis 90/die Grünen* brought the organizational diversification within the civic movement to an end, membership figures did not receive a boost. By 1994, *Bündnis 90/die Grünen* were still largely based in the West with some 41,000 supporters as opposed to a mere 2,800 in the East. In retrospect, the role of the civic movement in the Eastern *Länder* became clear. Although their activists initiated the downfall of the regime, they were mere "catalysts rather than leaders of a mass rebellion" (Poguntke and Schmitt-Beck 1994: 94). The movement's programmatic base soon eroded. The quest for freedom, human rights, and civic liberties was pushed out of the realm of relevance. With unification in October 1990, those goals were practically achieved. Other issues, such as unemployment, wages, and social security now dominated people's minds. The civic movement, however, was left with programmatic problems in attracting post-unification voters. So far, environmental and grass-roots politics found it hard to establish themselves in the East.

Not only political parties, but other interest-representing bodies also expanded their spheres of influence to the new *Länder*. Since no free interest aggregation had existed in the GDR, a network of groups and organizations had to be established. Subsequently, Western business and farm organizations, trade unions, the churches, and civic groups developed structures in the East. The State Treaty of May 1990 called for the adoption of the entire West German system of labor organization and collective bargaining. The *Bundesverband der deutschen Industrie* (BDI—Federation of German Industry), the *Bundesvereinigung der deutschen Arbeitgeberverbände* (BDA—Confederation of German Employers' Associations) and the *Deutsche Gewerkschaftsbund* (DGB—German Federation of Trade Unions) quickly set up offices in the new *Länder*. Trade unions had an immediate impact on the political situation in the Eastern *Länder*. They emerged as "the best advocates for the interests of East Germans," as well as the motor of the "equalization of life conditions" (von Beyme 1991: 163). With an aggressive policy of continuous threats of strikes, unions pushed for increases in wage levels. Although such action was beyond any economically responsible, inflation-concerned means (see Chapter 3), it helped in return to ease social tensions and to avoid political unrest. The unions achieved high levels of moral credibility and political competence (Tiemann 1994: 155) among Easterners. Their impressive achievements, however, were not rewarded with an increase in membership. Similar to political parties, unions suffered from a dramatic loss in membership. In 1992, more than 750,000 or 18 percent of the total membership in the Eastern *Länder* left the DGB. The Western branches documented only a minor fall in the ratio of organized employees—from 26 percent to 25 percent. In the East, the drop was staggering. Between 1991 and 1994, more than 1.5 million (or some 30 percent) left the unions. The loss in membership was regarded as a reaction to the economic situation in Eastern Germany. Redundancies on a massive scale caused by restructuring processes resulted in a decreasing base for recruitment of new members. Still, the percentage of employees with a union membership card was considerably higher in the East than in the West. This, however, was a relic of the artificially high level of labor organization in the GDR. After unification, the virtually compulsory membership of the SED-controlled FDGB came to an end. As a result, the number of organized employees dropped from 55 to 39 percent. Against the backdrop of tight individual budgets, a considerable number of Eastern workers preferred to save membership fees by leaving the unions. It remains to be seen at what state the still higher Eastern membership will consolidate. Only then can one assess whether it represents a dying habit taken over from the GDR past or an affirmative willingness to participate in the political process. Until the end of 1994, the dramatic downward trend did not come to an end. Declining membership figures were further aggravated by severe problems in the recruitment of activists (Boll 1994: 127). Unions suffered from the same phenomena that also rendered the work of political parties difficult: the Easterners' preference of "exit" over "voice."

Hence, in the aftermath of 1989, a variety of environmental groups emerged on the political scene. Out of the GDR mass organization GNU (*Gesellschaft für Natur und Umwelt*—Society for Nature and Environment), the *Bund für Natur und Umweltschutz* (BNU—Association for Nature and Environment) and the *Grüne Liga* (Green League) emerged. Additionally, the *Naturschutzbund der DDR* was established in March 1990 which subsequently merged with its Western counterpart. In October 1990, the West German *Bund für Umwelt und Naturschutz* (BUND—Association for the Environment and Protection of Nature) set up offices in the East and merged with several district branches of the BNU. Additionally, Greenpeace set up headquarters in Berlin.

Five years after unification membership remained low. While the *Grüne Liga* could count on some 4,000 Eastern activists (Boll 1994: 124), Table 4.12 shows the striking disparities between Eastern and Western membership figures. Prior to unification, ecological groups were vital organizations in the op-

Table 4.12
Membership in Civic Groups in 1994

	East	West
Greenpeace	8,000	499,000
BNU	10,500(^{1})	197,000(^{2})
Bund	3,500(^{1})	212,000(^{2})

(^{1})Including Berlin.

(^{2})Excluding Berlin.

Sources: Press offices of organizations.

position against the regime. An entire society was united and determined to bring down the regime. Opposition *per se* to the SED mattered, and not the particular content of it. This common political focus was lost after 1989. "Bread and butter" issues of unemployment and social security, as well as the general task of coming to terms with new political and economic structures were more pressing to East Germans. Environmental protection took second stage. To summarize, although the structure of interest representation, including a network of political parties, employers associations, trade unions, and civic groups was well developed in the East, it represented "little more than an organizational shell" (Boll 1994: 114). Although political interest and passive political participation reached satisfactory levels that almost equaled those of the West, they did not materialize in active political participation.

After unification, indifference and apathy toward participation in churches remained widespread throughout Eastern Germany. The differences in general church membership between East (50 percent) and West (80 percent) were profound (Eisel 1994: 155). The Evangelical church became subject to widespread criticism for quickly demanding the introduction of the Western state-supported taxation system. Allegations over the *Stasi* involvement of clerics certainly did not help to stop the decreasing level of sympathy. The church argued that relations with the security apparatus and hence with the state were unavoidable in a totalitarian regime and represented part of the arrangement with the authorities that still allowed for a respectable degree of independence. The Catholic church defended its close cooperation with the state security with the same rationale. If it wanted to achieve anything within the SED state, the Ministry of Security offered the most influential contact (Haese 1994: 132). Although the Catholic church maintained that it utilized the *Stasi* as a source of information, for clarification of church-state issues, and for complaints, *Stasi* files revealed the considerable material benefits that some clerics enjoyed out of their conspiracy (Haese 1994: 133). These attempts to rescue the churches' reputation were faced with severe skepticism by the public. Although in March 1992, 58 percent acknowledged that close contacts with the *Stasi* were vital for church leaders to maintain a *modus vivendi* with the state, a significant proportion of 39 percent rejected the notion altogether (*Politbarometer*). Also, the prevalent secularization of the GDR continued to have a persistent legacy in the new *Länder*. For decades religious habits and customs played an ever-decreasing role in the lives of East Germans. Five years after unification, religious loyalties were still moderate. In postwar West Germany, Catholic and Evangelical churches enjoyed a phenomenal revival. At that time they provided a mental refuge and source of hope and spirit in a depressed and derelict environment. In post-unification Eastern Germany the churches failed to generate emotional attachments. Despite the sweeping system changes, churches were not perceived as institutions to offer spiritual and mental support. Forty years of Socialism simply pushed them out of the sphere of practical relevance to the individual. In retrospect, the people's passivity toward the churches pointed toward the churches' function as a hollow protective shell for the opposition movement of the GDR. They were welcomed and utilized as the only autonomous organizations. The religious content, however, left the population largely unaffected. As the only political alternative to the streamlined SED society of the GDR, the churches were embraced for their participative opportunities. Religious belief, however, was secondary. With unification, opportunities for participation increased and the legacy of secularization in the GDR became visible.

State-Citizen Relations

At first glance, East Germans were rather skeptical toward the arrival of democracy. Between 1990 and 1994, the figures of *Politbarometer* hardly changed. With only around one-third of respondents being satisfied with the democratic system and a striking two-thirds dissatisfied, the adopted West German political system failed to attract a sizable following. In comparison, the numbers in the West were just the opposite. Here, around two-thirds of respondents were content with democracy.[6]

East Germans nonetheless appreciated the arrival of an open society. Freedom of expression or freedom to travel were overwhelmingly approved as a welcome departure from the rigid, oppressive, and restrictive life of the GDR. More than two-thirds of respondents were positive about the changes in personal freedom that unification brought about (see Table 4.13). The relationship of Easterners toward their new political system and its implications for the individual were therefore not as dismissive as the low approval rates for democracy would have suggested.

The staffing of key positions within the administration was complicated by severe limitations on human resources. Because of the hierarchical and oligarchic nature of the SED regime, East Germans hardly had opportunities to be-

Table 4.13
Perceived Personal Freedom in the East (percentages)

Question: Thinking of your personal freedom, do you fare better or worse as compared
to the days of the GDR or is there no difference?

	March 1992	1993(*)	August 1994
Better	76.2	69.7	72.2
Worse	3.9	6.5	6.1
No difference	19.9	23.8	21.7
N	1,079	2,053	1,059

(*)Cumulated data 04, 06–1993.

Source: Politbarometer.

come accustomed to such notions as individual responsibility and decision
making. The SED's ideological streamlining infiltrated the intellectual potential with a political dogmatism that was hardly adequate to the requirements of
a modern democratic administration. Since the Federal Republic's administrative institutions were not gradually established in the East but instead introduced almost overnight, the demand for efficient, experienced, and reliable
staff was pressing. As a result, Western civil servants were recruited in large
numbers to work in the East. Western officials predominantly held positions
within the higher civil service, as well as in the finance and justice departments.
In June 1992, 20,000 Western civil servants worked in Eastern administrative
bodies (Grundmann 1994: 34). In 1991, in the state of Brandenburg, 52 percent of officials within the higher civil service came from the old Federal Republic (Hansch 1993: 291), who worked most notably in the state chancellery
(72 percent), the Ministry of Justice (72 percent), and the Ministry of Finance
(67 percent). Asked in September 1990, the majority of 44 percent of Eastern
respondents strongly approved of Western bureaucrats taking positions in the
East. Only 6.7 percent rejected the measure altogether (Grundmann 1994:
35). Since the overwhelming majority of East Germans had just approved of
joining the political, economic, social, and administrative structures of West
Germany, such a largely positive vote came as a logical consequence. By 1992,
perceptions had changed drastically. In November of that year, only 14 percent
of respondents in Saxony-Anhalt and 20 percent in Eastern Berlin expressed
unanimous approval of Western officials. Resentment grew to 20 percent in
Saxony-Anhalt and to 13 percent in Eastern Berlin (Grundmann 1994: 37).

The approval of Western civil servants was in general "not very high" (Grundmann 1994: 38). The Western official who more or less voluntarily worked in the East experienced firsthand the cultural clash between East and West. For most civil servants, the East was formerly a distant and unknown world. Problems of integration and little interest in becoming familiar with Eastern problems were common. Mentality and living standards were too diverse to allow for a smooth integration, and friction was hard to avoid. The persistent post-unification rhetoric of denunciation of the SED regime—not only of its political failures and shortcomings but in general of every aspect of life in the GDR—helped to establish the notion of the victorious West in the fight for systemic supremacy between Capitalism and Communism. As a result, the perception of a political takeover was complemented by notions of an administrative subordination of the East.

In a further survey taken between January and March 1993, (see Table 4.14) around 1,500 respondents in Eastern Germany were asked to evaluate orientations toward public administration (Löwenhaupt 1995). In comparison with responses by Westerners taken in 1990, the public service was perceived in a more critical way. In particular, attitudes toward the general functioning of public administration (statement 1) were markedly different, with half of the population in the West being satisfied, as opposed to only one-

Table 4.14
Attitudes Toward Public Administration (percentages)

Question: Do you agree that . . .

	East 1993			West 1990		
	yes	no	neutral	yes	no	neutral
1. Public offices do NOT work satisfactorily	43.4	33.3	23.3	23.3	52.5	24.2
2. Public offices work more slowly than necessary	72.9	13.5	13.6	65.9	17.6	16.4
3. Citizens do not have many opportunities to protest	51.6	27.8	20.6	47.1	33.3	19.6
4. Citizens are treated like numbers	50.8	31.3	17.9	45.9	37.0	17.1
5. Civil servants are NOT friendly and helpful	28.8	45.6	25.6	23.9	51.3	24.8
6. It is better not to argue with the administration	34.0	48.4	17.6	39.9	45.7	14.4

Source: Löwenhaupt 1995: 158.

third in the East. When asked specifically about some deficiencies (statements 2 to 6), however, the differences between East and West were not as drastic, although they remained in general more negative in the East. Nonetheless, 73 percent of Eastern respondents were not satisfied with the speed of work, 52 percent saw little opportunity for protest against administrative action and a quite high 34 percent thought that it was better to remain quiet and refrain from challenging the authorities. Furthermore, the bureaucratic dilemma of being caught between the provision of an efficient service and anonymous, impersonal routine was perceived in a more pronounced manner in the East than in the West (statements 4 and 5).

The mass demonstrations during the autumn of 1989 impressively demonstrated the capacity for political mobilization in Eastern Germany. Hundreds of thousands of citizens took their anger and frustration to the streets and brought down the SED dictatorship. Undoubtedly without this massive public protest, the system transformation would not have been possible. With the near eclipse of the civic movement as the catalyst of the revolution one has to wonder whether such political activism was only short lived or generated into a prevalent standard within unified Germany. Table 4.15 shows that by 1992 the willingness to enforce demands through protest had not disappeared. Considerable numbers of respondents had already participated in various forms of

Table 4.15
Political Protest in the New Länder, 1992 (percentages)

	have done	would do	would possibly do	would never do	n
Approved demonstration	32.2	14.1	17.5	34.5	2,090
Discussion at public meeting	20.9	17.6	19.5	40.5	2,092
Sign petition	16.0	18.0	22.8	41.6	2,093
Participation in citizen initiative	8.1	18.9	26.9	44.4	2,090
Illegal demonstration	7.6	4.8	16.3	69.9	2,089
Violence against—police	0.9	4.7	16.8	75.8	2,086
—citizens	0.5	6.7	16.2	75.0	2,090
—politicians	0.5	4.8	11.7	81.2	2,086
Damage to property	0.3	2.8	6.9	88.2	2,089
Take possession of house, factory, or public office	0.3	4.2	13.0	80.7	2,086

Source: Gabriel 1995: 180.

protest, most notably approved demonstrations. Only between 35 and 44 percent flatly denied a general willingness to protest with constitutional means. Hence, the protest potential for such activities as approved demonstrations, discussion at public meetings, signing of petitions, and participation in citizen initiatives reached around 60 percent. Moreover, only a small fraction of respondents regarded participation in illegal and violent activities as a possible alternative or had already participated in them. The overwhelming majority was clearly opposed to such means. Thus, the protest potential in Eastern Germany had anything but disappeared after the *Wende*, while the channels for uttering demands followed constitutional means.

State-citizen relations were further complicated by the painful task of coming to terms with the former totalitarian regime. The unification treaty called for the establishment of an independent authority to reveal the extent and activities of the state-security apparatus. The "Gauck office"—named after the responsible state secretary Joachim Gauck—began its task as early as October 1990 and subsequently created a central archive of all available data from the security apparatus. The passing of the *Stasi-Unterlagen-Gesetz* (Law on *Stasi*-documents) in December 1991 complemented the comprehensive governmental action. As a consequence, Eastern Germany remained the only country of the former Communist bloc to fully open its files for inspection. The disclosure of the archives of a secret service represented a unique step—not only in Germany but probably in world history. Anyone who worked for the secret police had been barred from public office. This ensured that allegations over *Stasi*-involvement could now be based on fact rather than rumor and allowed East Germans to find out who was spying on them for all those years.

However, the "Gauck office" did not offer open access, either for individuals or for administrative bodies, research institutions, or intelligence purposes. Instead, applications had to be filled out and individuals including former *Stasi* officials were then given information for reasons of personal rehabilitation. Public institutions were provided with data on the involvement of their employees in the security apparatus to assess employment matters. Judicial bodies were given information only in cases of the prosecution of grave criminal offenses (Strotmann 1995: 808–812). Until May 1995 the office was flooded with applications. A total of 1.6 million requests for information on individual persons were made, in addition to 950,000 East Germans who asked to inspect their personal files (Strotmann 1995: 820). This striking interest documented the sensitive and complicated nature of addressing the legacy of the old regime. The official propaganda of the GDR as the first Socialist state on German ground proved to be a bitter lie. The revelations of the lifestyle of the political elite who owned luxurious mansions, hunting grounds, and even private islands turned the proclaimed egalitarian society into a retrospective farce. Disappointment and anger were directed particularly against the former political elite. The suspension of Erich Honecker's trial in January 1993 caused widespread irritation. Despite the former leader's incurable cancer, 63 percent were still opposed to the notion of letting Honecker escape without judicial consequences (*Politbarometer*).

The discovery of the extent and practicalities of the *Stasi* apparatus with a ratio of around one informant for 95 citizens (Golz 1994: 343) created a strong sense of shock and a "retroactive dissolution of trust" (Stern 1993: 115). Subsequently, any revealed connection to the repression apparatus caused suspicion. The list of prominent public figures who collaborated with the *Stasi* demonstrated the all-encompassing web of surveillance in the GDR. It included intellectuals, such as the writers Christa Wolff and Heiner Müller, the regime critic Monika Maron, and the popular Radio-DJ Lutz Bertram. Even the dissident Robert Havemann, an ardent idealist of Communism who vehemently criticized the SED state, collaborated with the *Stasi* between 1956 and 1963 (*Der Spiegel* 21–1995: 87). On the private level, formerly intact social circles came under stress, with the realization that one's friends or even a family member served as spies.

Not only the political elite but virtually every segment of society from writers to journalists and even to regime critics had its conspirators. Through secret meetings, the state managed to infiltrate the most inner life of its citizens to such an extent that privacy was nonexistent and total surveillance was guaranteed. Although all East Germans were quite aware of the apparatus, the qualitative and quantitative depth of the gathered information came as a sudden shock. The feeling of betrayal is indicated in Table 4.16. In 1992, 36 percent favored increased measures of interrogation in order to work out the *Stasi* past. The discovery of the regime's suspicion, of surveillance, of voyeurism for the sake of political stability, and of distrust sought for an emotional safety valve in order to achieve a sense of retrospective justice toward an unjust regime that categorically assumed its citizens to be disloyal.

Table 4.16
Handling the *Stasi* Past (cumulated data, percentages)

Question: Should more measures be taken in order to work out the Stasi past?

	1992	1994
Do more	36.4	18.8
Same extent	27.8	28.0
Close the issue	35.0	52.2
Undecided	0.8	1.0
N	6,519	3,212

Source: Politbarometer.

For those who were actively involved in the *Stasi*—as so-called unofficial informants or as permanent members of the staff—the demise of the regime left many in a state of severe moral crisis. The formerly familiar environment disappeared almost overnight. With unification, the individual was forced to adapt to new political and societal norms. However, most informants failed to recognize any moral deficiencies in of their former behavior. As a typical example, Lutz Bertram argued that he joined the *Stasi* without any feeling of injustice and stated that if he had not done it, somebody else would have. He never knowingly damaged anyone, adding that he merely passed on information while the responsibility of the application of it rested with the apparatus (*Der Spiegel* 22–1995: 96). In retrospect and from a Western perspective one would have assumed a conflict between the collaboration with an oppressive totalitarian regime and individual moral ethics. Such a conflict, however, was not necessarily present. Despite a certain level of discontent with the SED state, people such as Wolff or Maron nonetheless supported the raison d'être of the GDR. Criticism against the regime and subsequent spying for the regime were merely intended to improve the state of Communism in Germany. The official rhetoric of the GDR always emphasized the development of the Communist man and the evolution of Socialism toward Communism. Despite its repressive measures, the *Stasi* represented a tool for this process as a sort of secretive educational agency. Furthermore, the State Security was part of the political establishment and represented the political norm. Working with the *Stasi* meant working with the state, which fostered a sense of solidarity and togetherness among individuals who were united for the common goal of establishing a Communist society. For the benefit of this society, for the benefit of Socialism, informants were willing to spy, even on friends.

With unification, moral intentions were now judged as moral crimes. The climate of democracy, human rights, and individual liberties left no space for sentimental notions of Communist idealism. The collaboration with the SED regime turned from self-perceived virtue into publicly perceived reprehension. The sudden system changes hardly left time for reflection. New norms required immediate adaptation. Hence, the past was repressed, the necessary process of coming to terms with one's action was postponed. For former *Stasi* informants, the process of acknowledging immorality against the former Socialist-idealist conscience remained difficult if not impossible. Nonetheless, a certain level of sympathy and compassion among East Germans remained. After all, Table 4.16 also shows that in 1992, 35 percent of respondents wished the *Stasi* controversy to come to a close. East Germans experienced firsthand how hard it was to function within a system of constant surveillance and repression. Their own past was now examined along a thin line between ideological commitment and existential necessity. Hence, in 1990, the overwhelming majority of two-thirds of respondents supported a limited prosecution against only the leading officials of the *Stasi*. A mere 29 percent were in favor of drastic measures which would have placed the entire surveillance apparatus including official staff members and unofficial informants under judicial scrutiny (*Politbarometer*).

Manfred Stolpe, Minister President of *Brandenburg*, served as an archetypal example. As a former political activist in the Evangelical church of the GDR, he had to confront severe accusations over his role as an informant to the *Stasi*. Charges, however, were dropped and Stolpe justified his action by arguing that a minimal involvement with the SED regime was necessary in order to achieve political influence at all. At the height of the controversy in the autumn of 1992, 39 percent in the East believed that the allegations were justified, as opposed to 55 percent who rejected such accusations. Moreover, 63 percent held the opinion that he should remain in office, while 34 percent preferred his resignation (*Politbarometer*). The entire controversy, however, by no means damaged Stolpe's political career. In contrast, his popularity subsequently increased. At the *Länder* elections for the state of *Brandenburg* in September 1994, Stolpe's Social Democratic Party achieved an absolute majority of 54 percent, up from 38 percent four years before. Stolpe incarnated the dilemma that every Easterner had to face: on the one hand the cooperation with, or at least the adaptation to, the totalitarian state, and on the other, the craving for recognition and the adaptation to new societal, political, and moral standards. The majority of East Germans supported Stolpe in manifesting his position as an influential Eastern politician against the political takeover of the West. This pattern represented an envisaged blueprint of life for Easterners: the struggle in the initial aftermath of unification ought to be followed by overcoming the yoke of the GDR past and should eventually result in a new status of influence and respect within the united Germany.

Thus, by 1992, East Germans were divided into three camps that were roughly equal in size: those who favored stronger measures in coming to terms with the *Stasi* past, those who were satisfied with the current *modus vivendi*, and those who resented the issue altogether. However, two years later, public perceptions performed a drastic U-turn. Table 4.16 shows that the number of contented people stayed at 28 percent. But now, only 19 percent favored an increased discourse, with a majority of 52 percent wanting to finally close the issue.[7] A certain sense of over-saturation emerged that resulted from the constant media exposure of such issues. The results indicated an attitude that society should go on with life by looking ahead instead of interrogating the unpleasant, morally reprehensible, and increasingly distant aspects of a past existence. For collaborators and sympathizers to the regime, any emerging guilt could have been circumvented by avoiding the confrontation with one's former moral deficiencies. Hence, the collective memory of Eastern Germany looked for convenience and comfort that worked on a selective base that remembered the positive and repressed the negative. The *Stasi* and the involvement of a considerable number of GDR citizens certainly belonged to the latter.

CONCLUDING REMARKS

Despite their political antagonism, patterns of participation in the GDR and the FRG shared some essential features. Both systems encouraged active political participation and offered a variety of opportunities for the politically interested. In the West, the rise of the Greens broadened the existing party agenda of Christian, Social, and Liberal Democrats, while trade unions and citizen initiatives offered ample opportunities to voice political demands. In East Germany active and informed participation was regarded as a vital cornerstone of the official political culture. Individuals were expected to participate through membership in mass organizations and cast their votes at election time. A considerable number of citizens joined the SED or the block parties. From a quantitative perspective, East Germans were actually more involved in politics than their Western counterparts. However, participation in the GDR was streamlined and followed rigid top-down patterns. The party did not represent political interest but instead mediated it from the *Politbüro* and the Central Committee to the individual. With the exception of brief phases in the mid-1950s and mid-1960s, internal party democracy and factionalization were virtually impossible. Democratic Centralism ruled the GDR. Participation was coercive and state-mobilized. Interest representation suffered from a paradoxical antagonism. The regime encouraged participation but undermined expression of citizens' interest. Participation was welcomed as long as it followed the designed tracks of interest aggregation. Involvement in politics was encouraged as long as the citizen accepted the vanguard role of the party in policy making. The dictatorship allowed political activity only in those ways that strengthened the citizen's allegiance to the state but would not question its authority.

This infantilization of the individual, the suppression of individual demands under the common goal of society continued to shape political participation after unification. The SED regime promoted political activity and fostered political knowledge—albeit with strong dogmatic implications—among a public that eagerly observed West German politics through the help of Western TV and visits from relatives and friends. With the demise of the GDR, these norms of mass participation and knowledge did not disappear but instead significantly contributed to the strikingly high turnouts and interest in politics in early 1990. Although the participative euphoria was also caused by a thirst for free expression after four decades of totalitarian suppression, such astonishing turnouts of more than 90 percent would not have been possible without an already informed citizenry that was accustomed to participation. These virtues of information and participation were even strong enough to guarantee stabilization at a satisfactory level, despite the massive overexposure of unification issues in the media and the general easing of the revolutionary and highly politicized climate. What the GDR failed to teach, however, was the substance of democracy. Participation was not designed to aggregate individual interest and demands and ultimately to influence the government's course of policies and politics. Instead it represented a way for the government to influence its citizens. The rigid top-down hierarchy did not allow for the expression of individual concerns.

The development of West Germany after World War II showed that the citizen virtue of confidence can be a learning process. The participatory revolution of the 1970s dramatically changed the political climate. Since then, West Germans have developed into a participative, interested, and informed citizenry. Public interest groups expanded the political agenda to include post-materialist issues. Demonstrations, protests, and other direct action methods broadened the array of political activities. Political freedom and expression of political will turned into standards that were taken for granted. The West German citizen of the 1980s was more aware, more confident, and more critical than his or her counterpart of the 1950s. In contrast to this evolutionary process, Easterners were forced to develop their citizenship virtues in a crash course. While it took almost twenty years for Westerners to become actively involved in party politics and public-initiative groups, the rapid extension of the Western structures of interest mediation onto the Eastern *Länder* demanded a sudden commitment to active participation from the newly democratized citizens of the East. With the coercive nature of participation of the SED regime being swept aside, and with only rudimentary experience in confidently expressing individual demands it seemed only logical that active engagement and participation in politics were underdeveloped in the East. Trade unions, civic groups, and political parties in Eastern Germany quickly became aware of this in light of their rapidly declining membership figures. Unified Germany therefore faced the challenge of expanding the already existing prerequisites of democratic citizenship—political interest and knowledge—into active participation. Easterners needed to realize that active involvement in politics had its benefits, with individual demands resulting in policy changes and individual commitment improving the state of society.

In the first years since unification, however, East Germans had experienced exactly the opposite. The revolutionary upheavals during the autumn of 1989, the participation in demonstrations, and the civic movement represented highly positive individual commitments. The Monday marches in Leipzig called for freedom and civic liberties, for the individual's right to determine his or her destiny. One year later, people's destinies lay in the hands of the political elite, most notably from the West. The feeling of mis- and under-representation within unified Germany grew. Easterners sensed a political and administrative colonization by the West. The predominantly Western parties were logically regarded as the agents of change in the new *Länder*. Social, Christian, and to some extent Liberal Democrats designed the policies and were responsible for their implementation. The changes brought about by unification, however, were hard, sometimes devastating for the individual. Since hopes of "blossoming landscapes" did not materialize, criticism against—Western—political parties increased. They administered the change, but the change did not live up to its promise.

This negative attitude was further strengthened by the fact that the pro-grammatic bases of some political parties were simply out of touch with the fundamental concerns of East Germans. Inter-party turmoil between renewal-ists and the establishment, as well as persistent revelations of former *Stasi* ties of top Eastern politicians, certainly did not promote the legitimacy of the party system. It only stressed the sense of a lost cause. While the revolution was sup-posed to mark the dawn of a new era, it merely resulted in the continued in-volvement of Communist collaborators within the new Western political setting. The persistently weak party identification showed that political parties faced enormous difficulties in getting accepted as vital agents of political repre-sentation. Surprisingly, the number of people who dropped their identification with a Western party after unification outnumbered those who developed new affiliations. The Western party system was on the verge of destructive rejection. Consequently, the PDS was able to cash in on such negative attitudes. Gysi's *bunte Truppe* represented a lively contrast to the established party elites of the West. The PDS took the role of the advocate of the East and was supported by people with wide-ranging societal backgrounds. With local advisory groups, and an extensive local network, and backed by financial resources from its SED past, the party managed to stay in touch with the populace and therefore com-pensated for the problems of Western parties in establishing sound party affilia-tions in the East. By voting for the PDS, East Germans turned the notion of mis- and under-representation into an affirmative statement. Defamation by Western elites (the red-painted fascists) only strengthened support for the party. Despite its legacy as the successor organization of the SED and despite allegations over *Stasi* involvement of some of its leaders, the party was per-ceived by a considerable number as the only viable alternative. The PDS emerged as the catalyst for protest votes, exemplifying discontent with the Western party system and defiance against the perceived political colonization. Eventually, the initial euphoria surrounding unification, the naive idolizing of the West complemented by the denunciation and flat rejection of anything that was connected to the GDR, was replaced by a more realistic and critical under-standing of politics. Notions of confident pride in the East emerged. As the only exclusively Eastern party, the PDS served as a vital anchor for this emerg-ing mentality. Within the near future it remains unlikely that electoral support for the PDS will vanish. Although more protest vote than actual political orien-tation, the mere fact that 95 percent of PDS members used to own a SED party book accounts for an electoral potential of at least 15 percent in the Eastern *Länder*. Unless Western parties are able to establish more comprehensive af-filiations with the Eastern populace, the PDS will not disappear from the politi-cal scene.

The political agenda of the FRG and the GDR was to some extent compara-ble. Despite the system antagonism, concerns about peace and environmental protection were shared by East and West Germans. However, the economic development of the Federal Republic and the resulting affluence, as well as civic freedom and pluralism, accounted for a fundamentally different outlook on politics. In the West, post-materialism and the "New Politics" emerged by the late 1960s, embracing a departure from such former principles as stability and security, as well as new forms of interest representation, for instance extra-parliamentary opposition or citizen initiatives. In the East, politics had been strictly confined to the static patterns of interest aggregation that were controlled by the SED. The expression of political opposition was a careful undertaking in order not to alienate the authorities. Real dissent, however, was never tolerated. Only the protective function of the church provided some form of autonomy from state and party. Hence, individual expression which lay outside of the official agenda bore the potential of system criticism. To argue for peace as a private citizen or to point out ecological exploitation represented ultimate challenges to the regime. Hence, "New Politics" in East and West had fundamentally different prerogatives. In the FRG, they were evolutionary, developing out of the gradual maturity of society. In the GDR the same principles were revolutionary (Dalton 1993: 263). With the demise of the regime and the transitional processes within unified Germany, the revolution, however, gave way to the adaptation to Western political, social, and economic standards. Principles of "New Politics" lost in significance. Materialist notions of social and job security, rising prices or wage levels dominated people's thoughts. In the GDR, "New Politics" was a form of protest against the regime. With the regime consigned to history, "New Politics" ultimately lost its rationale. Thus, citizen initiatives or ecological organizations had to face severe difficulties in generating a political impact in the Eastern *Länder*. The churches were confronted with additional problems. Their functions as protective umbrellas for opposition and interest articulation disappeared after unification. No longer useful as political instruments, the true level of secularization in the East became visible.

The experiences of the Federal Republic after the mid-1960s resulted in dramatically different state-citizen relations between East and West. Apart from the participatory revolution and growing interest in politics, West Germans displayed an ever-increasing civic confidence, indicated by the emergence of citizen initiative groups and the growing readiness to protest or demonstrate against unjust administrative actions and policies. In return, the constitutional consensus over democracy as the best form of political organization became solid and unchallenged. Declining cleavages along the lines of class, religion, or profession accounted for a strong centrist drive in politics. Integration within the West, social security, economic stability and industrial harmony functioned as stable policy anchors. The appeal of the two *Volksparteien* SPD and CDU stabilized the party system and pushed extremism out of the realm of relevance. The approval rate of parliamentarism and the institutions of democracy consolidated at high levels, which provided for a buffer of support in times of economic crises or political terrorism. The former recipient and obedient mentality progressed toward an active, participative, confident, and informed citizenry.

In contrast, state-citizen relations in the GDR represented a succession of negative experiences. The upheavals of 1953 were answered with Soviet tanks and imprisonment. Not only was active participation and the expression of individual demands crushed to the ground but, most importantly, the legitimacy of the state was fundamentally eroded. The citizen was forced to comply with the system. If one did not agree with the *modus vivendi* of Stalinist principles and policies, he or she could choose only intellectual, internal emigration and a retreat into the private sphere. Although system-conformist behavior was required for professional advancement and social status, it hardly emerged out of a conscience that approved of the SED state. Only as long as the regime was able to offer a minimum of material benefits and social security was the individual willing to obey totalitarian rules. Infantilization of the individual and the general distrust by the authorities toward a more participative and politically emancipated role for their citizens finally backfired in 1989. Captured by decades of political indifference, East Germans had apathetically accepted restrictions imposed on individual liberties. They needed a catalyst to transform imminent dissatisfaction with the regime into concrete political action. Gorbachev's "perestroika," the subsequent opening of the Iron Curtain in Hungary, and the SED's reactionary response to Tiananmen finally got the East German revolution off the ground. By the autumn of 1989, the whole of East Germany was in a state of high political mobilization. The civic movement showed promising democratic virtues. Participation in demonstrations and the signing of petitions underlined notions of an actively involved citizenry. Demands for open discourse, free elections, and human rights confidently expressed fundamental democratic principles. The highly charged political atmosphere that began in the summer of 1989 continued even after the demise of the SED regime in early 1990. East Germans eagerly followed the political campaigns surrounding the *Volkskammer* elections of March 1990, as well as the preceding roundtable discussions between representatives of the civic movement and the government. The optimistic attitude prevailed that the future held the prospect of compensating for the wasted years under Communism.

This euphoria, however, was only short-lived. Although the arrival of an open society with its freedom of expression and freedom to travel was overwhelmingly appreciated, the new system of democracy failed to gain unanimous support. A variety of factors accounted for the Eastern public's largely skeptical attitude. First, hardly any East German—as well as hardly any Western politician—could foresee the hardship that unification would bring to some citizens. The loss of the all-encompassing welfare state, the subsidy system, and employment security confronted many Easterners with a notion of instability for the first time in their lives. Democracy, which had caused these ruptures, was consequently perceived in a more negative way. Secondly, in retrospect the feeling of colonization by the West turned the people's revolution into an obsolete effort. One superimposed system—although democratic—had replaced another superimposed one. For decades Soviet-type Stalinism ruled the GDR. Now West German principles of government ruled the Eastern *Länder*. Instead of unification, Easterners were annexed. The brave and risky undertaking of ousting a totalitarian regime generated hopes of reforming the rundown society. Until the end of 1989, unification was regarded as only an eventual step somewhere in the not-so-distant future. The emphasis, however, was on reforming Socialism. Although the roundtable talks of early 1990 addressed the question of unification, emphasis was still on reform, which was indicated by the lengthy constitutional draft for a unified Germany. In the end, envisaged reform turned into the implementation of the Western mode of government. Although the overwhelming majority of Easterners initially supported quick unification with the West, the subsequent experiences of the transition processes showed a severe lack of democratic legitimation that consequently weakened the emotional attachment to this newfound democratic unity. In the third place, although the East Germans were rightfully proud to have initiated and participated in the only successful revolution ever on German ground, their subsequent political behavior within a new political environment demonstrated that the civic democratic virtues of the Easterners were only weakly developed as a result of the forty-year-long oppression of civic liberties. The high levels of participative involvement in the SED state were artificial, with hardly any cognitive support. After unification, the dramatic decline in membership in political parties and interest groups showed the hollow mode of participation. For East Germans, democracy still had to be filled with meaning and content. Although a willingness to protest was widespread and although Easterners felt underrepresented within the post-unification political process, a reluctance to become actively involved was nonetheless prevalent. In contrast to the revolution of 1989, which offered a prime example of direct citizen action (Dalton 1993: 189), East Germans returned to their former indifferent and incapacitated attitudes. A recipient mentality re-emerged that took life as a given destiny and undermined the confident and self-reliant effort of improving one's situation.

Hence, in contrast to the postwar Federal Republic, the new system of democracy faced enormous difficulties in generating positive and affirmative orientations. The arrival of democracy was held responsible for individual economic and social hardship. The extension of the West German form of government ridiculed the revolutionary experience, while the subservient and obedient behavioral standards of the GDR era rendered an active and confident expression of demands and interests difficult. Within a relatively short period satisfaction with administrative action reached acceptable standards. The large majority of Easterners were content with bureaucratic measures that represented a good sign against the backdrop of the vast changes in this area. However, the critical perceptions toward Western officials gave reason to worry. Work relations within public administration served as telling examples of the persistent mentality clashes between East and West. Westerners were perceived as arrogant. Easterners were perceived as incompetent. The Western missionary collided with the Eastern pupil. Diverging socialization and cultural experiences, as well as considerable differences in living standards, further exemplified the rift between two societies that had not yet merged together.

These clashes however, possessed an important buffer that safeguarded the democratic development of the Eastern *Länder*. A stable democracy also relies on stable institutions. In contrast to other East European societies, the solid and time-tested democratic structures of West Germany were implemented in the former GDR. The proven ability of the *Bonn* Republic to defend its system against anti-democratic principles renders a reversal of the democratic transition difficult. In that respect, even if political orientations of East Germans would tend toward a return to authoritarian rule, they have less opportunity and chances to do so, in comparison to other post-Communist states. Eastern Germany is therefore privileged by being exempt from institutional conflicts.

These complicated state-citizen relations were further aggravated by revelations of the practicalities of the totalitarian elite. The GDR state betrayed its citizens. The discovery of the extent of the *Stasi* apparatus came as a sudden shock and split the Eastern society. On the one hand, *Stasi* informants and permanent staff showed severe problems in acknowledging their unjust behavior. There was hardly a feeling of guilt since one worked for the Communist cause or left the responsibility with higher authorities. On the other hand, anger and bitterness prevailed among those who perceived themselves as victims of a oppressive regime. Ideological commitment or existentialist necessity clashed with indignation and outrage. The state—the political system that organizes the citizens' lives—gave the citizen yet another reason for caution and skepticism. The state deceived the individual, showing disloyalty and indifference toward people's needs, concerns, and demands. Over the course of the past few years, however, this societal rift in Eastern Germany seemed to have healed. The majority showed sympathy for *Stasi* collaborators, while a desire to close the issue of the *Stasi* controversy became widespread. Here lies a potential danger for leaving permanent scars. Without a confrontation with the *Stasi* past, a mental departure from the GDR will never be possible. Repressing the inhuman aspects of the oppressive regime resulted in a selective memory that disproportionally remembered the positive aspects—for instance, social welfare or job security. For the actual *Stasi* collaborator, repressing the involvement within the apparatus made him or her subject to dependence, threat, and blackmail. In post-unification Germany, the *Stasi* legacy affects only the Eastern psyche. However, without a clear working out of the *Stasi* past in both East and West, Westerners will not be capable of understanding the psychological trauma that haunts large numbers of Easterners. Without it, East Germans will not be forced to understand and acknowledge past failures and moral shortcomings.

NOTES

1. For a more thorough discussion on the concept of citizenship see, for example, Heater 1990, Janowitz 1983, Oppenheim 1977.

2. The Catholic church never achieved a level of importance and influence comparable to that of its evangelical counterpart and largely refrained from politics altogether. Former officials of the *Stasi* department for church relations acknowledged that the apparatus regarded the Catholic church as a minority church which tried to maintain the highest possible distance from the state, while possessing a mostly apolitical attitude (Insider Komitee 1994: 377). Hence, the goal of the *Stasi* was to prevent the Catholic church from acquiring an equal status of political involvement and interest as the evangelical one—a policy that undoubtedly succeeded.

3. For a gripping account on the mass protests in Leipzig, see Zwahr 1993.

4. Even according to age groups the numbers stayed at similar levels. Only the younger generations were slightly more hesitant to identify themselves with a political party. In November 1994, 54 percent below thirty had no party identification as compared to 49.6 percent of the total population.

5. In 1990, the Federal Constitutional Court ordered the introduction of separate 5 percent thresholds for East and West. When in 1994 the all-German threshold was reinstated, the peculiarities of the German electoral system which combines majority and representative elements gave the PDS 30 seats in the *Bundestag*.

6. In the East, PDS supporters were particularly critical. In 1994, 89 percent of respondents with a strong PDS identification were dissatisfied with democracy. For those with a moderate or weak PDS identification, the level of dissatisfaction was still strikingly high at 79 percent. According to age cohorts, respondents under 24 and between ages 40 and 49 were slightly more skeptical, while people over 60 shared an evaluation that a was little above average.

7. According to age brackets, the figures offered nearly identical proportions.

5

Mass Culture

As the final anchor of civic identity, a common mass public culture had been defined as "common historical memories, myths, symbols and traditions," generated by a "set of common understandings and aspirations, sentiments and ideas" (Smith 1991: 11). Mass culture, however, goes well beyond this conceptualization. It defines itself not merely in reference to the past—from history, myths, and symbols—which are then expressed in traditions and common understandings, but furthermore refers to a society's reaction to modern technological, economic, political, or social developments in the process of establishing prevalent attitudes, standards, and behavior that fill one's life with meaning. Meaning in this sense simply implies how individuals organize and conceptualize their lives. Where to go on holiday, what to do after work, where to live, how to define career, work, and social relations, or what to consume, are questions of mass-cultural relevance that could also be described as lifestyle.

During the five decades before unification, West Germany had established distinctly different mass-cultural features in comparison to the GDR. One can argue that after World War II, West Germany underwent a transformation into a postmodern society. In general, postmodernism indicates the belief that a new age has begun that transcends modernity with a distinctly different set of behavior, experiences, and attitudes. The postmodern society shows such features as the development of an information and consumer society, a much looser form of organization and discipline, or new attitudes toward expenditure, work, and leisure that are fostered by growing levels of consumption, affluence, and the desire for immediate gratification (Gibbins 1989: 15). East Germany was thrown into this new age without the slow and gradual development that West Germany had experienced since 1945. With unification, mass-cultural characteristics that had become standard features of life in the Federal Republic splashed over the new *Länder* in a gigantic wave that drastically changed the lives of most individuals and therefore, fundamentally shaped people's perceptions toward the unified reality. East Germans opted for the social, political, and economic order of the Federal Republic, but, in return, mass culture was included in the package when Easterners favored unification over reforming the Socialist GDR.

Three mass-cultural phenomena in particular fundamentally changed the East German existence, whereas an adaptation of (or at least a trend towards) these mass-cultural standards would indicate the development of a common national identity. They include consumerism, life and leisure, and the media. During the first months following the opening of several border crossings, scenes of a massive consumer migration dominated the news agenda in Germany. On the *Autobahn* and in numerous towns along the border, convoys of East German "*Trabis*" and "*Wartburgs*" brought the traffic to a standstill. East Germans were flooding West German shops. Supermarkets and department stores had to close down temporarily because of the unexpected rush for Western goods. Ingenious Western entrepreneurs traveled eastward in trucks packed with oranges and bananas, and returned with empty crates and full wallets. The 100 Deutschmark "welcome gift" that every Easterner was entitled to collect upon arrival in the West was quickly spent on such long-wanted consumer products as tropical fruit, jeans, or sneakers. Millions had their first taste of life in the West. The consumer world with its affluence and choice was taken as a vital performance indicator for the market economy of the Federal Republic. In the eyes of most East Germans, consumer products manifested the superiority of the West and functioned as focal points for their own individual needs and desires. After a day-out in the West, the return to the gray reality of the GDR came as a shock that drastically highlighted the material deficiencies of one's daily existence. An analysis of identity-creating processes within the unified Germany has to take such a spectacular mass phenomenon into account. The exclusion of an assessment of consumer patterns and preferences would mean the exclusion of formative experiences of East Germans after the fall of wires and fences. The unexpected opening of the Iron Curtain on the evening of November 9, 1989, represented the "true caesura" (H. Weber 1993: 106) of the East German revolution. Suddenly, people were exposed to the vast gaps between the differing consumer societies and their respective living standards. It was then that the notion of reforming the old system gradually gave way to an anonymous support for a rapid unification. As individuals in the hostile consumer environment of the GDR, Easterners voted with force for the Western consumer society.

Aside from this spectacular mass hysteria, two further mass-cultural phenomena shaped East German perceptions toward the unified existence. The admittedly generalizing heading of "Life and Leisure" addresses the fundamental changes caused by modernization, restoration, and renovation programs in Eastern cities and villages. For years, buildings and road and rail networks in the GDR had been largely neglected. After unification, Easterners gradually were able to enjoy the comfort and convenience of modern housing and the redevelopment of urban landscapes. Unification also brought the highly welcomed freedom to travel. The pent-up desire to visit the "other Germany" and to experience foreign countries other than those of the Communist bloc resulted in a tourist boom. In addition, the increase in leisure opportunities brought Easterners a wider choice of how to spend their spare time. The rather limited range of leisure activities in the GDR gave way to a wide selection that was capable of satisfying any taste—from eclectic and uncensored forms of art to new waves of sport, such as tennis, squash, or bodybuilding. They exemplified the introduction of new societal standards of individuality, independence, and free will.

Finally, the extension of the Western dual system of private and public media stood in sharp contrast to the parsimonious media diet that had been offered by the SED state. As a telling example of the vast changes, this chapter examines the arrival of the new age of television as an indicator of the dramatic mass-cultural change in this sector. Although West German television had been received even before 1990, the Eastern consumer could now choose among some 25 channels and was exposed to new standards of information, entertainment, and presentation.

THE GERMAN DEMOCRATIC REPUBLIC

Compared to other countries of the Comecon, the GDR was a prosperous and successful industrial state. By the mid-1970s East Germany had established a "functioning economic system" (H. Weber 1993: 83) and showed a respectable growth in general living standards. Despite the worldwide recession, the GDR was proud to present full employment and stable prices for essential food items, as well as a sizable growth of the average monthly income (from 755 Mark in 1970 to 860 Mark 1974), while the provision of consumer goods grew steadily. Low prices for basic goods were financed through the disproportionate costs of luxury items. Prices for cars, refrigerators, washing machines, and television sets stood in no relation to the average monthly income. The purchase of such products was a long-term investment that required years of saving. The often scarce production of luxury items resulted in long waiting lists that stretched out over several years. Eventually, persistence and thriftiness paid off, and by the 1970s nearly every household enjoyed the convenience of modern appliances (see Table 5.1). The luxury goods were no longer the exception but became a standard feature—albeit with a delay of at least ten years as compared to West Germany.

Despite a period of economic stabilization and success in the early 1970s, the gap in living standards with the Western rival did not decrease but widened. By the late 1970s, the economic tide turned and living standards began to stagnate (H. Weber 1993: 83, 91). During the last decade of its existence, the GDR was permanently confronted with the prospect of financial bankruptcy. Only substantial loans from West Germany kept it alive (see Chapter 3).

Table 5.1
Provision of Consumer Products in the GDR (percentages per household)

	1955	1965	1975	1985	1988
Car	0.2	8.2	26.2	48.2	54.7
Refrigerator	0.4	25.9	84.7	137.5	159.6
Washing machine	0.5	27.7	73.0	99.3	107.3
Television set	1.2	53.7	87.9	117.6	125.2

Source: Statistical Yearbook 1989: 53.

Hence, the shortage of supply and often poor quality of consumer goods re-emerged as constant features of life in the GDR.

In contrast to common Western marketing slogans that confidently praise the virtues of a product, East German goods were presented in a plain matter-of-fact style. Both language and design were dull and lacked any appeal (H.W. Schmidt 1994: 367). This was all the more logical, since the planned Socialist economy did not promote such concepts as advertising, marketing, or competition. The GDR product was not challenged by the prerogative of any market economy to sell at maximum profit. Every article was offered at a fixed price with a fixed quality. Production was geared toward the satisfaction of often only basic demands. Stimulation of demand was absent, and innovation toward the improvement of standard products was severely lacking. Demand for consumption products in the GDR quite often exceeded the supply and consequently even the most unattractive product eventually found its buyer (H.W. Schmidt 1994: 367). The public's experiences of shortages and scarcity were further emphasized by the vast affluence and luxury that was prevalent in the West. Western television in particular transmitted advertising images of a consumer paradise and generated consumer wishes that could by no means be met by the Communist authorities. With the easing of restrictions on cross-border travel (see Chapter 2), personal hands-on experiences of Western lifestyles gradually became possible for larger segments of society. These occasional Western experiences—travel to the West, Western friends and families staying in the East, the Christmas package filled with Western goods—were highly appreciated and treasured exceptions from the streamlined Socialist consumer reality that drastically revealed the deficiencies of the GDR.

The traumatic reality of the Wall and barbed wires, as well as the complicated and time-consuming application procedure to travel to the West, gave consumer products a powerful position as additional communicators, as "ambassadors" (Diesener and Gries 1993: 23) of a different and affluent world. Not only were Western goods the topic of much conversation but furthermore they became relics, while their possession quite often meant an elevated social status. West Germany provided an immensely important focal point for choice, variety, and quality of consumer products and for affluent living standards. East Germans were in fact "fixated" (H. Weber, 1993: 91) on the more prosperous Federal Republic and the persisting gap between East and West. Thus, consumerism generated political attitudes. Since television, telecommunications, and the gradual easing of travel restrictions gave East Germans increasing opportunities to experience a share of life in the West, Western products and the Western consumer world acquired a normative status. They constantly reminded the population of how life could be. During daily shopping trips, however, East Germans were confronted with the Socialist reality of suppressed consumer wishes, lack of choice, shortage of goods, and long queues. These deficiencies of the planned economy generated into judgmental variables where the gap between potentiality—as seen in the West—and reality became increasingly unbearable.

Life and Leisure

In comparison to Western societies, life in the GDR was characterized by a distinctly slower pace and was visibly less stressful and hectic (Woods 1993: 59–60). With a limited choice of leisure activities, people focused on their social environments of friends and family. When asked about their priorities in life, respondents mentioned "harmony within the family" and "happy marriages" as the most important goals (Lemke 1989: 88). At work, permanent gaps in the provision of material allowed for several breaks. Attitudes toward time and performance at work were markedly relaxed. Apart from its productive function, the Socialist collective also had an individual, personality-enhancing ambition (Belwe 1989: 97). The working environment represented an essential focus for one's social life. After work, colleagues jointly participated in sport, organized picnics, and went on holidays together. Such tight social networks were widely regarded as highly positive achievements of the Socialist society (Belwe 1989: 103). Ninety percent of all workers in the GDR thought highly of harmonious working environments, as well as of companionable relations to their fellow workers (Sailer 1989: 148). Advanced social services including guaranteed employment and pensions, subsidized housing, child and health care, complemented the widespread sense of security.

Cultural exchanges with other societies were hardly possible. While abroad, East Germans were only allowed to experience another Socialist reality. On the shores of Lake Balaton or the Black Sea, the cultural broadening of horizons was severely limited by talking to your East European comrade who lived under similar ideological principles and a similar one-party rule, and experienced a similar Socialist lifestyle. In addition to being confined to travel only to Socialist countries, the regime's restrictive currency policy further hampered cultural exchanges. East Germans were only allowed to buy foreign Socialist currency in such low amounts that often even simple hotel expenses could not be paid for. With little money to spend, East Germans were regarded as second-class tourists who were only reluctantly served. Consequently, Easterners often grouped together at campgrounds as their affordable choice of accommodation. Thus, even in a foreign country, travelers of the GDR often spent their holidays with their compatriots. Experienced cultural differences could be regarded as marginal.

The SED instrumentalized art as a pedagogic means for the general political and social education of the individual (Stiller 1989: 148–150). Artists were obliged to close the gap between "art and real life" (H. Weber 1993: 52) by expressing images of Socialist reality. Decadent notions were politically unsound, while abstract art opposed the fundamental imperative of tangibility. Hence, the SED preferred, encouraged, and implemented Socialist realism as the binding form of artistic expression. Consequently, the regime did not only criticize the "trivial" art of light entertainment but furthermore attacked all forms of Capitalist/Western art which, according to the SED rhetoric, lacked class consciousness and depicted decadence. Authorities arrested artists or expelled them to the FRG, canceled events, or censored books, while conjuring up morality and tradition (Stiller 1989: 148). Theater, film, and literature found it difficult to contribute to a spirit of discourse and confrontation. On the contrary, art in East Germany was heavily supervised, controlled, and largely streamlined. By 1980, the reservations against Western and light entertainment gradually decreased. The SED adopted a more pragmatic approach and slowly abandoned its idea of establishing a Socialist form of culture. In fact, art and culture turned into consumption goods (Stiller 1989: 147). To counter the danger of simply copying Western patterns, the SED fostered its own version of contemporary, mass-oriented forms of entertainment by initiating an FDJ movement for traditional German songs and by concentrating on German folklore. Eventually, by the mid 1980s, diversity and quantity of entertainment increased. The party finally acknowledged the "compensatory function" (Stiller 1989: 152) of simple entertainment as a welcome diversion and relief from daily pressures. Still the emphasis on the symbiosis of culture and education remained, albeit the former rigid prerogative of a high culture of fine arts was significantly softened. Now, even Western rock music found its way onto East German stages. Between supply and demand, however, a gap was still apparent. While the high-cultural offerings, such as theater, classical concerts, and belles-lettres literature were quite sufficient, "lower" forms of entertainment were still characterized by a shortage in provision.

In accordance with the SED's demanding ambition of establishing a Communist society, the regime expected from its citizens the pursuit of political activities in their spare time and encouraged participation in political parties and mass organizations (see Chapter 4). In practice, however, leisure preferences differed strongly from this theoretical imperative and were instead in line with other industrial nations. According to a sociological survey in 1966, 68 percent chose to watch television in their spare time, complemented by walks (50 percent), reading newspapers and magazines (47 percent) and reading books (42 percent). Thirty-five percent preferred to spend time with their children, while political activities were attractive to only 16 percent (H. Weber 1993: 65). An additional favorite pastime was sport. The membership figures of the "German Association for Sport and Gymnastics" grew steadily from 8.4 percent of the population in 1960 to 21.9 percent in 1988 (Statistical Yearbook 1989: 330). Despite the powerful social impact of political parties and mass organizations, East Germans showed a strong urge to design their life individually. People looked for a partial escape from the ever-present and often annoying official political rhetoric by retreating into private spheres, into individual, nonpolitical entities, where state and party did not exert any influence. Over the years the system fostered a society of niches, where five-year plans, the collective, party propaganda, and Communist rhetoric were left outside.

The most prominent aspect of this retreat was the *Lauben* culture. The idea of a community of small garden lots originated in the German industrial revolution of the mid-nineteenth century. The entrepreneur Schreber, a protagonist for a more healthy environment, offered his employees a parcel of land for individual use. Over the years, this concept developed into a vital cornerstone of social life, both in West and East Germany. Membership figures for the association of allotment-gardeners in the GDR grew from 940,000 in 1965 to 1.5 million in 1988 (Statistical Yearbook 1989: 414). In East Berlin, 40 percent of families owned a garden (Rytlewski 1988: 639), most of them equipped with a *Laube* (cottage). Gardeners emerged as a mass organization and the private entity of the *Laube* transformed into an escape from daily life and represented the focus of leisure and activity on the weekend. Party pragmatists silently tolerated such escapism. It functioned as an important safety valve within the closed and totalitarian society (Sontheimer 1990: 72) and furthermore represented the nucleus of social existence in the GDR: a society of little unpolitical cells.

Apart from the *Laube*, the car constituted the other unofficial ambition of private leisure and activity. The demand for individual transportation remained constantly high. The annual production of *Trabants* and *Wartburgs* increased steadily, from 64,000 in 1960 to 218,000 in 1988 (Statistical Yearbook 1989: 27). But production could by no means meet the consistently high demand. The waiting list for a new *Trabant* increased to an impossibly long period of twelve years. It therefore came as no surprise that the car acquired the status of a fetish. In 1984, East Germans spent an astonishing 28 percent of their total expenditure on items associated with an automobile (Rytlewski 1988: 639). The car truly represented the most precious possession.

Media

After the demise of the Nazi dictatorship, the Soviet military administration gradually passed the authority of the media sector to the East German Communists. With the subsequent establishment of a one-party rule, the SED enjoyed a "monopoly on opinion" (H. Weber 1993: 25) by controlling radio, publishing houses, and newspapers. Over the years, the regime not only functionalized the media as a propagandistic means for the political legitimation of its totalitarian rule but also as an instrument for the psychological mobilization and political indoctrination of the population (Meyer 1989: 41). Abstract ideological and political issues were rather underrepresented. Instead, the media of the GDR focused on the documentation of tangible achievements and successes of the system. At the center stood the general relationship between state and citizen which the SED regarded as a mutual contract of service and performance. Thus, the media reported on concrete deeds and accomplishments of both the population and the Communist authorities (Meyer 1989: 41). Society was portrayed as a large family where state and party provided security in return for the personal commitment of the individual to the goals of Socialism. Particularly before elections, party congresses, or political holidays, the amount of mobilizing campaigns, appeals, proclamations, and political discussions increased significantly in trying to present the image of a united and dynamic society (Meyer 1989: 42). But even without such events, the political orientation of the GDR media was obvious, by its portraying the superiority and accomplishments of the Socialist system. The constant exposure to the achievements and successes of Socialism in general and the SED state in particular constituted a permanent indoctrinary irrigation for the population.

The official news agency ADN (*Allgemeiner Deutscher Nachrichtendienst*) possessed the monopoly on foreign news. Apart from ADN, only the key SED publication "*Neues Deutschland*" employed foreign correspondents. As a state agency, ADN directly responded to instructions and guidelines of the SED and the Central Committee. Hence, "news" was often reformulated, censored, extended, or shortened by party executives in the "Department for Agitation" within the Central Committee and occasionally directly by the *Politbüro*. Reports that were formulated by radio or the TV news broadcast *Aktuelle Kamera* were strictly ordered to report the ADN version of the story, which gave the agency the status of the "prime collective provider of information" (Olivier 1995: 246). According to a former senior employee, the overwhelming majority of journalists accepted and adapted to the role of functional weapons in establishing the Communist society (Olivier 1995: 248), which gave ADN the key position as the central henchman for the regime in the process of ideologically streamlining the population. Critical journalism was almost absent. Even without the direct intervention of party and state officials, journalists and reporters internalized the mere threat of censorship and avoided conflict by circumventing issues and interpretations that could have aroused official criticism. After decades of tutelage, the "scissors in the mind" (Olivier 1995: 250) worked in a pragmatic manner.

In 1988, 99 percent of households in the GDR possessed a radio and 96 percent owned a television (Statistical Yearbook 1989: 291). Television represented the most important source for information and entertainment. With an estimated weekly spare time of some 25 hours devoted to media consumption, Easterners spent 13 hours watching television, 10 hours listening to the radio, and 1.5 hours reading newspapers, magazines, or books (Warnecke 1989: 87), which qualitatively and quantitatively placed the GDR in line with other European societies. Television, radio, and newspapers in the GDR were characterized by a constant flow of political messages. While listening to the GDR state radio, one was permanently confronted with such issues as a collective's overachievement of a production plan or the stunning fertility of this year's potato crop. This impression was supported by the statistical shares of the respective programs as shown in Table 5.2. Since "music" accounted for roughly half of the output of the five national and twelve regional radio stations, it seemed striking that "politics and economics" were allocated around 70 percent of the remaining air time. Consequently, "culture, drama, and entertainment" achieved only an insignificant status, with some 5 percent of the total broadcast hours.

Unfortunately, the official data on the two television channels was not as telling as that on radio. In particular, the vague category of "television journalism" made compelling conclusions on the degree of politicization of East German television difficult. Nonetheless, between 1965 and 1988, the category "informative political broadcasts" combined with the category "television journalism" accounted for a minimum of 24.1 percent in 1988, and for a maximum of 29.2 percent in 1965 (Statistical Yearbook 1989: 325). The largest percentage belonged to "drama and entertainment" (between 33.8 and 42.5 percent), which usually consisted of ideologically correct movies, soaps, or theater productions. Hence, the politicization of television was comparable to that of radio. Both media devoted considerable time to light entertainment—music on the radio, and film/theater/soaps on television. Political broadcasting, however, still exerted a significant impact on the media timetables.

Table 5.2
Radio Broadcasts in the GDR (percentages)

Year	Politics and Economics	Sport	News	Culture, Drama, Entertainment	Music
1965	38.8	0.8	5.2	5.7	49.4
1975	38.2	0.9	6.2	5.4	47.8
1980	38.2	1.2	7.0	4.8	47.1
1985	38.3	0.9	6.7	5.0	46.9
1988	34.0	1.2	6.1	5.5	51.1

Source: Statistical Yearbook 1989: 325.

Western television and radio represented welcome and widely appreciated changes from the streamlined media diet. With the exception of the greater area around Dresden,[1] at least the two major West German public channels could be received through standard aerials. According to estimates, some 80 percent of East Germans were able to receive Western channels (Wilke 1989). In the end, the GDR represented a hometurf for West German television, its news, and political magazines, as well as soaps and game shows. Table 5.3 demonstrates the permanent presence of Western television. Although the survey was taken among a small number of emigrants, it still provides a telling look at the Western penetration of Eastern mass culture. All respondents at least watched Western news programs sometimes. The most popular news broadcast in the West—the "*Tagesschau*"—was watched by two-thirds on a regular basis. The entertainment sector also enjoyed respectable numbers of followers, since around two-thirds were familiar with American television series and West German game shows.

Official efforts to stop the downward trend of consumers of Eastern media included an emphasis on drama and movies geared for mass tastes, or the launching of the youth radio station DT 64. Such efforts, however, could only soften the landslide. Instead, West German media acquired the status of a normative reference point for information, truth and entertainment as an escape from the often monotonous, streamlined, and propagandistic SED-recipe. It furthermore exposed Easterners to the vast differences between the two Germanys regarding lifestyle and political attitudes.

Table 5.3
East Germans Watching Western Television (percentages)

Broadcast		Regularly	Sometimes	Never
News	Tagesschau (8:00 P.M.)	65	35	--
	Tagesthemen (10:30 P.M.)	28	64	8
	Heute (7:00 P.M.)	46	64	11
	Heute-Journal (9:45 P.M.)	24	59	17
Soaps	Dallas	29	33	38
	Dynasty	26	26	48
Game shows	Dalli-Dalli	23	44	33
	Der Grosse Preis	22	47	31

N = 162 emigrants from GDR who received West German television.

Source: Hesse 1988: 43.

THE FEDERAL REPUBLIC

The first years after the capitulation of the Third Reich were characterized by severe material privation. Towns lay in ruins, food was rationed, and energy supplies were limited. The daily struggle to survive and to organize bare existential necessities left a traumatic mark on most West Germans. For the next two decades, material security dominated the public's consciousness, and the gradual improvement of living standards was at the top of the agenda of every household (see Table 5.4). By the mid-1950s, the booming economy gradually brought prosperity to broader segments of society. A wave of gluttony swept over the country, and West Germans seemed to compensate for the years of scarcity and self-denial of the preceding decade. To own a "*Volkswagen* Beetle" became the aspiration of the common man, and the car's cheap and robust design gradually allowed for the motorization of the entire society. "*Es geht wieder aufwärts*" (Things are looking up again)—a slogan widely used by media, politicians, and commentators—aptly characterized the public psyche. "Made in West Germany" was not only a label guaranteeing the quality and endurance of industrial products, but furthermore constituted a source of pride in the recently established consumer society.

Table 5.4
Consumer Products in West German Households (percentages)

| | 1972 | | 1989 | |
	Type II	Type III	Type II	Type III
Car	65.6	88.0	96.4	99.3
Color TV	9.1	12.9	95.2	93.8
Black and white TV	86.8	84.7	30.6	36.5
Refrigerator	98.1	99.0	80.6	82.0
Freezer	28.2	30.6	74.7	79.9
Combined refrigerator-freezer	—	—	25.3	30.5
Dishwasher	2.7	18.2	52.6	88.5

Type I (not included): two-person household including pensioners and social security recipients with low income.

Type II: four-person household, medium income.

Type III: four-person household, higher income.

Source: Statistical Yearbook 1991: 540; 1976: 496.

The unprecedented choice and variety of consumer products, and gradually the ability to purchase them, became vital agents for the enhancement of low self-esteem. After the demise of National Socialism and severe material privation, the Federal Republic offered West Germans a form of political and economic organization that was able to generate increasing and widespread prosperity, and consumerism emerged as a vital systemic bastion for the approval of the young democracy. By the 1970s, and merely 25 years after the total collapse of the Third Reich, West Germany developed into a highly affluent society. Widespread prosperity was all too obvious. Nearly every household sported a comprehensive range of modern appliances. With 425 cars per 1,000 capita in 1988, only the United States (561) and Luxembourg (453) fared better in international comparison (Statistical Yearbook 1990: 685). The GDP per capita increased from 5,466 Deutschmark in 1960 to DM 11,141 (1970) and to DM 34,528 in 1988 (Statistical Yearbook 1990: 566). Salaries rose persistently and made the West German labor force one of the best paid in the world. By the mid-1980s, the 35-hour working week was gradually introduced. The number of annual holidays was unparalleled and reflected the country's enormous economic success, with the average employee being entitled to thirty days vaction on top of eleven to thirteen church or public holidays.

Life and Leisure

Postwar West Germany experienced the "erosion of traditional political and social milieus" (Rudzio 1991: 480). Formerly, people had organized their lives around social, political, or religious affiliations, such as proletarian-Socialist, Catholic, bourgeois-liberal, or agrarian-conservative. These strong societal divisions gradually broke down and allowed for the emergence of distinctly classless and egalitarian elements. The expansion of the service industry resulted in an increase in white-collar jobs and contributed to the manifestation of the *Mittelstand,* a class of independent, small-business owners. The media bridged traditional milieus and catered to broader societal segments. With the exception of some Catholic boarding schools, educational affiliations to specific milieus disappeared, and neighborhoods gradually had a more mixed social composition. Eventually, West Germany became a more flexible and mobile society. Tribal, social, and religious homogeneity diminished, while the formerly close communal networks of family, church, and neighborhood were gradually eroded.

These processes were dramatically boosted by the cultural revolution. By the late 1960s, norms of personal and group behavior became less disciplined and authoritarian, as well as visibly more relaxed in comparison to the Adenauer era (see Chapter 4). By the mid-1960s the material orientation to build up one's life from the ruins left behind by World War II were gradually replaced by a consumer mentality which forever sought new outlets and satisfactions (Bark and Gress 1993: 70). In particular the younger generations no longer accorded work, career, and material security the same priority as their parents, whose thoughts and behavior were engrossed by years of reconstruction. These changing material perceptions, combined with the ongoing social developments of urbanization and increasing personal mobility and prosperity drew attention to new issues, including environmental concerns and citizenship initiatives, but also leisure and quality of life. The generation gap in West Germany was particularly pronounced because of the loss of millions of members of the now-middle generation who had died during the war. Since the young hardly had any recollection of the immediate aftermath of the Third Reich, generation differences were more defined than ever before in recent German history. Within these social trends, student radicals were able to set the agenda and to transform the political culture (see Chapter 4). Subsequently hierarchical patterns in schools and universities, at work and in the family were subject to severe scrutiny. Notions of "independence and free will" (Mertes 1994: 20) and a general objection to authoritarian standards became increasingly popular. The student revolts were in fact both cause and consequence (Mertes 1994: 20) of a cultural revolution that transformed West Germany into a new era and in retrospect represented the strongest caesura in the country's postwar history. Life in West Germany became freer and more open, while breaking with the former rigid patterns that characterized work, family, and leisure.

By the 1980s accumulated prosperity, short working hours, and long holidays supported a marked rise in leisure activities, both quantitatively and qualitatively. Between 1980 and 1989, the average four-person household with a medium income spent between 7 and 8 percent of their net income on costs related to a car, between 13 and 14 percent on general leisure activities, and around 3.5 percent on travel.[2] With increases in the GDP per capita of 31 percent (1980) and 50 percent (1988) as compared to 1970, West Germans were able to spend more money in absolute terms on travel, or sport or in restaurants. Throughout the 1980s the sports industry enjoyed a remarkable boom. Membership in the *Deutscher Sportbund*—the central umbrella organization for all sports clubs—more than doubled from 8.3 million (14 percent of the total population) in 1970 to 18.4 million (30 percent) in 1989 (Statistical Yearbook 1990: 394; 1983: 375). Sporting activities became more diversified. The traditional German passion for football and hiking was gradually complemented by more sophisticated physical undertakings, such as aerobics, bodybuilding, mountain climbing, windsurfing, and foremost by tennis.

Spending on travel increased steadily and destinations became ever more extravagant. According to the *Deutscher Reisebüro-Verband* (Association of Travel Agents) in 1960, 69 percent of West Germans spent their holidays within Germany. By 1989, the figures had reversed, and a markedly high 71 percent preferred to spend the most precious weeks of the year abroad. Average spending on holidays increased from some 700 Deutschmark per person in

Table 5.5
Travel Expenses (in Deutschmark) and Destinations, West Germany

	1960	1970	1980	1989
Austria	560	2,206	6,183	7,123
Italy	467	1,930	6,417	6,533
Spain	67	749	2,770	5,470
France	207	692	2,593	3,514
Switzerland	512	1,152	2,468	3,211
Netherlands	228	791	1,711	2,351
United States	288	640	1,050	2,070
Great Britain	90	279	906	1,276
Yugoslavia	21	409	1,055	1,038
Belgium-Luxembourg	50	208	469	608
Others	161	1,174	5,849	11,086
Total	2,651	10,230	31,471	44,280

Source: Deutsche Bundesbank, Press Office, 1995.

1970 to over DM 1,300 in 1989. As demonstrated in Table 5.5, the most popular foreign holiday destinations of 1960—Austria, Switzerland, and Italy—combined for a total travel spending of 58 percent. By 1989, the top three countries—Austria, Italy, and Spain—only attracted 43 percent, while the share of countries not listed in the table rose to 25 percent as compared to only 6 percent three decades earlier. Clearly, the summer rushes to the Alps and the teutonic bathtubs along the Italian coast were eventually regarded as rather philistine, and West Germans gradually conquered the remaining continents. By 1989, spending in foreign countries amounted to an astonishing 44 billion Deutschmark or some DM 650 per capita.

Media

Prior to the founding of the *Bonn* Republic in 1949, the Western occupying forces had already established a dual principle of media organization, consisting of private press and public radio and television. The system remained virtually unchanged for some three decades.[3] West German households received three public television channels through traditional terrestrial transmitters. In regions bordering other *Länder* or foreign countries these increased to four to five. Public radio stations, which roughly followed the federal structure of the *Länder*, broadcast between two and four programs. By the early 1980s proposals that were largely inspired by the CDU/CSU called for radio and television licenses for private operators, arguing that more programs would result in more variety and hence more freedom and consumer choice (Schatz et al. 1990: 352). With the demise of the SPD/FDP coalition in 1982, the media landscape in West Germany gradually became subject to massive changes. By 1990, all *Länder* with the exception of Hesse and Bremen had altered legislation to allow for the establishment of private radio and television. Aided by the new technical infrastructure of cable and satellite, the number of television channels jumped to around twenty-five within a period of only five years. In urban areas, numerous private radio stations competed with public providers. The former dual principle was transformed into a one-and-a-half duality of private press, as well as private and public radio and television.

However, program variety turned out to be rather minimal. Supply multiplied quantitatively but not qualitatively. In contrast to public channels, which benefited from significant licensing fees and tax revenues, private television was solely dependent on advertisement revenues. Private stations therefore hardly established distinctive profiles, since most geared toward the satisfaction of mainstream tastes. Specialized programs remained surprisingly rare, and a mediocre mixture of sports, soap operas, game shows, and the movies that totaled some 75 percent of their output (Schatz et al. 1990: 352) emerged as the streamlined recipe for attracting consumers. Educational and informative programs, however, were notably rare on the new television agenda and were neglected in favor of readily consumable simple-mindedness and the "eternal repetition of sameness" (Frei 1989: 454). As a consequence of the free flow of market forces, broadcasting became increasingly sensational to gear toward the public's inherent lust for the digestible extraordinary. News programs adopted a casual style of presentation. Talk shows that formerly addressed political issues now gave center stage to the ordinary citizen and his or her unusual experiences. Clamorous reports about crime and sex, or "shocking revelations" from celebrities introduced the West German public to a new form of tabloid journalism on television.

With increasing numbers of cable households and satellite dishes, more and more West Germans turned to private television. In 1990, private providers had a 40 percent share of the national television audience. In households with cable hook-ups the figures were even higher at 57 percent (Humphreys 1994: 272). Although partly financed by taxes, public channels still depended on advertising revenues to balance their budgets. Since the popularity of private stations grew constantly, public television tried to regain viewers by providing the same mix. Consequently, the number of soaps and sports broadcasts increased, while documentaries and political analyses were pushed to late-night slots. Only in the realms of news and information was the public sector able to maintain its position as an unsurpassed bastion of quality and reliability, although a "private" element of infotainment visibly crept into its standard of presentation. Hence, the argument of variety regarding both programming and providers which swung the debate in favor of privatization in the early 1980s remained an unfulfilled promise. Nonetheless, West Germans did not seem to mind the arrival of the new media age. Between 1985 and 1989 the average daily time spent in front of television sets increased from 147 to 160 minutes (Darschin and Frank 1994: 98–110). The downward trend of the early 1980s clearly had been reversed. Over a period of less than ten years, West German television was "Americanized." More channels offered less variety. Quality standards dropped, with the emphasis being on cheap and quick productions. Deliberate "channel surfing" over longer hours replaced selective viewing, and the former prerogative of television as a source of information and education was undermined by the desire for instant gratification of entertainment needs, using low standards as the common denominator of mainstream tastes.

THE NEW LÄNDER

Despite incredible advances since unification, material preconditions for participation in the consumer society were still markedly different between East and West. As seen in Chapter 3, general income and living standards were improving, but for Easterners they did not reach satisfying levels. An overwhelming majority were discontent and expressed widespread bewilderment with the slow approximation of living standards between the old and new *Länder* that was caused by the evident gap in salaries and wages. Although lower than in the West, income and wages nonetheless offered enough financial resources to participate in the free market consumer world. By 1994, East German households generated a financial surplus (capital after standing charges) of 439 Deutschmark per month, which represented a significant increase from DM 304 three years earlier (Allensbacher Berichte 27/1994: 1). Gradually, the gap in wages between East and West narrowed; income levels began to rise and people had more money to spend.

Table 5.6 demonstrates the dramatic rush on consumer products between 1991 and 1994. By 1994, car ownership had reached equal levels in East and West. Easterners quickly sold *Trabants* and *Wartburgs* and invested heavily in new automobiles. Between 1991 and 1994, the percentage of "type II" households who bought a brand new car rose from 39 to 43 percent. The figures of "type III" households increased even more, from 45 to 54 percent. Leaving more basic products such as washing machines or television sets out of the equation (since their demand had already been satisfied prior to 1989), East Germans hardly wasted time in purchasing items that some years earlier were either unavailable or outrageously expensive. Gaps between East and West regarding video cameras and recorders had largely been closed by 1994. Although provison levels of dishwashers and microwaves still showed distinct disparities, the increase in purchases of these products was nevertheless striking

Table 5.6
Consumer Products in Households, East and West (percentages)

		1991		1994	
		East	*West*	*East*	*West*
Type II([1])	Car	93.8	96.5	97.3	95.8
	Video Recorder	39.9	58.5	67.7	73.4
	Video camera	3.3	11.9	21.6	26.1
	Dishwasher	1.1	61.8	9.3	68.7
	Microwave	4.8	49.1	25.7	61.6
Type III([2])	Car	93.1	98.5	97.9	98.0
	Video recorder	40.2	54.8	71.5	72.8
	Video camera	6.9	14.2	25.3	33.7
	Dishwasher	3.1	85.3	13.6	85.3
	Microwave	11.9	47.7	33.8	57.6

Type I (not included): two-person household including pensioners and social security recipients with low income.

(1) Type II: four-person household, medium income.

(2) Type III: four-person household, higher income.

Source: Statistical Yearbook 1995: 543, 544.

in both medium and higher income households. Hence, five years after unification and despite lower financial resources, the trend toward prosperous consumerism was firmly established in the new *Länder*.

Further insights into perceptions toward the arrival of the Western consumer culture were offered by a closer look at consumer patterns and preferences. After the currency union in July 1990, Western products overwhelmingly dominated the Eastern market. Years of material scarcity, limited choice, and often questionable quality, as well as pent-up consumer wishes, now found their expression in an unequivocal thirst for Western products. In particular, established and comparatively expensive brand products benefited from this trend (Diesener and Gries 1993: 21). It was not the no-name product that attracted the consumer but, in contrast, the brand that was already familiar to most Easterners. Over the years, advertisements on Western television had generated a product socialization that now provided the competitive edge in the newly liberalized consumer market. Despite often limited financial resources, Easterners followed the promising yet costly advertising messages, while showing "a lack of consumer competence" (Diesener and Gries 1993: 21) that otherwise would have properly evaluated the products' value for the money.

During this consumer euphoria, Eastern products hardly stood a chance against their Western rivals. They were stigmatized as representatives of an inefficient economy of short supply: outdated, unaesthetic, and unattractive. Gradually, Eastern products vanished from the shelves of supermarkets and shop owners were eager to sell the remaining stock at dumping-price levels (H.W. Schmidt 1994: 371). Nonetheless, Easterners increasingly had their first unpleasant experiences with the new consumer society. Dubious Western business opportunists claimed the East as the new frontier of Capitalism, and East Germans came to be acquainted with credit sharks, overpriced used cars, or disproportionate insurance policies. The markets of Eastern towns were packed with stands offering clothes and food products whose value-for-money ratings were all too often simply ridiculous. The appreciation of and curiosity toward Western consumer products and the often sheer helplessness when confronted with the newfound choice and diversity, gradually turned into bewilderment and skepticism. For some, these first experiences of Western-style consumerism left a bitter aftertaste that determined their future consumer preferences.

Hence, within an astonishingly short period of time, a clear reversal trend toward the appreciation of Eastern products became visible. By December 1991 almost three-quarters out of one hundred surveyed households deliberately chose Eastern over Western products, which represented a sharp rise from 50 percent in December 1990 and 65 percent in mid-1991 (Gries 1994: 1045). By the end of 1993, 82 percent of surveyed consumers stated that they preferred Eastern over Western products (*Der Spiegel* 52/1993: 46). Furthermore, in a survey carried out in February 1993, when respondents had been asked whether they bought Eastern products during their regular shopping trips, 65 percent answered "often," 31 percent with "sometimes" and only 3 percent replied "hardly" or "never" (Gries 1994: 1045). Western advertising images, language, and symbols faced increasing difficulties in reaching Eastern consumers. Uniform marketing campaigns which simply transferred Western slogans to the East failed to generate a successful impact. Market strategists were forced to respond to this new consumer orientation and began to design specifically Eastern strategies. Former GDR products underwent rapid transformations regarding design, quality, or presentation but kept the brand name of the former Socialist article.

The cigarette market served as an intriguing example. After unification, the tobacco giant Philip Morris incorporated the *Dresdner Tabakwerke*, with their brands "*F6*," "*Juwel*" and "*Karo*" into its corporate structure. The Western strategists at Philip Morris in Munich managed to run a strikingly successful campaign. "*F6*," which is exclusively sold in the new lands, was advertised as a product that stood for the good and the familiar, as a symbol of tradition and persistence in a time of sweeping changes, and as a vital representative of East German cultural history.[4] "*F6*" declined to change its design and the distinctively strong taste which differed strikingly from the much preferred "light" types of the West, remained. Philip Morris avoided Western advertising clichés, such as sophistication and affluence, and instead stressed tradition and authenticity that gave the impression that valuable achievements of the GDR still had a right to exist. Slogans, such as "the taste stays the same," "the original from *Dresden*," or "our classic" made further reference to the era prior to unification. The strategy had remarkable success. At the end of 1989, "*F6*" already possessed a dominant share of the Eastern market of 13 percent. A year later the make reached an astonishing peak at 33 percent, which subsequently dropped slightly to 31 percent in 1994 and to 27 percent in 1996.[5]

The sweet and artificial-tasting "*Rotkäppchen*" sparkling wine enjoyed a surprising resurgence. Prior to 1989, the company had sold some 15 million bottles annually. By 1991, sales had dropped to 2.9 million, only to increase dramatically to 5.7 million in 1992. In 1994, the company sold 17 million bottles, but only 50,000 in the West (*Der Spiegel* 27/1995: 59). Further examples included the former GDR cola "*Club*" which trumpeted: "Hooray, I'm still alive. Club Cola—our Cola." "*Burger Knäcke*," a crispbread from Saxony-Anhalt, achieved an astonishing market share of 65 percent in the East by 1993 (in contrast to 15 percent in the West). An essential product in the GDR diet, "*Burger Knäcke*" ran a successful campaign promoting the product as a "crispy piece of *Heimat*" (Gries 1994: 1052–1053). In addition, labels and stickers, such as "fabricated in Thuringia," or "brewed in the *Vogtland*," as well as the display of the emblems of the new *Länder* acknowledged local and regional loyalties.

Life and Leisure

When wandering through the towns of Eastern Germany only a few years after unification, the visible changes in the cityscapes were striking. The vast difference from the gray and dull impression that was so prevalent during the Communist era became even more breathtaking by comparing the advances of Eastern Germany to those of other post-Communist societies. Even the more prosperous Hungary, Poland, or the Czech Republic represented no comparison to the already accomplished massive transformation processes in the former GDR. The entire region resembled one gigantic construction site. Roads were being modernized, traffic bypasses built, historic buildings and entire blocks of houses restored or renovated. In particular, in the center of towns a difference between East and West became hard to depict. The Western corporate culture, including shops and advertisements, quickly established itself and eventually represented an almost perfect mirror-image of the West. Even small businesses like cafes, restaurants, or pubs showed a striking similarity to Western standards.

Despite the presence of horrific satellite towns that continued to dominate the outskirts of every urban area, the Communist period offered a paradoxical yet highly potential chance for urban and architectural improvement. For decades, urban planning and modernization was almost absent because of the lack of financial resources and commitment, which left historic buildings and entire towns at the status quo of 1945. In return, Eastern Germany was spared the modernizing sins of the postwar era which Western communities now struggle with. In the East, historic lines of streets remained intact, and life in inner cities was still relatively unaffected by four-lane highways, inhospitable "match-box" apartments, and large office complexes. Federal, *Länder*, and local authorities in Eastern Germany seized this unique opportunity and began a wide range of restoration programs that had the potential of establishing highly satisfying urban landscapes, not only regarding their historical aesthetics but also in terms of maintaining and fostering a socially advantageous neighborhood community. But how did East Germans respond to these developments? When queried about beauty within one's general living environment, different conceptualizations between East and West prevailed. As shown in Table 5.7, modernity, affluence, and technical innovation were on top of the Eastern agenda, which indicated that the recent arrival of the Western consumer society was widely appreciated. Born out of decades of material scarcity and con-

Table 5.7
Attitudes Toward Beauty, East and West, 1991 (percentages)

Question: On this list (presentation of options) are there certain items that you have recently noticed and which you find beautiful? (Multiple answers possible.)

	East	West
Shop window displays	49	30
Modern houses and office complexes	37	15
Expensive cars	34	17
Old houses	29	36
Neon advertising	18	6
Bunch of flowers	36	32
Nice gardens	35	36
Tall old trees	25	36
Sunset, sunrise	24	33

Source: Allensbacher Archiv, IfD-Umfrage 5059, December 1991.

sumer privation, Easterners envisioned their living environments with shop window displays, expensive cars, and modern houses.

In sharp contrast, Westerners favored idyllic and romantic things. On top of their agenda were such antipodes to modernity and technological progress as old houses, gardens, and trees. Forty years of diverging experiences therefore generated fundamentally different aesthetics. In the East, modernity was embraced. The West, however, had already experienced the downside of modernity, with inhospitable city centers, traffic congestion, or urban alienation and instead favored a retreat into the idyllic as an escape from Chaplin's vision of "Modern Times." While West Germans might have despised shopping malls as ugly and anonymous architectural monstrosities, East Germans appreciated their convenience and vast display of choice and affluence.

Also, while West German observers were enchanted by the restoration of medieval towns, Easterners placed more emphasis on the provision of central heating or well functioning plumbing. This seemed only a logical reaction since the state of housing in the old GDR left much to be desired. Half of all houses were built before 1945. In early 1990, the average apartment size comprised only 61 square meters as compared to 84 in the FRG. Forty percent had grave structural deficiencies. Eleven percent were completely unsuitable for housing, and a further forty percent had minor defects. Only ten percent of apartments in the GDR were in satisfactory condition. The provision of heating, hot water, interior WC, bathroom, and kitchen reached 75 percent in new apartments, but a mere 30 percent in old houses (Crow and Hennig 1995: 101, 102). Hence, after four decades of Communist parsimony, East Germans eagerly absorbed "modernity" with such notions as convenience, comfort, change, progress, and innovation. In this respect, they displayed comparable intentions to their Western counterparts in the immediate postwar era. The retroactive distancing from modernity with the contemplation of such notions as tranquillity, sensuality, or peacefulness had yet to reach the new *Länder*.

Life in general became harder and faster in Eastern Germany. Working environments and requirements changed. Progressive social services were abolished and old routines broke down. The individual was asked to adjust and comply to new economic, political, and social principles. The transformation stressed notions of initiative, individuality, and independence that were in marked contrast to the old totalitarian system, which had nurtured obedience, hierarchy, and apathy (see Chapter 3). These pressures had a profound impact on every individual's life, and East Germans evaluated the new social climate in a strongly negative fashion. In 1994, more than half of the respondents' social relations to their neighbors had worsened in comparison to the GDR. The middle generation (people aged 40 to 49) was particularly disillusioned, with numbers reaching 69 percent (*Politbarometer*).

These strikingly negative perceptions showed the level of security—both mentally and materially—that the Communist system was able to offer its citizens. These figures also demonstrate the vast social ruptures since unification that will require years of adjustment. Despite improved material conditions, despite increased comfort, convenience and choice, people were nonetheless ill-prepared for the sudden arrival of Capitalism, and they found it hard to adopt the underlying prerogatives of prosperity and affluence within a market economy: competition, performance, and individual responsibility.

Although East Germans were all too aware of the negative side-effects of prosperity, they nonetheless showed a confident demand toward their positive connotations. Hence, the choice of leisure activities could not keep pace with people's expectations. In early 1993, only 8 percent of Easterners were satis-fied with the variety of leisure opportunities in their neighborhood or close by, as compared to 57 percent in the West (*Der Spiegel* January 18, 1993: 56). More specifically, the *Allensbacher Institut für Demoskopie* queried people aged 16 to 29 about leisure choices. Table 5.8 shows the drastic disparities between East and West in almost every leisure sector.

Apart from the diverging leisure infrastructures, the prevalent economic disparities that affected broad societal segments in the new *Länder* accounted for different leisure preferences and activities for East and West Germans. A survey among some 51,000 respondents (Baldauf and Klingler 1994: 409) showed that handicrafts, hiking, and sports received almost identical responses. However, clubbing and eating out, as well as going to theaters, concerts, and movies, were markedly more common on the leisure agenda of West Germans, while more East Germans never participated in such activities at all. The persis-tent economic instability made inexpensive leisure activities ever more attrac-tive to most Easterners. Affluent leisure pursuits were regarded as expensive

Table 5.8
Leisure Opportunities, East and West, 16–29 Years (percentages)

	East	West
Sports club, sports ground	65	89
Swimming pool	44	73
Parks	46	63
Disco	63	55
Youth clubs	29	57
Clubs, unions, etc.	16	55
Fitness gym	36	59
Cinemas	37	59

Source: Allensbacher Archiv, IfD-Umfrage 5070, October 1992.

extravaganzas. The drastic price increases in restaurants and for theater, concert, and cinema tickets further contributed to the reluctant acceptance of Western patterns of leisure consumption. While these were substantially subsidized in the old GDR, the sudden introduction of market principles prompted many East Germans to simply erase them from their leisure agenda.

Shortly after unification, East Germans showed a marked interest in travel. This came as no surprise since in the autumn of 1989, demands for the lifting of travel restrictions were prominent features of various demonstrations. Banners even depicted "*DDR*" (the German abbreviation for GDR) as "*die dauernde Reiselust*" (persistent desire to travel). By 1991, average annual travel expenses per capita had reached DM 787. The figure trailed significantly behind the Western level of DM 1,468, but nonetheless represented a 60 percent increase in comparison to 1990 (Deutscher Reisebüro-Verband 1996). Against the backdrop of the considerable economic disparities between East and West and the substantial material insecurity of East Germans, most Easterners preferred to spend their holidays in Germany. Travel to the old *Länder* satisfied a pent-up desire to experience life on the other side of the former Iron Curtain. Table 5.9 also shows the marked lack of interest of West Germans in visiting the new *Länder*. Although the data only referred to main holidays (usually in the summer), the meager shares of 2.5 and 2.7 percent stood neither in relation to the attrac-

Table 5.9
Destination of Main Holiday, East and West Germans (percentages)

| | East | | West | |
	1990	*1991*	*1990*	*1991*
Germany old Länder	31.9	33.4	27.2	27.9
Germany new Länder	43.4	20.8	2.5	2.7
Foreign countries total	24.8	45.5	70.3	69.4
Spain	3.0	7.4	13.0	13.7
Italy	2.5	4.9	10.2	10.5
Austria	4.3	9.7	7.0	8.8
France	1.4	2.2	5.9	5.8
Eastern Europe	9.6	10.8	3.8	3.4
European	0.5	3.0	9.8	10.3
Other	3.5	7.5	20.6	16.9
Total	100	100	100	100

Source: Deutscher Reisebüro-Verband, Press Office, 1995.

tive tourist offerings of Eastern Germany, nor the opportunity to freely visit a part of the country without the former hassles of border controls or visa restrictions. Even the often rudimentary state of Eastern tourist facilities at the outset of unification could not explain such indifference on behalf of West Germans.

As with the West, Spain, Austria, and Italy emerged as popular foreign holiday spots. When looking only at foreign destinations, 40 percent of East Germans in 1990 and 49 percent in 1991 traveled to these three countries. The figures were in marked similarity to the West, with 43 percent in 1990 and 48 percent in 1991. The former "Comecon bathtubs" in Hungary, Romania, or Bulgaria still featured prominently on the East German travel agenda. In 1990, 39 percent of all foreign holidays did not take advantage of the new freedom to experience other countries that was largely prompted by attractive low price levels and currency advantages in Eastern Europe. The often-reported indifference toward new and more exotic holiday experiences, however, represented a false conclusion. By 1991, only 24 percent of foreign holidays were spent in the former Communist states, and more and more East Germans traveled to southern, Western, northern, and non-European countries.

Media

With unification, political authorities wasted no time in radically transforming the Eastern media landscape along the lines of the established West German system. In the public sector, the Hamburg-based *Norddeutscher Rundfunk* expanded to Mecklenburg-Westpomerania. The *Sender Freies Berlin* now catered also to the eastern part of the city. Two further public stations, the *Mitteldeutscher Rundfunk* (covering Saxony, Saxony-Anhalt, and Thuringia) and the *Ostdeutscher Rundfunk Brandenburg* filled the void left behind by the demise of the state-owned radio and television network of the GDR. Private television stations highly welcomed the arrival of millions of new customers. By 1993, 93 percent of all households in Germany were able to receive more than four channels, 60 percent could choose between 16 or more stations, and only 7 percent were still limited to the public television diet. While in the West most households had already been connected to the cable system, Eastern viewers installed satellite dishes until their neighborhood was connected. Differences between East and West regarding the reception of private stations were therefore only marginal (Darschin and Frank 1994: 98).

Patterns of media consumption displayed marked differences between East and West. Although television viewing increased between 1991 and 1994 in both the old and new *Länder*, Easterners spent significantly more time in front of the "box" (see Table 5.10). Adults over the age of fourteen watched some 20 percent more, children occasionally (1991) even 40 percent more, which was largely the result of increased consumption of light entertainment programs (Darschin and Frank 1995: 160).

Table 5.10
Television Consumption, East and West (minutes per day)

	East		West	
	Adults	*Children 6–13 years*	*Adults*	*Children 6–13 years*
1991	189	132	160	93
1992	199	124	160	97
1993	209	125	168	100
1994	207	114	170	95

Source: Darschin and Frank 1995: 154; 1994: 98.

While Western viewers continued to prefer the two public channels *ARD* and *ZDF*, Easterners showed a marked preference for private stations. In 1994, viewing shares for *ARD* and *ZDF* in the West totaled 17.5 and 18 percent, respectively. In the East, however, numbers amounted to only 12.5 and 13.5 percent. In contrast, viewing shares for the private station *SAT.1* were 14 percent in the West and 17 percent in the East, while *RTL-plus* accounted for 16.5 percent of Western and 20 percent of Eastern air time (Darschin and Frank 1995: 156). The figures for 1994 were only marginally different from 1993, which indicated a consolidation of differing consumer behavior. In particular, the Eastern television audience was more receptive to the sensationalist news journalism of private channels. While in 1994, the most popular news show *Tagesschau* (from the public *ARD*) was watched by 15 percent of West Germans, it only interested a total of 11 percent in the East. In contrast *RTL Aktuell* reached 4 percent of Westerners and 8 percent of Easterners. Also, public news magazines attracted fewer viewers than did their private counterparts. The most popular *ZDF* show, *Bonn direkt*, was watched by 11 percent in the West and by 10 percent in the East. However, 19 percent of Easterners tuned in to the *RTL* infotainment show *Explosiv*, as compared to only 9 percent of Westerners (Darschin and Frank 1995: 162). It seemed that the casual, tabloid type of presentation struck a popular chord with East Germans. More than in the West, informative broadcasts fulfilled additional functions as sources of entertainment and diversion.

CONCLUDING REMARKS

Despite the persistent disparities regarding prosperity between East and West, East Germans generated enough money to participate in the Western-style consumer society. Within a short period, the Western consumer world was embraced by Easterners. These first consumer experiences within unified

Germany were in marked resemblance to the West German economic boom of the 1950s where a wave of gluttony and consumerism compensated for years of material deprivation. The consumer euphoria in the new *Länder* exemplified similar positive orientations toward the arrival of Western-style consumerism. Participation in and approval of it served as a buffer of support within the general and often demanding and unsettling transformation processes. This initial open embracing, however, transformed into a unique consumer mentality. Although affluence and choice as offered by the new market economy were not rejected, Easterners defined them differently and filled consumerism with political meaning. The product of consumption thereby acquired the status of a miniature plebiscite that reflected on the general transformation processes in the aftermath of unification. As argued in Chapters 3 and 4, attitudes prevailed that unification merely represented a corporate takeover and colonization by the West since the political, economic, social, and administrative structures of the *Bonn* Republic were simply extended to the Eastern *Länder*.

The resurgence of Eastern products—whether newly introduced or rejuvenated from the GDR past—expressed the widespread resentment against these developments. In buying "East," Easterners articulated notions of defiance against the general eradicating processes of unification that perceived anything East German as unsuitable for the new system of democracy and capitalism. East Germans sensed that the West was not always the best, that the East had achieved and produced worthy assets as well. Defiance was furthered by growing skepticism and bewilderment. As one of the first lessons of market economics, Easterners realized that glamorous and polished products did not always keep their advertised promises. Subsequently, the normative consumer paradise of the West that had prevailed in the parsimonious days of the GDR was demystified. Coded political messages, such as "I am still alive" or "Against the taste of unification," captured the *Zeitgeist* of the Eastern *Länder*.

The orientation toward Eastern consumer goods also became an indicator for emerging regional pride. Once spotted, differences in consumer behavior and preferences between East and West were cultivated and turned into relics of self-esteem. Easterners responded to the streamlining processes of transition and the perceptions of a second-class citizenry by proudly heralding the quality, beauty, or performance of "their" products. Eastern goods were attributed with highly positive characteristics, such as value for money, trust, integrity, or honesty that confidently expressed the difference from the presumably untrustworthy and sleazy West and thereby acquired a vital identity-creating function. In addition, notions of escapism and nostalgia became apparent. During the massive transformation processes, people were longing for a piece of familiarity, for a stable constant in a time of sweeping changes. Such emotional coziness was offered by former GDR products that had kept their old brand names. They reminded East Germans of the past prior to unification—not necessarily of its totalitarian implication but simply of a time when life was not as complicated and demanding. They stood in sharp contrast to the daily experiences of post-unification, including job insecurity or challenged social status and the urgency to adapt to new social, political, and economic demands.

Catching up with the reference culture of the old *Länder* was on the mind of many Easterners. As an indication of the much desired approximation to the West, Easterners complained about the still insufficient provision of leisure choices. The marked interest in travel, and in particular holiday destinations that largely resembled those of the West, furthermore pointed toward the internalization of Western mass-cultural standards. Differences regarding the pursuit of leisure activities or travel patterns were not the result of different preferences but instead were caused by the still-existing gaps in the material standards between East and West. However, certain diverging conceptualizations of life and leisure remained. East Germans overwhelmingly complained about the deteriorating social climate. The pressures of transition, the urge to perform at work, the stress on social circles caused by material insecurity and changing social status, as well as the general speed and depth of the massive system transformations left many in a state of imbalance. The incoming Western culture emphasized fundamentally different notions. The single-mindedness of the Adenauer-era with its orientation toward stability and material security gave way to a desire for new outlets for satisfaction. The corrupting influence of affluence sought for ever-increasing and ever-changing material and spiritual gratification. Growing material prosperity allowed for increased and diversified spending. Leisure activities grew qualitatively and quantitatively. Affluent travel became a common feature, while life in general became faster and more complex.

Easterners had yet to accommodate these cultural standards. The former stable and foreseeable patterns and circles of life became subject to sudden changes. Former rigid regulators of life, such as state, party, and ideology disappeared and a complex web of multiple determinants emerged. Suddenly the individual was confronted with freedom of choice. Questions, such as where to go on holiday, what consumer goods to buy, or what to do after work were enriched by vastly increasing opportunities. The freedom to choose and to freely determine one's life, however, did not always constitute a positive asset, but instead often a confusing and demanding imperative. Life in a freer, faster, more complex and less anchored society was sometimes daunting. This sudden flexibility and fluidity of life made Easterners pessimistic about the state of their rapidly altered social climate.

Media consumption in the new *Länder* strongly accommodated Western mass-cultural standards. Despite the radical extension of the Western media system after 1990, the arrival and subsequent extensive use of private television did not represent a caesura, but instead a continuation of consumption patterns of the GDR era. Before unification, Western radio and in particular Western television constituted integral parts of life in Eastern Germany as normative references of information, truth, and entertainment and were widely used as alternatives to the politicized Eastern media. East Germans were therefore quite familiar with the new developments in the media sector of the Federal Republic in the 1980s. In the West, the arrival of the new media age brought an unprecedented choice of channels but only minimal programming variety, resulting in the "Americanization" of West German television. The enthusiastic response of East Germans to these trends had its roots in the GDR past and in the regime's dissatisfying offerings in the entertainment sector. Television and radio were politicized and functioned as propaganda tools, as well as means of political indoctrination. The function of simple entertainment as a compensation for daily pressures, although it was acknowledged by the SED, but nonetheless never accordingly acted upon.

With unification, this "vacuum of fun" could suddenly be filled. More than their Western compatriots, East Germans watched more television and in particular preferred the light forms of entertainment. Sensationalist news reports, banal stories, and in general a distinctively casual form of presentation answered a need for easy entertainment. With other entertainment sources, such as cinema, theater, or books suffering from drastic price increases, and leisure opportunities still relatively underdeveloped, television acquired to an even greater extent the escapist function of a retreat into the private sphere where one was able to relax and unwind and to tune out of the daily pressures of unification.

NOTES

1. Ironically, the SED had to install extra transmitters throughout Saxony to prevent people from moving.

2. Data according to Statistical Yearbook, 1990: 487, 1987: 472, 1983: 453, 1990: 566.

3. Exceptions included Adenauer's unsuccessful attempt to install a government-run television channel in 1961, the launch of a second public TV station a year later, and the introduction of "Third Channels" operated by the individual corporations of the *Länder* in the mid-1960s.

4. Information according to the Press Office at Philip Morris, March 1995.

5. Information according to the Press Office at Philip Morris, January 1997.

6

Ethnicity

Anthony Smith (1991: 20) describes an ethnic group as "a type of cultural collectivity, one that emphasises the role of myths of descent and historical memories, and that is recognised by one or more cultural differences like religion, customs, language or institutions." In this respect, not only objective factors of laws, regulations, and civic standards, of economic resources and practices, of borders and territorial properties constitute vital anchors for a national identity. Subjective factors, "permanent cultural attributes of memory, value, myth and symbolism" (Smith 1986: 3), the historic glory of a nation, legends, historical figures and events, or a mythical homeland shape the emotional attachments of members of a community. Although ethnic identities are generated by objective indicators, such as language, religion, customs, or skin color, they are also derived from meanings which developed over generations on "cultural, spatial and temporal properties" (Smith 1986: 22). Smith terms this ethnic conception of the nation non-western (1991: 11). Whereas most western nations emphasize a historic territory, a legal-political community, the legal-political equality of members, and a common civic culture and ideology, the ethnic conception is grounded in the belief that the nation has its roots in a common ancestry, therefore stressing notions of a community based on birth and a shared native culture.

Against this theoretical backdrop, Germany represented a highly peculiar case. By the mid-nineteenth century, E.T.A. Hoffmann's political slogan of *"Deutschland, Deutschland über alles,"* which subsequently became the lyrics of the national anthem, suggested the paramount goal of uniting the several kingdoms and duchies into one coherent nation. Germans were scattered out over various states, while the envisaged unification found its rationale in fostering ethnic-national loyalties to a common nation. With the first unification of 1871 the united Germany found its identity in shared cultural heritage, in a common language, and in common descent, while other nations, such as Britain or France, had already developed a sense of common citizenship in the western terminology as applied by Smith. As a reminder of the past, even today

German citizenship is granted on the principles of *jus sanguinis* (citizenship based on descent) rather than on *jus soli* (country of birth).

The rhetoric of the Third Reich perverted such loyalties. *"Deutschland, Deutschland über alles"* now implied German racial, political, and military supremacy. Ethnic attributes of Aryan glorification were complemented by digging deep into historical myths of the "Roman Reich of German Nations." Against this vigorous and fanatical overemphasis on ethnic components, the civic-western conception of a national identity hardly stood a chance. With the demise of Hitler and the country's division, the ethnic element effectively disappeared from the public psyche. In the West, any expressions of pride in being German were seen to have ethnic connotations and were regarded as antidemocratic or even Fascist. The legacy of the Third Reich gave German ethnicity an almost immoral attribute. Indeed, German ethnicity largely vanished from the political rhetoric. *"Verfassungspatriotismus"* (Sternberger 1979), namely civic loyalties to the new system of democracy, and *"Deutschmarknationalismus"* (Habermas 1990), the emerging pride in economic achievements, served as an additional antipode to the Third Reich.

For the young GDR, the raison d'être lay in the state's postulated identity as the Socialist alternative within the German nation. Fundamentally different modes of politics, of economics, and of citizen's responsibilities pushed the ethnic component into oblivion. Under Ulbricht, the regime drew its legitimacy from the establishment of Socialism in the sovereign Socialist German state. Although unification was still perceived as an eventual political goal—albeit under the Communist guidance of the SED—ethnic orientations to the common German nation were nonetheless superseded by orientations to Socialism and the state that culminated in the doctrine of the peaceful coexistence of two states within one nation. Under Honecker, modest attempts to integrate German ethnicity to further the new officially propagated notion of two German nations were often awkward. Although German ethnicity, history, and myths were addressed in memorials, speeches, and in school curricula, the dogmatic Socialist reading of the past was one-dimensional and failed to generate significant emotional attachment among the population.

The Cold War antagonism emphasized political-ideological differences between Communism and democracy. Caught between these systemic rivalries, the identity markers for the young Federal Republic and the GDR lay in spheres other than ethnicity. Both states placed considerable effort on integration within their respective political and economic camps. NATO and Warsaw Pact, market economy and Socialism, Democracy, and Communism dominated the public psyche and further blocked any notions of addressing ethnic factors. Hence, both the GDR and the FRG were what Max Weber (1958) had termed "incomplete nation." Ethnic pride was absent from the official rhetoric, as well as from the public psyche.

Given this striking insignificance of ethnic identities prior to 1989, one could have assumed that unification would have provided ample opportunity for demonstrating ethnic loyalties. After all, the German ethnicity in the FRG and in the GDR was finally reunited, and neither the Cold War nor systemic antagonism stood in the way of expressing references to historical memories and myths, or ethnic attributes, such as common language or common descent. However, forty years of neglecting ethnic identities—of repression in the FRG and of one-dimensional distortion in the GDR—did not fail to exert a considerable impact. When visiting the united Germany on the third of October (the country's national holiday), foreign observers were amazed by the distinct absence of a festive mood. Hardly any flags, public speeches, or rallies (with the notable exception of Berlin) were visible as reminders of the presumably glorious day in 1990 when the nation was finally reunited. At major sport events, the reluctance of the crowds to join in singing the national anthem stood in sharp contrast to such occasions held in France, the United States, Great Britain, or Italy. It took the persuasive power of the national soccer team and the likes of such sports heroes as Klinsmann or Beckenbauer to introduce the public to the concept of singing the Federal Republic's anthem, *"Einigkeit und Recht und Freiheit."* The obvious discomfort of some team members strongly reflected the awkwardness which most Germans felt during the occasion. Until the end of 1995 and six years after the fall of the Wall, cultural attributes to German history, myths, symbols, ancestry, or descent did anything but constitute significant identity markers for the recently unified nation.[1]

Such reluctance in expressing ethnic loyalties renders an analysis on diverging ethnic identities between East and West difficult. Against this background, Fredrik Barth's typology of internal and external boundaries (1969) offers a cogent approach. As seen in Chapter 1, the mechanisms of boundary creation are used as the overall theoretical framework for this study in order to analyze the existence of common and/or diverging identities in East and West toward the unified nation. Apart from this broad perspective, the typology is also able to shed light on the nature of ethnic identities. In general, ethnic boundaries canalize social life and organize inter-ethnic relations. Internal boundaries serve the purpose of identifying others as members, while external boundaries dichotomize others as strangers. "Prescriptions" govern and "proscriptions" prevent inter-ethnic interaction.

The post-unification period offered plenty of evidence for Barth's conceptualization. "Prescriptions"—the positive expression of ethnic loyalties to the nation—remained almost absent. "Proscriptions"—the establishment of external boundaries, whereas the individual was denied access to the ethnic community—were widely documented. Germans demonstrated to ethnic outsiders—to foreigners, immigrants, or refugees—that a dividing line still existed between Germans and non-Germans. By 1991, the international media reported various incidents of violent attacks on hostels for asylum applicants. Documentaries on the neo-Nazi scenes, in both Eastern and Western Germany, stirred up emotions and raised parallels to the Third Reich. Bewildered politicians urged tolerance and civility, fearing xenophobia and violence against foreigners.

This chapter therefore addresses ethnicity in its negative understanding. An interrogation into ethnic markers of identity leaves positive, prescriptive expressions aside and analyzes negative, proscriptive notions, asking why and to what extent did East and West Germans establish ethnic external boundaries. Hence, the emphasis lies on xenophobia, on racial intolerance and ethnic chauvinism as distinct characteristics of preserving an ethnic identity by preventing outsiders from entering the German ethnic community. These notions have to be viewed in a wider historical context in order to assess contemporary attitudes in the post-unification era. Throughout its history, Germany never experienced a multicultural society. The short period of colonization prior to World War I had hardly any cultural or social impact on the Wilhelminian Reich. In the aftermath of 1918, other nations, such as Britain or France, maintained their colonial ties, which even after the decolonization waves of the 1950s and 1960s granted them a better exposition to, and understanding of, foreign cultures and customs. In contrast, from Bismarck to Hitler and to the FRG and GDR, German societies remained truly homogeneous. After unification, such multiculturalism—appreciation of cultural diversity, as well as ethnic tolerance—could have provided for a regulating mechanism in a time when growing numbers of refugees and asylum seekers altered the *modus vivendi* of social relations.

The moral and political legacies of the Third Reich were handled in a fundamentally different manner in East and West Germany. The *Bonn* Republic accepted responsibility for the genocide and pogroms of the Nazi era. A confrontation with the past was reluctantly, but nonetheless painstakingly, pursued. In contrast, the SED regime avoided a thorough interrogation into National Socialism. Anti-Fascism emerged as a state doctrine without addressing the moral failures of Hitler's regime but by merely offering political and economic antipodes to capitalism. While *Auschwitz* remained an essential part of the political conscience of West Germans, East Germans were given absolution from the crimes of the Third Reich.

Finally, the old FRG and the GDR acknowledged the divided nation in a fundamentally different manner (see Chapter 2). In the West, the division was largely accepted as a irrevocable fact. Integration within the community of Western States, democracy, and economic achievements compensated for the cognitive void caused by the division, and the separated eastern part of the nation gradually disappeared from the public's conscience. In contrast, East Germans continued to uphold the notion of one common nation. Marxism, Communist brotherhood, and Socialist internationalism could not provide the identity markers as envisaged by the regime. Instead, the prospect of reunification maintained the status of a powerful source of emotional attachments. Hence, this chapter explains the establishment of ethnic external boundaries not merely out of their political, economic, or social contemporary context.

Instead, it traces the historical-cultural timelines of these attitudes by analyzing differences in East and West regarding the legacy of the Third Reich, the different accommodation of the fact of the division in the understanding of German ethnicity, as well as implications for post-unification Germany caused by the prevalent cultural homogeneity of the GDR and the *Bonn* Republic.

THE GERMAN DEMOCRATIC REPUBLIC

After the founding of the GDR, the official political rhetoric focused on the ideological notion of the creation of a Marxist-Leninist state. Intentions to propagate a national identity which incorporated German ethnicity and heritage were largely ignored. Nonetheless, unification was still regarded as an essential political undertaking. For the SED and the Communist Party of the Soviet Union, the German question remained open to negotiation, albeit under the condition of preserving the established political system of the GDR (Meuschel 1992: 144). For Ulbricht, the progressive development of the GDR would have eventually resulted in the establishment of a superior system that was highly attractive to the workers, farmers, and intelligentsia of West Germany (Meuschel 1992: 145). In 1954, he therefore referred to German unification as an "incontestable inherent law" (H. Weber 1993: 44).

However, the FRG's accession to NATO, the subsequent incorporation of the GDR into the Warsaw Pact, as well as its sovereign status, by 1954 drastically reduced the importance of German unification on the political agenda. By 1955, unification was finally laid to rest by Khrushchev's insistence on the maintenance of two separate German states. It now became clear that the Soviet Union would never allow its westernmost Communist bastion to depart from its hegemonial sphere of influence. Unification was only possible if Socialist principles and Soviet influence were safeguarded (H. Weber 1993: 45).

In the processes of the growing systemic antagonism of the Cold War, the GDR gradually emerged from the shadow of the divided nation and subsequently stressed its status as a sovereign state. Its identity and legitimacy were now represented in the doctrine of two states within one nation. The development of two antagonistic systems which were firmly rooted within their respective ideological camps was confidently acknowledged by stressing peaceful coexistence with the FRG. Consequently, Article 1 of the constitution promulgated that "the GDR is a Socialist state of the German nation." With the replacement of Walter Ulbricht in 1971, the self-perception of the GDR took a decisive turn. Ulbricht's successor, Erich Honecker, manifested the notion of two separate German nations, while propagating the Socialist German nation-state. From this perspective, two different German identities were the logical consequence. The revised constitution of 1974 therefore stated that "the GDR is a Socialist state of workers and farmers," while all references to German unification were eliminated.

This growing confidence allowed for a gradual recall of the German past. Interpreted under the Communist dialectic, German history was resumed and incorporated into the official political rhetoric. National identity, national community, and national history of the GDR and its citizens and not the history of Germans (Meuschel 1992: 285) stood at the center of historical analyses. From the peasant uprising in 1525 to the war of liberation against Napoleon in 1813, from the history of the German labor movement to the proletarian resistance against Hitler, history was reconstructed in a patriotic fashion (Meuschel 1992: 68) along the progressive lines of the Communist dialectic. The year 1983 was declared the "Luther year," and Honecker explicitly honored the religious reformer as a role model. The regime also paid respect to Frederick the Great and even Bismarck (H. Weber 1993: 96). In combining two principles, the GDR tried to implement a Communist-national conscience by emphasizing its German heritage and emergence out of German history, as well as the notion of a Socialist state with the ideological concept of the establishment of a utopian Communist society.

The regime's aspiration to artificially create a new legitimacy as a German nation-state was not convincingly adopted by the population. As seen in Chapter 2, notions of the GDR and the whole of Germany as one's "fatherland" existed side by side. The same applied to emotional orientations to being German and being a GDR citizen. The overwhelming majority in 1984 did not follow Honecker's dictum of two separate nations. Instead, 80 percent upheld the notion of one common people (Köhler 1992: 76). The official rhetoric of a separate German ethnicity—of the Capitalist West German and the Socialist East German—was far from corresponding to real attitudes among the people.

Anti-Fascist Legitimacy

The GDR considered itself as a genuinely new German Socialist and anti-Fascist state. In line with the declaration of the Komintern in 1937, the SED defined Fascism as the terrorist dictatorship of reactionary, chauvinist, and imperialist elements of the finance capital. National Socialism was merely regarded as the utmost form of Fascism. Anti-Semitism, racial supremacy and the systematic extermination of Jews, however, were only minor parts of the official political rhetoric and even disappeared as soon as the SED joined the East bloc campaigns against Zionism (Meuschel 1992: 30).

From the beginning, anti-Fascism became an alternative form of politics and constituted a fundamental raison d'être for the young GDR. The failures and shortcomings of the past provided the moral and political legitimization for the new regime. Anti-Fascism offered a political and moral integrity that represented a radical departure from National Socialism. Unity of the working class, peace and cooperation with the Soviet Union, land reform, equality, and the destruction of the political power and influence of finance capital represented decisive markers for the dawn of a new era, where the GDR offered those who had resisted National Socialism a spiritual home. Hence, the official interpretation of anti-Fascism offered the convenient political and moral advantages of presenting the GDR and its citizens as victims of and winners over National Socialism. They were victims of a Nazi-regime that had ultimately emerged as the logical consequence of a capitalist society. They were winners out of the GDR's legitimacy as a workers' and peasants' state that overcame the exploitation of the masses and the imperialist expansion of capitalism in its quest to create the Communist society. From this understanding, the Federal Republic represented a mere restoration of a bourgeois-capitalist society. As with National Socialism, the suppression of the working class, the power of the bourgeoisie, of the land-owning class, and of capital continued to represent fundamental characteristics of the *Bonn* Republic. According to the official rhetoric of the SED, the imperialist bourgeoisie maintained its grip on power in West Germany. In sharp contrast to the GDR, a departure from the Nazi past was absent. Hence, the SED perceived the National Socialist regime as an exclusively West German issue and problem.

Prior to the founding of the GDR in 1949, the Soviet military administration implemented a thorough denazification program in its zone of occupation. During the first two years after the capitulation of 1945, 520,000 people lost their jobs, most notably in the public sector. Sixteen thousand former members of the NSDAP, the SS, or the Gestapo were put on trial (H. Weber 1993: 10, 14). The Soviet authorities filled the existing gaps with German Communists, in particular in such sectors as the police, justice, administration, and education, which considerably strengthened the political power and influence of the Soviet Union over its new satellite state. Soviet denazification was the most profound among the four occupying forces. While the western zones increasingly reinstalled former civil servants within the administrative or judicial systems, the eastern zone in comparison was given the cleanest break with the Nazi past.

In contrast to this promising point of departure, the forty-year long history of the GDR largely refrained from any historic debate about guilt and responsibility for the crimes of the Hitler era. Issues connected to the Third Reich almost represented taboos (Schulz 1994: 408). Instead, from early on there was an institutionalized—yet selective—form of historical remembrance. The GDR developed a cult of anti-Fascism. It uncritically hero-worshipped the Communist resistance, while avoiding a discourse on the historic background of Nazism, its cause and consequences. Such a handling of the past was one-dimensional and very convenient. It circumvented any personal confrontation or responsibility with German National Socialism. The silent majority that experienced and sustained the Third Reich was not forced to work out its past. As Christoph Kleßmann (1993: 198) noted, "there was never a comprehensive biography of Hitler in the GDR—nor were the millions of his followers, not least among the workers, ever subjected to close scrutiny." Nor was there a historic or political analysis of Fascism or National Socialism. An interrogation into the *modus vivendi* of Hitler's dictatorship ultimately would have resulted in the condemnation of the *Führer* principle, the one-party system, blind obedience, violence against and repression of citizens. Such underlying characteristics of the National Socialist regime, however, bore a direct significance to the established political status quo of the totalitarian Communist dictatorship of the GDR. The Ministry for State Security, judicial arbitrariness, the monolithic power of the SED, as well as the party's tutelage in all economic, political, and societal aspects of life would have made coherent parallels to the NS regime all too obvious. From this perspective it therefore came as no surprise that Fascism and National Socialism were addressed in such generalizing terms. In the end, East Germans were able to quickly move on in their daily lives. A critical and probably painful confrontation with an immoral past was suppressed by giving absolution and a collective psychological guilt-free stamp to the population.

The rather limited importance of the Nazi past to the collective perceptions was documented in a survey by the Western *Institut für Demoskopie*. In December 1990, people were questioned as to whether German history possessed unique features that were particularly German and that distinguished Germany from other nations. An overwhelming majority of 67 percent answered positively. Out of these, only 4 percent mentioned the Third Reich. Only 1 percent named Nazi crimes. These answers were markedly different from the Western survey, where responses totaled 52 percent for the Third Reich and 13 percent for Nazi crimes (Noelle-Neumann 1991: 203).

Homogeneity of Society

The official ideology of the SED promulgated international friendship and understanding while supporting emancipatory ambitions within the Third World. Yet, the GDR did not allow its citizens to cross its own western border. Apart from highly restricted visits to West Germany, the experiences of East Germans in getting to know foreign cultures and peoples were limited to visits to other Socialist states. Even then, tourist stays were a tiresome and complicated undertaking, with time-consuming application procedures and restrictions on the amount of East German money to be spent abroad. Also, the regime's cosmopolitan rhetoric was not reflected in the attitudes of the population. Instead, a broadening of horizons and fostering of understanding was almost impossible in the "ghetto-situation" (Kleßmann 1993: 207) of East Germany. When talking to Easterners in the aftermath of unification, the former feeling of superiority over other East bloc countries, based on the—by Communist standards—GDR's respectable material wealth, became quite obvious. The notions that their own economic achievements were largely passed on to the Soviet Union or used to sustain other Communist countries were widespread. The officially imposed friendship with Communist Poland never reached beyond the status of artificiality. Cognitive reconciliation along the officially declared "peace border" was a myth. In 1973, an open-border experiment had to be terminated after a few months, since resentment grew to dangerous proportions. Suspicion and arrogance toward the "lazy Poles, who buy up all our meat" prevailed and were highlighted by the territorial loss of Silesia after World War II.

Only one percent of the population of the GDR was foreign (*Der Spiegel,* August 31, 1992: 21), mostly students and workers from various Socialist countries. As many as 90,000 employees worked in the GDR as parts of bilateral agreements (Golz 1995: 7). East Germans, however, maintained a profound indifference toward foreign cultures and peoples. Relationships towards fellow workers from Vietnam, Angola, Mozambique, or Cuba were frosty. Foreign students were housed in special hostels and therefore tightly separated. Cultural approximation stopped short outside of factory and classroom, while foreigners in the GDR were isolated and excluded from socialization, culminating in the widespread racist jargon of "*Fijis,*" which referred to people with a differently colored skin. Fundamental characteristics of the Nazi era were by no means given a clean break in the GDR. The prevalent ethnocentrism of National Socialism was able to flourish in East Germany because of a lack of multicultural exposures, as well as because of the impact of a combined 56 years of totalitarian rule that suppressed open-mindedness. The SED regime avoided a full exploration of the genocide of the Third Reich. School curricula failed to address such issues as anti-Semitism, racism, or hostility toward other nations. Education in tolerance was absent. Overt racial violence was only suppressed by the totalitarian nature of the GDR with its rigid judicial and surveillance apparatus. Nonetheless, by the 1980s the first signs of Skinhead and neo-Nazi movements became visible (Merkl 1995: 434–435). However, instead of looking inward in order to analyze the causes that prompted juveniles to turn their backs on Socialism, the regime merely attributed their actions to seduction by the deranged West.

THE FEDERAL REPUBLIC

The collaboration with or at least the silent approval of the Nazi regime and the refusal to take action against the genocidal barbarism drastically formed the West German psyche after the demise of the dictatorship. From the outset, the *Bonn* Republic was morally handicapped by the collective guilt of its people. The FRG and its newly democratic citizens carried the burden of succeeding from a political system that trampled on humanity and morality, and that abandoned tolerance, respect, and intellectual enlightenment for the cause of racial supremacy and military superiority. School curricula, literature, film and political rhetoric reflected this consciousness and persistently had the Third Reich as an issue. Even forty years into the existence of the *Bonn* Republic, it was virtually impossible for West Germans to escape a confrontation with the past.

Nonetheless, confrontation with National Socialism was marked by four distinctly different phases. In the immediate aftermath of the capitulation, the occupying powers arranged compulsory tours of concentration camps in several towns and municipalities. Denazification programs were implemented to screen the population of Nazi supporters and collaborators. Lectures and films represented further attempts to educate the public about the horrors caused by the Hitler regime. Most notably, in the immediate postwar years, the Nuremberg trials of 1945/1946 dominated the political discourse. However, the controversy surrounding war crimes and anti-Semitism were undertaken in a generalizing and abstract fashion (Wilenga 1994: 1060). Apart from "Nuremberg," criminal charges against Nazis were hardly put forward. The denazification processes turned into a cunning attempt to outwit allied authorities. The public was placed into five categories according to their alleged involvement in the NS regime, ranging from "highly guilty" to "unincriminated." Category IV termed *Mitläufer* (follower) was the threshold for moral reinstatement and employment within the public service. Hence, denazification was termed the "Persil permit"—a proverb which drew parallels to the detergent that washes everything whiter. Instead of a coherent confrontation with the past, denazification turned into repression. Although the collective guilt of Nazi Germany was accepted by West Germans (Wilenga 1994: 1060), the mental process of acknowledging one's personal involvement in the unjust NS regime faded against the task of proving that one complied with the new moral standards of a political system that advocated *Rechtsstaat* principles and human rights. Moreover, in the chaotic first years after 1945, the public was preoccupied with mere survival. Emigration, expulsion, food, or housing dominated people's thoughts. Against these material and political insecurities, the mental and moral confrontation with the past had only secondary importance. West Germans looked for relief—from material hardship, as well as from former moral deficiencies.

Repression was even further accentuated in the Adenauer era. Western integration, economic resurgence, and increased material standards pushed the past further away from the realm of relevance. The initial discourse over guilt, war crimes, and denazification came to a gradual close. Between 1945 and 1950 some 5,000 verdicts had been passed in relation to Nazi crimes. Between 1950 and 1955 the number dropped to twenty per year (Wilenga 1994: 1062). The focus was on the present: rebuilding devastated towns, producing the economic miracle, or safeguarding international stability. West Germans just gradually got accustomed to the new principles of democracy and the social market economy. A confrontation with the past would have been only a disturbing backlash to these new affirmative processes.

A thorough confrontation with National Socialism had to wait until the 1960s. The wave of anti-authoritarianism generated by the student revolts, accompanied by growing civic confidence, allowed for a critical interrogation into personal responsibilities for contributing to the moral barbarism of the Nazi regime. The personal backgrounds of the protest generation were free from guilt, participation in, or approval of the NS regime that made the confrontation with the Hitler era such a colossal burden for their parents. In addition, growing interest in politics, the participatory revolution of the 1960s, and a more open political discourse contributed in paving the way for an uninhibited and unbiased mental confrontation with National Socialism. The judicial system increasingly tackled Nazi matters. Between 1961 and 1965, the number of trials related to the NS regime doubled in comparison to the period from 1951 to 1960 (Wilenga 1994: 1062). Günther Grass's novel *die Blechtrommel* (the Tin Drum), published in 1959, sparked a wide-ranging public discourse. The Eichmann trial in Jerusalem in 1961/1962 drew further attention. On several occasions, the *Bundestag* extended the statutory period of limitation for murder until it was finally scrapped in 1979.

By the end of the 1980s, the governments of Schmidt and Kohl had attempted a moderate return to normality. The "moralizing impulse of the 1960's" (Wilenga 1994: 1064) was followed by a consciousness that confidently expressed the democratic achievements of the Federal Republic. Nonetheless, the horrors of the Nazi era continued to form the West German psyche. Every now and then, a movie, a television documentary, or a judicial trial confronted West Germans with their past. Numerous public commemorations (fifty years since the rise of Hitler in 1983, forty years since the end of World War II in 1985, fifty years since the *Reichskristallnacht* in 1988) kept historical memories of the Third Reich on the political agenda. In contrast to the 1950s, denial or repression were no longer possible. Instead, the barbarism of National Socialism, the moral failures to stop genocide, and other war crimes continued to form an integral part of the Federal Republic's identity.

Repressing German Ethnicity

The close mental link of "Germanness" to Nazi Germany resulted in the almost complete absence of an affective orientation toward the nation. Even the simple intention of expressing one's pride in being German was labeled as Fascist or right-extremist. For the public, national symbols had a minor if not repressed importance. In 1961, 38 percent could not remember having heard the national anthem since 1945. Furthermore, in 1961, as well as in 1981, roughly one-fifth did not know the first line of the Federal Republic's anthem (*"Einigkeit und Recht und Freiheit"*), while 46 percent in 1961 and still 37 percent in 1981 referred to *"Deutschland, Deutschland über alles,"* (Noelle-Neumann 1991: 29, 42). West Germans developed an "anti-German" identity. In the 1950s the country's strong drive toward the lyrics that were used until 1945 integration within the West (NATO, the Common Market), as well as emerging pride in economic achievements, served as new anchors for a national identity during a time when national pride was crushed due to the traumatic legacy of the Third Reich. By the 1970s these were complemented by those principles that the Nazi dictatorship denounced in such a fierce manner: democracy, humanity, and morality. Such values and orientations served as "a counterpoint to *Auschwitz*" (Le Gloannec 1994: 137). These notions, however, did not relate to "German" ethnicity. Instead, they were cognitive principles of citizenship virtues. Since "German" still bore the attribute of the Nazi past, the denial of "German" could easily be accommodated into this new agenda of national identity. Paradoxically, a good West German, therefore, was the individual who denounced anything "German." The new patriot for humanity, morality, cooperation, and democracy represented an antipode to the past, in fact an anti-German patriot.

This schizophrenic attitude toward one's own country led to the description of West Germany as "the world's most dialectical nation" (Ash 1994: 75). On the one hand, the Federal Republic established itself as a stable democracy, with a high degree of harmony, inner peace, openness, and civility, complemented by a firm and secure anchoring in the West. On the other hand, however, the traumatic past of the NS regime continued to haunt West Germans, resulting in insecurity and guilt when dealing with other nations and their people.

Ethnocentrism

West Germany, like most European states, had traditionally been a country of net emigration. Postwar governments therefore paid little attention to ethnic integration or arising demographic pressures (Chandler 1995: 344). The Basic Law was characterized by a highly liberal protection from political persecution. Article 16(2) gave "every politically persecuted person . . . the right to asylum." Article 16(1) guaranteed the right of return for ethnic Germans who after 1945 found themselves outside the now-reduced German territory. The provision was later extended to include ethnic Germans under Communist rule. Within the first ten years after the founding of the Federal Republic, some nine million refugees and expellees moved to West Germany, most notably from Silesia, East Prussia, and the *Sudetenland*. Between 1950 and 1991, some 2.6 million ethnic Germans outside of prewar German territory (mainly the Soviet Union and Romania) migrated into the Federal Republic (Fijalkowski 1993: 851). Despite the constitutional provisions, West Germany remained a largely homogenous society. *Jus sanguinis* (citizenship based on blood) made it difficult if not impossible for immigrants to gain German citizenship.[2] A notable exception, however, was represented in the cases of the vast numbers of *Gastarbeiter* (guest workers). After the economic boom of the 1950s, a shortage of labor endangered economic prosperity. Beginning in 1955, various bilateral agreements between *Bonn* and several southern European states allowed for the recruitment of workers on limited-term contracts. West Germany highly welcomed the foreign influx of workers who supplied cheap, ununionized, and easily exploitable labor (Fulbrook 1994: 226) to fill semiskilled and unskilled positions. Italians were followed by Turks and guest workers from the former Yugoslavia. Millions of *Gastarbeiter* took up permanent residence. For the first time, West Germans were exposed to foreign cultures on a wide scale which brought with them different traditions and religious practices.

Gastarbeiter were perceived as temporary economic solutions to the lack of manpower. However, successive governments failed to recognize the human aspect of this massive transformation of labor. The fact that migrants would eventually seek to establish social and family roots in their host country was not given much attention. Until the late 1980s, the established principles of the Adenauer era toward *Gastarbeiter* remained virtually unchallenged. Politics of guest workers were politics of employment. By 1977, net immigration became a political reality. With the oil crises and subsequent recessions of the 1970s, the former shortage of labor increasingly turned into severe unemployment problems. Incentives to persuade Italians, Portuguese, Greeks, Spaniards, or Turks to return to their home countries were introduced. In 1973, the SPD/FDP coalition issued a ban on further recruitment. Nonetheless, the number of foreigners continued to increase, since many who were born or had been living in West Germany for many years decided to stay, partially out of economic reasons, but also because of the continuing social integrative processes within their new environments. Family members arrived and the second generation of guest workers was born. As a result, by 1990 their ranks had reached 8.4 percent as compared to 4.3 percent twenty years earlier (Statistical Yearbook 1995: 67). In particular, Turkish migrants came in higher numbers. Their figures rose from 7,900 in 1979 to 58,000 in 1980 (Leenen 1995: 606). By 1990, Turks constituted one-third of all foreigners, followed by Italians and Yugoslavs, who each represented one-tenth.

By the 1980s, *Gastarbeiter* were no longer welcomed. In 1982, 62 percent agreed that there were too many foreigners in the country, while a further 50 percent argued that they should be forced to go back to their home country (Fulbrook 1994: 227). Against the backdrop of persistent inequality in employment opportunities, few foreigners had been able to rise into professional or managerial positions. Some opened small enterprises such as restaurants or grocery shops. Nonetheless, foreign workers contributed considerably to West Germany's impressive GDP and economic strength (Braunthal 1995: 207), but few West Germans acknowledged this achievement. Many complained about guest workers and their spouses who received equally comprehensive social benefits as West Germans, including social and unemployment insurance or subsidized housing. Often guest workers, immigrants, or refugees were confronted with a wall of social isolation, resulting from prejudice, rejection, and discrimination.

Heightened economic pressure and instability looked for a safety valve. Twenty years after the moderate successes of the right-wing *Nationale Demokratische Partei Deutschlands* (NPD) between 1966 and 1968, a further right-wing grouping shocked the political establishment. By the late 1980s, the *Republikaner* enjoyed increasing support. The party made asylum and foreigners its central campaign motives. Political asylum and immigration as issues of controversy functioned as focal points for heightened discontent that extremist parties were able to capitalize on (Leenen 1992: 1042). Their polemical political rhetoric finally woke up the established parties and firmly placed immigration and ethnocentrism on the political agenda. The *Landtage* elections of the early 1990s[3] demonstrated that the *Republikaner* hit an electoral nerve and further showed the voter's readiness to express dissatisfaction with the political establishment.

Despite a wave of tourism that exposed West Germans to foreign cultures, and despite an increasing hands-on experience within their own country, multicultural attitudes developed only reluctantly. Although *Politbarometer* noted in 1988 that 25 percent of respondents had personal contacts with foreigners through friends or acquaintances, and 46 percent stated that foreigners lived in their neighborhoods, the appreciation of foreign cultures hardly went beyond culinary delicatessen or tourist sights. Foreigners were tolerated but not accepted. Survey data (Leenen 1992: 1049) analyzed critical attitudes toward foreigners in West Germany between 1980 and 1990. Response categories included "*Gastarbeiter* should adapt their lifestyles to German standards" (adaptation), "*Gastarbeiter* should be sent back," "*Gastarbeiter* should be denied any political activity" (political abstinence), as well as "*Gastarbeiter* should marry only within their ethnic group" (endogamy). Throughout the 1980s, support for all four categories decreased considerably. The racist notion of "endogamy" dropped from 44 percent in 1980 to 24 percent ten years later, while the number of respondents who thought that guest workers should be sent back dropped from 52 to 31 percent. In 1990, "political abstinence" was supported by only 36 percent, which represented a 15 percent drop since 1980. However, a majority continued to insist on the cultural adaptation of lifestyles (from 66 percent in 1980 to 51 percent in 1990). While in 1980 most foreigners in West Germany came largely from southern European countries, the influx of large numbers of Turks, who shared distinctly different, non-western customs and religious practices, made the cultural clash of immigrants and native West Germans more obvious than the preceding contacts with Italians or Spaniards. The persistent support for "cultural adaptation" which was prevalent in spite of the growing levels of tolerance in the remaining three categories indicated that multicultural experiences were welcomed only as long as they did not threaten or undermine prevalent German customs and traditions.

In addition, foreigners were occasionally victims of violent attacks. Limited outbreaks of foreign hostility first occurred during the first postwar recession of 1966/1967 with the parallel success of the neo-Nazi NPD in several *Länder* parliaments. The 1970s saw some violence particularly against Turks in context with economic slow-down and growing unemployment. Between 1983 and 1990, the number of violent legal offenses with a right-extremist background rose from 76 to 306 (Bundesministerium des Inneren 1993: 71). Still, xenophobic incidents were only "sporadic" (Chandler 1995: 351). Despite the reluctance in accommodating foreign cultures, the prevalent ethnocentrism in the *Bonn* Republic ought therefore not to be confused with xenophobia. Many West Germans may have disapproved of the growing number of foreigners, but nevertheless rejected the idea of racial violence. Research revealed that right-extremism in West Germany was not much different from its counterparts in other EC-countries regarding quantity, socioeconomic correlates, or concentration in political parties (Bauer and Niedermayer 1990: 15–26). Throughout Western Europe, xenophobic violence emerged as a worrying phenomenon in the 1980s. West Germany made no exception to this trend, but it was also not at the forefront of a new extremist movement.

THE NEW LÄNDER

By the end of 1993, the number of foreigners living in Germany had increased to some 6.9 million as compared to 5.9 million two years earlier. In international comparison, the ratio of foreigners of 8.5 percent of the total population ranked well above that of France (6.3 percent), the Netherlands (5 percent), or Great Britain (4.3 percent; Golz 1995: 4). Only 22 percent were citizens of EU member states. Turks constituted by far the largest foreign ethnicity, representing some 30 percent of the overall foreign population (see Table 6.1).

The share of foreigners varied dramatically according to regions. In 1992, 97 percent lived in the old *Länder* and in the western part of Berlin. Western cities like Frankfurt (28 percent), Stuttgart (23 percent), Munich (22 percent) or Cologne (18 percent) accommodated significantly higher numbers of foreigners than did their eastern counterparts. For instance, in Leipzig, Rostock,

Table 6.1
Foreigners in the Federal Republic (1990–1993) (percentages)

	Total Number (in 1,000)	Share Population*	Italy	Greece	Spain	Portugal	Turkey	Former Yugoslavia	Poland
1990**	5,342.5	8.4	10.3	6.0	2.5	1.6	31.7	12.4	4.5
1991	5,882.2	7.3	9.5	5.7	2.3	1.6	30.3	13.2	4.6
1992	6,495.8	8.0	8.6	5.3	2.1	1.5	28.6	15.7	4.4
1993	6,878.1	8.5	8.2	5.1	1.9	1.5	27.9	18.0	3.8

*Countries: percentages of total foreignes.

**1990: only old Länder.

Source: Statistical Yearbook 1995: 67.

Dresden, and Halle the presence of foreigners was under 2 percent (Golz 1995: 4). The considerable increase was largely caused by the dramatic transformation processes in Eastern Europe, as well as the civil war in Yugoslavia. Between 1989 and 1992, the number of applicants for asylum rose from 121,000 to 450,000. The vast numbers of asylum applications resulted in a tremendous administrative backlog. In addition, ethnic Germans from Eastern Europe and the former Soviet Union came in increasing numbers. In 1989, 377,000 moved to Germany, followed by 397,000 in 1990 and 220,000 in both 1991 and 1992.

The demand for legislative modification became pressing. After lengthy negotiations among CDU, CSU, SPD, and FDP a constitutional compromise emerged which stated that the asylum title of the German constitution may not refer to those who enter German territory from another EC member state or another country that provides asylum under the provisons of the Geneva conventions or the European Convention of Human Rights. Legislative organs now determined the countries where political and inhuman treatment or punishment were excluded from domestic political life. Hence, applications originating in these countries could be recognized as unfounded and immediate expulsion could be ordered. The constitutional changes took effect in July 1993. Since then, the number of asylum applicants decreased drastically. In the first six months of 1994, the authorities registered only 62,000 cases (Golz 1995: 6).

In 1992, the overwhelming majority of both Easterners and Westerners supported restrictions on immigration regardless of the cause or the country of origin (see Table 6.2). Ethnic Germans faced the least and non-EU citizens the most criticism, which had to be interpreted as a reaction to the highly publicized wave of political refugees and asylum applicants and the subsequent heated debate over the reform of immigration laws in 1992. It showed that attitudes toward foreigners were significantly influenced by the prospect of im-

Table 6.2
Attitudes Toward Immigration, East and West, 1992 (percentages)

	Ethnic Germans		Asylum Applicants		EU Citizens		Non-EU Citizens	
	West	*East*	*West*	*East*	*West*	*East*	*West*	*East*
Free immigration	19	15	12	15	35	13	10	5
Restricted immigration	71	74	64	67	56	63	62	59
No immigration	10	11	24	18	9	24	29	36

Source: Allbus; in Kühnel and Terwey 1994: 89.

migrants seeking economic and material advantages by taking up residence in Germany.

The relatively small numbers of respondents in the old *Länder* who completely rejected immigration continued the positive trend that had started in the mid-1980s with increasing tolerance toward guest workers (Kühnel and Terwey 1994: 89). In Eastern Germany, attitudes toward immigration were not necessarily more negative. Disapproval of ethnic Germans showed similar levels between East and West, while immigration of asylum applicants faced even less criticism. Attitudes toward immigrants from EU and non-EU countries, however, displayed marked differences. EU citizens were significantly more accepted in the West, which represented a reaction to the fundamentally different experiences within Europe. Indeed, some fifty years of West German European integration were hardly comparable to the short period since unification in which Easterners were exposed to the concept of Europe as a spiritual home. Finally, the rejection of non-EU immigrants was more pronounced in the East. It seemed that insecurity over employment and material status further accentuated resentment against foreigners who merely entered Germany in the hope of benefiting from its high economic standards and social security.

Spreading Xenophobia

Right-wing extremism emerged as a worrying phenomenon. Racist violence by neo-Nazi splinter groups was widely documented in the media. The *Verfassungsschutz* (Germany's intelligence agency) spoke of a right-extremist potential of 40,000 in 1991 and of 36,000 in 1994. The numbers did not even include the *Republikaner* with some 20,000 members. Membership in militant right-extremist groups (in particular Skinheads) rose from 4,200 in 1991 to 6,400 a year later and consolidated with 5,400 in 1994 (Bundesministerium des Inneren 1995: 77).[4] Between 1991 and 1992, the number of violent legal offenses with right-extremist backgrounds nearly doubled from 1,400 to 2,600 (Bundesministerium des Inneren 1993: 70, 1992: 76). With one-fifth of the population, one-third of such offenses occurred in the new *Länder*. In international comparison, this member of xenophobic acts did not represent an outstandingly high figure. The state of New Jersey alone regularly reported some one thousand crimes every year. In 1991, an astonishingly high 7,780 racial hate crimes were committed in England and Wales (Merkl 1995: 430). Nonetheless, the dramatic rise in xenophobic acts in Germany over the course of just two years was without any parallel in the country's postwar history.

After 1992, official statistics reported on general anti-foreign legal offenses without elaborating on violent attacks. The number of cases jumped from 2,426 cases in 1991 to 6,721 in 1993. By 1994, tension decreased significantly with a reported figure of 3,491 (a drop of 52 percent). Regarding offenses per capita, the East stayed markedly behind Western levels. With one-fifth of the population, the number of cases in the East amounted to one-twelfth in 1993 and one-sixth in 1994 (Bundesministerium des Inneren 1995: 85, 1994: 101).

The data therefore suggested that xenophobia was not an exclusively Eastern phenomenon.

Four key events shaped the political psyche of Germany. Over five days in September 1991, rioting youth firebombed a hostel for asylum applicants in the north-Saxonian town of Hoyerswerda. Several hundreds of people—mostly local residents of the area—openly declared their solidarity with the delinquents by disrupting police forces in their attempts to calm the situation. In August 1992, the northeastern town of Rostock witnessed the worst outbreak of racist violence. Over six days, some one thousand young extremists attacked another hostel for asylum applicants, while an enthusiastic crowd of thousands of spectators—young and old—were unwilling to interfere. On November 25, 1992, public attention shifted to the West, where three Turkish nationals were murdered in a firebombed private house in the town of Moelln near Hamburg. The attack prompted even further perplexity since the victims were neither refugees nor lived in a hostel. The same was true for the incident in the Westphalian town of Solingen, where in May 1993, five Turks died in an arson attack on a family home.

Public attitudes toward foreigners were largely influenced by these four incidents. As indicated by Table 6.3 the levels of acceptance toward foreigners were markedly different between East and West. In the aftermath of the riots in Rostock (August 28, 1992) more than half of the respondents in Eastern Germany disapproved of the many foreigners living in Germany. A year later and against the backdrop of the arson attack in Solingen (May 29, 1993) attitudes were considerably more positive but still remained significantly behind Western levels.

Moreover, attitudes in the East were consistently less tolerant throughout the period between 1991 and 1993. Before the riots in Hoyerswerda (September 22, 1991) support was slightly below 40 percent (West: slightly below 50 percent). In the run-up to the events of Rostock, support dropped from a high

Table 6.3
Attitudes Toward Foreigners in Germany, East and West

Questions: Many foreigners live in Germany. Do you think this is . . .

	October 1992		July 1993	
	East	*West*	*East*	*West*
All right	39.8	60.1	56.9	70.1
Not all right	59.5	34.9	42.6	26.8
Do not know	0.7	5.0	0.5	3.1

Source: Politbarometer.

of 58 percent down to 35 percent (West: consistently around 60 percent). Leaving racist violence and legal offenses aside (since these were committed by a very small minority), the attitudes of the general public in East and West toward foreigners, and consequently the notion of tolerance and respect for foreign cultures and customs, showed considerable disparities.

The new legislation that came into effect in July 1993 undoubtedly had a calming effect. With fewer foreigners and in particular asylum applicants, the political controversy lost a vital edge, media presentation decreased, and tension among the population eased. Public counterdemonstrations against racial hatred sparked a profound reorientation. Political commentators drew parallels to the xenophobia of the Third Reich. In particular the incidents in Moelln and Solingen functioned as moral wake-up calls. Subsequently, public initiatives and solidarity committees were founded. Candle marches were organized by unions, churches, or schools and held in hundreds of towns. Between November 1992 (Moelln) and January 1993, some three million people participated in such demonstrations (Leenen 1995: 623). Dismay, compassion, and solidarity grew.

By 1994, political discourse, solidarity marches, and public appeals showed moderate educative effects on the population. Nonetheless, differences between East and West regarding foreign tolerance prevailed. Eighteen months after Solingen, only 17 percent of the Eastern respondents categorized "more understanding for foreigners" as a very important priority. Here, the West was considerably more sensitized, with 27 percent. The difference between old and new *Länder* became more visible when looking at the top two response categories. Although in both East and West the majority regarded understanding for foreigners at least as a "fairly important" issue, the numbers in the West (72 percent) were considerably higher than those in the East (61 percent).

This moderate ethnic tolerance, however, did not imply that Germany should continue to open its gates to foreign cultures. Both Eastern and Western respondents agreed on the importance of preventing further immigration from non-EU citizens (see Table 6.4). The margins between East and West showed only small differences. In the West, 67 percent agreed to the top two response categories, in comparison to 64 percent in the East. Such pronounced rejection of a multi-ethnic society was further documented by the very low numbers of respondents who regarded dual citizenship for foreigners as a pressing concern. In the West, the top two categories attracted 44 percent, while Easterners were even more reluctant with 37 percent.

The political influence of the neo-Nazi movement remained very moderate. Only 4 percent of perpetrators of right-extremist attacks were members of right-extremist organizations (Klinger 1994: 157). Only 10 to 15 percent were politically right-wing motivated (Fijalkowski 1993: 856). The scene was highly fragmented. Six years into German unification, neo-Nazi groups and parties had failed to function as a forum for hopes and needs of societal segments. Despite some occasional successes at *Länder* or local elections, the *Re-*

Table 6.4
Attitudes Toward International Understanding and Their Importance for
Society, East and West (1994)

	More understanding for foreigners in our society (percentages)		Stop further immigration of non-EU foreigners (percentages)		Dual citizenship for foreigners who have been living in Germany for a long time (percentages)	
	East	*West*	*East*	*West*	*East*	*West*
Very important	17	27	32	37	9	14
Fairly important	44	45	34	30	28	30
Little importance	31	24	26	23	38	32
Not important	7	5	8	10	24	23

N: 1,532 (East); 6,013 (West).

Source: Gruner und Jahr 1995: 54–58.

publikaner never emerged as the sole political representative of the far right. The party found it impossible to take over its competitors, such as the *Deutsche Volksunion* (DVU), the *Nationale Demokratische Partei Deutschlands* (NPD), or the *Freiheitliche Arbeiter Partei* (Free Workers Party; FAP). Neo-Nazism had virtually no impact on the academic or intellectual scene. As a political program, the resurgence of Nazi ideology, Nazi symbolism, or the revision of the "*Auschwitz* lie" were restricted to a rigidly limited number of followers. This political de-ideologization of xenophobia was further documented by the spontaneous nature of Rostock or Hoyerswerda, where even weak traces of organized right-wing extremism could not be identified (Klinger 1994: 152).

Reasons for Xenophobia

The violent potential did not suddenly emerge after unification but was already present in the GDR. Violence and hooliganism, however, did not reach the surface of public attention because of the strong repression apparatus of police and state security. Surveillance and repression in the totalitarian system generated notions of helplessness and renunciation toward state authority and its monopoly on political power. The state, and in particular the police and the *Stasi*, entailed a historically negative image among Easterners. After unification, the potential for violence, however, was given ample opportunity to erupt. Repression and surveillance, as well as the official rhetoric of internationalism and Socialist brotherhood, became notions of the past. The reorganized police forces of the new *Länder* were often understaffed and lacking in experience in handling incidents of such dimensions as Rostock or Hoyerswerda. These organizational deficiencies were regarded by the rioters as a welcome weakness of the "enemy." Therefore, the violent clashes with the police in Hoyerswerda and Rostock also represented moments of reckoning with the totalitarian past, where a mixture of a "continuity of violence and a distance to the state" (Klinger 1994: 151) fueled the riots.

From an organizational point of view, the Eastern *Länder* were simply not prepared to provide accommodation for thousands of asylum applicants. After unification, the federal Minister of the Interior, Wolfgang Schäuble, decided that accommodation had to follow strictly according to the population ratio between East and West. Hence, local councils in the new *Länder* were asked to provide housing for some 20 percent of the incoming applicants against the backdrop of precarious housing markets. Occasionally, sports complexes, school yards and youth centers were transformed into provisional hostels. For East Germans, this sudden exposure to foreigners had a distinctly negative undertone. Foreigners were barely a social feature of life in the GDR, but Schäuble's decision resulted in a significant concentration of asylum applicants in one area, often accompanied by the sight of overcrowding and filth.[5] For many, the speed of immigration which happened almost overnight was too much to bear, and people were overstrained in accommodating notions of compassion or understanding.

Aggressive ethnocentrism and xenophobia also had their roots in internal aspects of society. As seen in the preceding chapters, the transformation processes of unification had a dramatic impact on the new *Länder*. With the demise of the GDR, social networks that formerly provided for stability, security, and emotional shelter were subject to severe pressure. Unemployment was widespread. Reduction in social services affected many. The break-up of supportive and integrative social ties resulted in general disorientation, individualization, a feeling of social exclusion (Merkl 1995: 454). Life was off-balance, and the decline of former patterns of a regulated and organized life became threatening to those who were unable to replace them with new contents.

In conflicts of distribution over scarce jobs, affordable housing, or unemployment benefits, the abstract political issue of asylum application and migration turned into a concrete phenomenon of practical xenophobia. While East Germans had to struggle to come to terms with the new realities of the market economy, asylum applicants were perceived as free-riders who were instantly given accommodation and a weekly allowance. Dissolution and uncertainty over the future led to insecurity and aggression. People who were marginalized because of their material disadvantages projected their own inadequate status on the foreigner, while claiming a lack of solidarity among fellow Germans and criticizing the preferential treatment of foreigners. These crises of self-esteem caused many to adopt a racist rhetoric or even to commit xenophobic attacks.

Suddenly, foreigners were utilized by both Easterners and Westerners as convenient scapegoats for the economic malaise. Against the backdrop of the raging civil war in Yugoslavia and the political upheavals in Eastern Europe, such generalizations revealed weak civic virtues of compassion and tolerance, which were clearly sidelined by the prevalent material concerns over one's immediate future.

A generalizing, irresponsible, and insensitive media spread further fear and discontent. By 1991, press and television widely reported on the dramatic increase in asylum applications. Metaphors of a "tidal wave of free-riders" or a "full boat that cannot carry further passengers" entered the public arena. In the immediate aftermath of Hoyerswerda, Rostock, Moelln, and Solingen, the number of xenophobic crimes increased drastically (Leenen 1995: 619). Hence, media presentation of these incidents not only fostered a public discourse and moral reconsideration. It also generated violence from segments of society who were in need of a catalyst, to whom the media offered a ready blueprint for action. A convenient emotional safety valve emerged: asylum seekers in hostels and non-European foreigners in general were convenient scapegoats in a world of economic struggles and social reorientation. The painful perception of most East Germans that they were years away from harvesting the promised benefits of the transition made it all the more easy to project inferiority, anger, and disappointment on foreigners. Whereas in the West media reports aroused anger against foreigners, they prompted mass hysteria in the East. Journalistic sensationalism and voyeurism were treated at face value in an attempt to find answers in the complex and complicated world of unified Germany.

The young in particular violently expressed their frustration. Growing individualization of society and the dissolution of traditional milieus of friends and family accounted for a severe lack of orientation and support. Faced with material pressure, unemployment, and a general societal drive toward performance and competition, the simplistic scapegoating of foreigners who were held responsible for individual economic and social shortcomings provided a convenient solution for one's mental balance. "Simplistic rules of violence and simplistic reasoning of cause and effect" (Leenen 1992: 1045) tempted many into racial hatred. The evaluation of one's deprived material and social status resulted in overt aggression against ethnic minorities as a reflection of the growing antagonisms within society.

At this point one should keep in mind that xenophobia was not exclusively prevalent among the young. Although 75 percent of criminal offenders with foreigners as their victims were under age twenty and 95 percent were male (Fijalkowski 1993: 856), surveys indicated that negative attitudes toward foreigners were also common among elder generations. The cheering, if not enthusiastic approval, of bystanders in Rostock or Hoyerswerda indicated that the criminal action against asylum hostels struck a chord not only with the young. When talking about the rioting youth, "adults" never explicitly or unanimously distanced themselves. Although they did not excuse the action, they nonetheless failed to condemn it (Klinger 1994: 150). Quite often, the scope of resentment merely altered: from active readiness for violence to passive tolerance of it.

CONCLUDING REMARKS

A coherent national identity that incorporated German ethnicity would have been able to provide a buffer of tolerance for the influx of foreigners. A confident notion of "Germanness" established over decades would not have seen the increasing numbers of foreigners as a threat but as a challenge and enrichment to the national identity. In fact, the cultural impact of the incoming wave of foreigners of the 1990s was very limited. Ethnic Germans from the Volga or the Danube hardly introduced their customs and traditions to the German folklore. Political refugees and asylum applicants stayed segregated in hostels and shelters until they were returned to their countries or given permission to settle in Germany. In either case, the German way of life hardly came under attack.

However, no political system can sustain schizophrenic policies for a long period. Both the FRG and the GDR compromised the very notion of the nation and largely marginalized any ethnic identity markers. Intolerance toward foreigners was further enhanced by deficient multicultural experiences. Although West Germans developed a supportive civic identity to the Federal Republic (a strong constitutional consensus, citizenship virtues of participation, interest, and tolerance, accompanied by affirmative experiences in the sphere of economics), the political system never demanded that this civic identity had to accommodate multiculturalism. Multicultural exposure at home remained limited and selective. Despite highly liberal constitutional provisions that provided for the generous immigration of ethnic Germans and political refugees and despite the growing influx of *Gastarbeiter*, West Germany remained a largely homogenous society. *Jus sanguinis* did not only rule German citizenship law, it also ruled the attitudes of many West Germans. Unless one was of German descent, neither tax and insurance contributions, nor professional status, nor lengthy residence could offer comprehensive integration into society. In the GDR, severe travel restrictions and a very limited number of foreigners accounted for an even more restricted multicultural exposure. Ethnic chauvinism against Russians, Poles, or Czechs was widespread. Foreign workers and students remained segregated and socially isolated. In a society whose regime coerced its citizens into obedience and infantilized the individual for the intellectual supremacy of state and party, notions of tolerance and respect found an inhospitable environment. As a result, the ethnic jingoism of the Third Reich was never given a clean break and was able to continue to flourish throughout the existence of the GDR.

Against these historical developments, the organizational failures of the political authorities after 1989 represented disastrous mistakes. The federal government in Bonn, as well as local and *Länder* executive bodies, ignored the writing on the wall. Neo-Nazis and Skinheads had already emerged in both East and West by the 1980s and had been surveyed by police and intelligence services. Racist violence was already on the political agenda in such countries as France and Great Britain, which would have given ample opportunity to further study the cause of xenophobia. Nonetheless, the distribution of asylum applicants in strict accordance to East-West population quotas displayed a profound incompetence. Not only the almost complete absence of multicultural experiences, but especially the speed and extent with which asylum applicants were sheltered in the new *Länder*, provided a logical hotbed for racism. The long overdue reform of the immigration law resulted in a rapid decrease in racist attacks. It demonstrated the potential of political action in preventing social unrest. Unfortunately, measures were implemented after Hoyerswerda and Rostock had already shocked the public in Germany and abroad.

Overt racism could also have been reduced by coherent educational policies. The social challenge of integrating foreign ethnicities was simply ignored. After unification, ignorance prevailed. School curricula did not give much attention to the history and culture of ethnic minorities within Germany—a telling example of how *jus sanguinis* dominated the mind. In the media, foreigner-related issues were still treated with an aura of exceptionality over matter-of-fact presentation that was hardly apt in a country where almost one of ten residents was foreign. Temples and synagogues were still not perceived as common features of cityscapes, but as cultural oddities. Educational enlightenment was badly needed—a challenge that politicians failed to address.

Although the outlined reasons for the establishment of external boundaries were shared by Easterners and Westerners, fundamentally different experiences and historic legacies account for the markedly more rigid boundary creation by East Germans. Firstly, civic values were less developed in the East. In the old Federal Republic, virtues of civility and morality emerged, enhanced by successful democratic experiences that stressed discourse, reason, and rationality. Faced with the collective guilt of an entire society, West Germans agreed that genocide and racial jingoism should never again originate from German soil. Although West Germans did not develop into utmost tolerant, multiculture-embracing cosmopolitans, forty years of democracy and increasing travel opportunities at least implemented a certain respect for foreign customs, traditions, and ethnicities. West Germans did not necessarily assimilate foreign cultural standards but they tolerated them, as long as these did not fundamentally challenge the German way of life. In the East, the totalitarian regime generated fundamentally different experiences. A public discourse on the moral shortcomings of the Third Reich, on genocide and ethnic jingoism was never encouraged. The very nature of the totalitarian SED state undermined notions of civility and morality. East Germans were never treated as responsible, mature citizens. In a society where the authority of state and party was never questioned, the relationship between ruler and ruled was strictly hierarchical. The state generated a negative, oppressive, and dictatorial image among the population. Citizens were degraded to mere tools in the overall process of manifesting the SED's supremacy and were never given the opportunity to freely express their will in the political, economic or social spheres. Civic values did not emerge out of affirmative experiences in a process of interdependence and trust between state and citizen, but were simply delegated from above. Socialism as interpreted by the SED provided the GDR with a moral order, with a set of values to which people were forced to adjust. With unification, this regulatory role of state and party vanished. In contrast to the West, the acquired civic virtues of tolerance and respect were weak. They were neither fostered nor part of the moral code of the GDR. Instead, after 1989 ethnic chauvinism and cultural indifference were free to roam.

Ethnic exclusion in the new *Länder* emerged as a result of the continuous decline of other identities. Economically, unemployment, financial insecurity, and material gaps between East and West gave Easterners a sense of inferiority. Perceptions of political colonization by the arrogant and condescending West resulted in feelings of being second-class citizens. With these identity markers under attack, the vigorous defense of ethnicity provided an obvious solution for East Germans in their search for ego-boosting affirmative orientations. Ethnicity represented a ready repository of identity that was not directly challenged by the processes of unification. Attacking foreign elements compensated for the weak and hurt self-esteem of Easterners in an attempt to safeguard German ethnicity as one of the last remainders of one's emotional attachments. One solution would have been to rejuvenate the ethnic factor from within. But the distorted notion of German ethnicity of the SED regime and the prevalent neglect of positive prescriptions in unified Germany gave way to a morally questionable remedy: the rigid establishment of external barriers against foreigners.

Germans in general, but Easterners in particular have to come to terms with the fact that the influx of foreigners cannot be held solely responsible for the limited importance of ethnicity in public life. Despite the significant waves of immigrants, their social, economic, and cultural impact was too limited to pose a severe threat to the integrity of German cultural values and traditions, language, or blood. Instead, German ethnicity was undermined by an overemphasis on other identity markers. In the old Federal Republic, growing prosperity, social security, consumerism, Western integration, and the remarkable performance of the *Grundgesetz* served as new formative anchors for the *Bonn* Republic's consciousness. In the GDR, the SED tried to generate loyalties through the envisaged establishment of a Socialist society that would offer equal chances to all citizens, complemented by notions of Communist brotherhood and internationalism. Both civic identities, however, were too weak in coping with the increasing ethnic variety of post-unification Germany. Ethnic identity markers in the FRG and GDR were largely ignored in the quest for establishing new civic identities in the aftermath of National Socialism. By 1989, German ethnicity therefore represented an already ailing patient that blamed the incoming waves of foreigners as culprits for its identity deficiencies. Hence, the problem lay within the self-perception of the nation. With the end of the systemic antagonism of the Cold War and fifty years after *Auschwitz*, the world's most dialectical nation still had to find a coherent balance, where ethnic pride was reintegrated properly into a national identity. Germany ought to establish "prescriptions"; to fill the empty shell of German ethnicity with meaning by carefully addressing the German ethnic heritage without falling back on the ethnic chauvinism of the Third Reich.

NOTES

1. In striking contrast, during the European Soccer Championship of June 1996, German games were preceded by a vibrant and noisy chorus of thousands of fans who filled stadiums such as Wembley or Old Trafford with "*Einigkeit und Recht und Freiheit.*" The German Soccer Cup Final in Berlin a month earlier had already witnessed the participation of the large majority of the crowd in singing the national anthem. These incidents could mark the start of a new era where such ethnic-cultural expressions will indeed enter the public agenda in a more widespread and common fashion. This study however, is forced to exclude them, since the possible consolidation of this very recent trend has yet to be seen.

2. To receive German citizenship was a time-consuming undertaking. Naturalization was only possible after a permanent residence of at least ten years. A legal claim for naturalization was granted only after fifteen years, as long as financial security was safeguarded. People 16 to 23 years old could apply after eight years of residence in addition to at least six years of German schooling (Golz 1995: 4).

3. The 1991 elections in *Bremen* (7.7 percent together with a further extremist grouping, the *Deutsche Volksunion*) and *Schleswig-Holstein* (7.7 percent), as well as in *Baden-Württemberg* in 1992 (10.9 percent) formed an astonishing comeback from the electoral setbacks of 1990 when the party failed to enter the *Landtag* in the *Saarland*, Lower Saxony, and Northrhine-Westphalia.

4. Unfortunately, the official statistics on membership in right-extremist organizations did not differentiate between old and new *Länder*. However, in 1991, the Ministry of the Interior estimated the number of Skinheads at 3,000 in the West and 1,200 in the East (Leenen 1992: 1044).

5. In Rostock, some asylum applicants were forced to camp outside or on balconies. Subsequently, allegations arose that local politicians did everything to increase public outrage in order to draw attention to the scandalous state of affairs which in their view was caused by unsuitable federal and *Länder* regulations (Leenen 1995: 615).

7

Conclusion

With this century drawing to a close, images of Berliners chiseling away pieces of the Wall, tearful people embracing each other and partying together in the streets until the early hours, "*Trabis*" making their way from the wasteland of the *Potsdamer Platz* through a provisional hole in the soon-to-be dismantled Iron Curtain and onto the *Kurfürstendamm* represent some of the most vivid and moving memories of recent history. Those days in November 1989 highlighted the end of an era that had dominated world politics for over four decades: the systemic antagonism of the Cold War with the divided German nation as one of its most prominent victims. The subsequent years witnessed formerly unimaginable transformation processes and the successful structural integration of a former Communist society into a stable democracy. However, was the structural unification of the *Bonn* Republic and the GDR followed by the cognitive and emotional unification of Easterners and Westerners? Did Germans follow the call of former Chancellor Willy Brandt, who on November 10 stated "what belongs together has to grow together now"? Or were Germans more likely to adhere to Peter Schneider's image of the "Wall in the mind" (1983: 119)?

SHARED BOUNDARIES

At first glance, various identity markers shared by both East and West Germans pointed toward the establishment of a common national identity. "Affirmative economics" which were introduced by the West implied a positive orientation towards economics based on the successful experiences of the *Bonn* Republic—in particular, high productivity, industrial harmony, growth in living standards, and widespread prosperity. In the initial aftermath of unification, Easterners were shocked by the rundown state of the GDR economy. Overstaffed and inefficient companies and a deficient infrastructure resulted in low productivity. Businesses closed down and unemployment spread. Gradually, however, East Germans made their first positive experiences within the newly introduced market economy. For those with jobs, the financial situation improved significantly. The individual had more money to spend as a result of the generous conversion rate and advantageous wage negotiations by the trade unions that allowed for participation in the consumer society. Hence, East Germans were allowed to share this Western standard.

The standard of "active economics" also made advances in the new *Länder*. Virtues of initiative, self-reliance, and responsibility that represent vital qualities of any market economy were gradually adopted by many East Germans. This cognitive transition became even more impressive when looking at the economic legacy of the GDR whose planned, centralized, and outdated economy generated such attitudes as apathy, lethargy, and indifference. On a mass-cultural level, the arrival of the Western consumer society, its choice and variety of goods was largely approved by East Germans. From early on there was a rush on consumer products, in particular those that were formerly unavailable or overpriced, such as cars, electronics, or household appliances. Prior to 1989, the penetrative power of the Western media established the Federal Republic as a reference consumer culture that was in stark contrast to the parsimonious reality of the GDR. With unification East Germans did not waste any time in following in the footsteps of their Western compatriots who had experienced a similar wave of consumption in the 1950s that had made up for the years of material and consumer deprivation of the immediate postwar era. With the money surplus to participate, this embracing of the Western consumer world by East Germans represented a vital buffer of support for the challenges and hardship caused by the massive transformation processes. It convinced many Easterners that unification indeed had worthwhile and comforting assets to offer.

"Convenience and comfort" which implied modern housing and improved infrastructure, as well as Western consumer outlets, were highly appreciated. The arrival of these Western expressions of modernity hardly met any resistance against the formerly experienced rundown state of the GDR, including inhospitable housing, poor maintenance work, and repressed consumer wishes. Catching up with the Western levels of comfort and convenience stood on the agenda of many East German households. Regarding leisure, and in particular travel, qualitative and quantitative increases followed established Western standards. This came as no surprise against the backdrop of pent-up desires during the SED regime, which had effectively locked up its citizens from any non-Communist experiences and offered rather spartan leisure opportunities that stood in stark contrast to the sophisticated lifestyles as shown on (Western) television. Quantitative and qualitative differences between East and West nonetheless remained that were largely caused by the still-evident material gaps between the old and new *Länder*. The trend toward Western patterns of leisure, however, was undoubtedly present. In a similar vein, Easterners overwhelmingly adopted and even expanded Western patterns of media consumption. Easterners watched more television than did their Western counterparts and showed no signs of hesitation in consuming the increasingly

Americanized program structures. Post-unification viewing patterns represented the continuation of media consumption during the GDR era. The "vacuum of fun" and the politically distorted broadcast of the SED media diet was filled with Western television as a normative reference of truth and entertainment. After 1989 the already conditioned consumers of the new *Länder* saw no reason to break their existing habits. On the contrary, television provided a cheap and ready form of entertainment that provided a welcome leisure activity in a time of economic instability and financial insecurity.

In the civic-political sphere, the positive reception of the arrival of an open and free society represented a vital stabilizer for the recently introduced democratic structures. Easterners welcomed highly the departure of despotism and suppression, and the arrival of free expression and justice, while the sound and time-tested Western democratic structures provided an effective barrier against a potential return to totalitarian rule. In addition, the democratic transition from the Communist dictatorship was aided by the Eastern public's considerable interest in politics, as well as by satisfactory levels of electoral participation. Regarding these crucial democratic virtues, Easterners adapted thoroughly to Western standards. However, such fundamental basics of democratic citizenship—participation in elections and political interest—were already promoted by the SED regime which had possessed high norms of political participation and had fostered political knowledge, albeit in an ideologically streamlined manner. Political interest was further boosted by the highly politicized climate of the immediate months before and after November 1989. Broad segments of the Eastern society were involved in mass demonstrations, and the political, social, and economic future of Eastern Germany were the central topics of much private and public conversation. The repressive and coercive nature of political participation under the SED regime resulted in a thirst for free expression in the aftermath of 1989. These highly positive democratic virtues significantly contributed to the relatively smooth and rapid introduction of Western democratic structures of political representation.

WESTERN EXTERNAL BOUNDARIES

Apart from these mutually agreed standards that supported the establishment of common national identities shared by East and West Germans, a variety of exclusive barriers emerged that gave ample testimonies to the emerging "Wall in the mind." Territorially, Easterners had remained fixated on the Federal Republic throughout the existence of the GDR. While West Germans had largely accepted the fact of the division and found a new spiritual home within the community of Western states, Easterners continued to perceive of the unification of the nation as a political goal that would offer them freedom and prosperity. While for West Germans unification came as a welcome but not desperately pursued political opportunity, it was the fulfillment of a lifelong ambition for most Easterners.

From this ambivalent point of departure, a tidal wave of dividing experiences followed. Economically, the prospect and experience of unemployment came as a sudden shock for many East Germans. In sharp contrast to the GDR which gave the constitutional right of work to every citizen, the transition to a market economy resulted in an ever-decreasing work force. Unemployment became a widespread phenomenon and by far the issue of most concern to Easterners. Socialism had hardly prepared East Germans for this abrupt transformation. Overnight, work turned from a given without any particular financial or social value into one of the fundamental requisites of one's existence, on which social and financial status depended. Unemployment turned into a decisive barrier that separated East from West. The revolutionary upheavals of 1989 left many Easterners with the belief that years of consumer privation and lower living standards in comparison to the West would finally come to an end. On the contrary, however, many found themselves excluded from the material benefits unification had promised initially. A two-tier society emerged in the new *Länder*. On the one hand, those who regularly received their paychecks which offered satisfying participation in the newly established consumer society, as well as the pursuit of individual career ambitions—on the other hand, those who were excluded from the benefits of market economics. But even for those with employment, the prosperity gap between East and West represented an issue of much dissatisfaction. Although the large majority fared better economically than in the days of the old GDR, the advances after 1990 were regarded as insufficient. Images of the rich West and the poor East persisted and were counterproductive to the establishment of common economic identities of a unified nation based on material equality.

The formerly wide-ranging network of social services became subject to significant cuts. While the GDR comprehensively took care of its citizens, the West German *Sozialstaat* was tied to the country's economic competitiveness. East Germans now had to accommodate the fact that social security did not constitute an automatic given for individual demands. Hence, for most Easterners, living circumstances became unstable. The incoming Western culture stressed notions of individuality, performance, flexibility, and mobility. These stood in marked contrast to the slower pace of life in the GDR, with the pronounced emphasis on amiable and harmonious social relations, as well as state-guaranteed material and social safety. After 1990 tough competition for a limited number of jobs and the decline in rent and food subsidies or family allowances combined in a widespread feeling of insecurity. The vast demographic pressures, including the dramatic drop in marriage, divorce, and birth rates, the continuous support for the idea of Socialism, as well as the declining approval of Capitalism, represented telling indicators for a feeling of dissatisfaction with and confusion about the speed and extent of the economic transformation processes.

Such deep-felt ruptures to one's existence required a safety valve of aggression. The scapegoat was a conspiratorial apparatus of Western managers, Western politicians, and especially the *Treuhand* that were blamed for the economic malaise. In the GDR, the individual was the passive recipient of guaranteed work and social security. Notions of self-responsibility, independence, and initiative hardly stood a chance against powerful and centralized administrative apparatuses that organized virtually every aspect of life. Despite increased pressure to perform at work and to compete for jobs, economics continued to inhabit a passive and recipient undertone after unification. One superimposed system (West German Capitalism) had replaced another (Soviet-type Socialism). The generous currency conversion, as well as highly advantageous wage and pension levels, lulled Easterners into a subsidized prosperity. The individual was therefore often not forced to accept responsibility for the economic decline and to confront personal shortcomings and deficiencies. Instead, as with the old system of centralism and planning, people blamed abstract political and economic hierarchies that had caused such hardship. Notions of "exploitative" economics, of colonization by the West, became widespread. Opportunistic Western managers degraded the individual to a mere production tool, and enterprises to investment opportunities. Merciless Capitalism fought property battles, made jobs redundant, and threatened social safety. These perceptions of Western economic opportunism and superiority marked a further severe dividing line between East and West. Within such an atmosphere, East Germans felt reluctant to identify with the unified nation under Western economic leadership.

The frustration, shock, and anger caused by widespread unemployment, the decline of the former all-encompassing welfare state, and "exploitative" economics were further aggravated by alarming developments in the civic-political sphere. A paradoxical situation emerged. On the one hand, East Germans continued to give the large majority of their votes to Western parties. On the other hand, however, throughout the first four years after unification, around fifty perent could not identify with any Western political party. Easterners began to perceive unification as political takeover by Western parties and politicians. For many people, attitudes prevailed that the formidable effort of ousting a totalitarian regime merely resulted in the superimposition of another political system without any appropriate popular involvement. Indeed, with the exception of the PDS and the *Bündnis 90*, political parties that had their origins in the West took control of the Eastern *Länder*. The import of Western politicians and civil servants, as well as the limited impact of Eastern politicians on the national political scene further nurtured emerging attitudes of a Western political colonization and gave the political transformation processes a distinctly illegitimate characteristic. For many, political choices were limited and unsatisfactory. Western parties did not properly represent Eastern interests. The PDS still had the stigma of the successor party of the SED. *Bündnis 90* turned from a civic movement into a fringe party on the edge of the political agenda. As a consequence, active participation in politics, such as membership in political parties or trade unions, decreased consistently. Interest in politics—although still at respectable levels—nonetheless had dropped significantly since 1990. A growing indifference toward the political process emerged which regarded the newly-introduced mode of interest aggregation and representation as an alien Western system.

Revelations on the extent of the state security system and the astonishingly high numbers of private individuals and public officials who worked for the *Stasi* left a further dividing mark. The initial pride in the successful mass revolution was gradually replaced by a widespread feeling of disgrace. The imposition of Western economic, political, and social structures, the complete demolition of the entire GDR state and its particular way of life, and finally the scrutiny with which the *Stasi* past was interrogated, represented humiliating experiences for many East Germans. People were forced to justify their survival strategies of accommodating and adapting to a totalitarian regime to which many felt hardly any loyalty. The *Stasi* legacy divided the public psyche of the nation. Western-dominated media, Western laws, and the Western "Gauck office" called for an uncompromising interrogation. West Germany's own reluctance in confronting the people's involvement in the Nazi regime should not be repeated in the East. The West ordered utmost scrutiny. Not surprisingly, against this condescending Western standard, the East responded with escapism. Gradually, perceptions dominated which repressed the *Stasi* controversy and intended to draw the matter to a close. Understanding and compassion among West Germans for this complex and complicated issue, however, were severely lacking. After all, not every citizen of the GDR was either an ardent Communist supporter or involved in spy activities. Many were forced to collaborate out of coercion and existential necessity. The frantic and unrelenting manner with which media and public officials handled the matter pushed East Germans into an uncomfortable corner. Repression and denial were the only options for exiting this dilemma which prevented a thorough working-out of the past. Instead, excluding barriers developed between Western plaintiffs and Eastern defendants, between those who accused and those who justified their actions.

With these developments in mind, Easterners overemphasized the one remaining identity marker that was still shared by East and West: ethnicity. Throughout the existence of the GDR, East Germans never surrendered to the officially propagated notion of two German nations. In the Federal Republic the shameful legacy of *Auschwitz* and the gradual confrontation with the Nazi past resulted in a distinctly un-ethnic identity. However, national unity and the goal of the unified nation which offered freedom and prosperity were firmly on the Eastern public's mind. Indeed the desire for unification with the West was largely based on ethnicity. East Germany could very well have remained a separate state. A democratized GDR would have been possible, just like the democratized Poland, Hungary, and Czechoslovakia emerged out of the ashes of Communism. However, the common German ethnic identity tipped the balance in favor of unification within a single German state. While Communism had stressed internationalism and Socialist brotherhood, unification brought a political system which—although not expressly encouraged—nonetheless allowed the identification with ethnic elements. With the continuous decline of other identity markers, ethnicity for East Germans represented one of the last remaining bastions of self-esteem. Xenophobia and ethnic chauvinism offered ready compensation for widespread feelings of frustration and inferiority. Although the desire to preserve the German ethnic homogeneity was also undoubtedly present in the old *Länder*, the higher degrees of racist violence and general resentment against foreigners in the East pointed toward the functionalization of ethnic chauvinism and xenophobia as pressure valves. Condescending attitudes toward foreigners, foreign cultures and customs offered a considerable boost to one's badly hurt self-esteem in a time of existentialist pressures.

EASTERN EXTERNAL BOUNDARIES

Against these dividing barriers, East Germans soon began to establish their own excluding boundaries which marked their identities off from that of Western Germany. These new boundaries overcame the strong sense of inferiority and instilled desperately needed pride. As the widely noticed marker of this newly found self-esteem, the PDS enjoyed spectacular success. Votes for, as well as party identification with the neo-Communists increased continuously. As the advocate of the East, the party represented the catalyst for the defiant Eastern protest vote against political and economic colonization by the West. The PDS was able to instill a sense of community and it emerged as a regional identity party that attracted support not necessarily for its programs and ideas but moreover for its defiance against the political—Western—establishment.

The PDS was also able to benefit from an increasing nostalgic and selective reference to the GDR. As the successor party to the SED, East Germans related the party to a past (the so-called "*Friedenszeiten*," time of peace) that offered more stability, more security, and more harmony; when life was not subject to such sudden and colossal changes. While in the first year after unification the political and economic rhetoric of the elites and the media denounced practically all economic, political, and cultural developments that had ever emerged from the East as unworthy, the reverse trend became more and more evident by 1992. Now, Easterners put the past into a selective perspective. Although hardly any East German wanted a return to totalitarian rule, certain routines and lifestyles of the GDR era were now fondly treasured. "*Trabis*" were restored and driven with pride. GDR consumer products, such as "*Rotkäppchen*" or "*F6*" enjoyed an astonishing resurgence. Saluting the past represented miniature plebiscites against the speed and extent of the general transformation processes. They expressed one's defiance against the Western takeover, as well as pride in one's achievements and personal history. The transition with its sudden changes implicitly expected East Germans to start a new existence and to accommodate to new values, standards, and demands. Nostalgia, however, proudly stated that life did not simply start in 1990 but had its worthwhile and memorable assets before the time when the Wall came down. Here was the confident resistance against the streamlining processes of unification that had initially threatened to suffocate any particularly Eastern cultural, political, social, and economic expressions. Nostalgia was the proud establishment of an external boundary that no Westerner was able to cross. It was an exclusively Eastern standard that formed a distinct "Us-against-them" attitude in the entire region of the new *Länder*.

These dramatic responses of East Germans to the transformation processes pointed toward the conclusion that people reacted out of self-defense. The speed and extent of the transition, the imposition of new standards and the subsequent adaptation to them did not allow any time for reflection. In 1989 East Germans possessed clearly defined aspirations: civic liberties, freedom, and material prosperity. After unification, a confused storage of Communist experiences, new demands and expectations emerged. The past had just been invalidated by the nature of the transition that despised all former hierarchies, structures, and emotional anchors to one's past existence. With one sweep, unification sought to erase Eastern identities and streamline them into common all-German identities of Western origin. This however, was not an acceptable option for most East Germans. Confused standards of a fondly remembered past (which also held traumatic experiences of repression and curtailed liberties) and a complicated and demanding present full of abrupt cognitive changes left the individual struggling to find his or her place within the radically changed environment.

THE FUTURE OF GERMAN IDENTITY

The acceptance by East Germans of numerous Western standards offered plentiful evidence for the emergence of common national identities. "Affirmative" and "active economics," the establishment of the Western consumer society, media consumption, leisure and travel patterns, the approval of the arrival of a free and open society, as well as the basic civic virtues of participation and political interest had all reached comparable levels in East and West. Nonetheless, unification never constituted a project for both East and West. The transformation processes were implemented with hardly any public involvement. Westerners had no choice but to accept the incorporation of the Eastern *Länder* into the Federal Republic. Tax burdens, solidarity tokens, and a spreading economic recession gave the euphoric days of 1989 a sour aftertaste. In the East, the cognitive discrepancy between the active mass involvement of 1989, as well as the confident constitutional proposals of the "round table" discussions, on the one hand, and the economic and political superimposition of Western structures on the other could not have been more drastic. Many Easterners felt betrayed twice—first by the totalitarian lie of "real existing Socialism" and now by the hasty promises of "blossoming landscapes." In the end, the imposed unity, its speed and extent represented a burden that often threatened to undermine the public's psychological balance in both East and West. Sharing and growing together turned out to be more complicated than the preceding decades of coexistence. Inner unity often was a mere utopia, the establishment of which was hampered by a yoke of skepticism and intolerance.

Numerous excluding boundaries, whether of Eastern or Western origin, severely disturbed communication and reconciliation between the two German societies and continued to drive Germans apart. Instead of focusing on common grounds, Easterners and Westerners built new loyalties around excluding standards and only very reluctantly attempted to integrate the compatriots across the former demarcation line into one another's identity. Instead, the development of post-unification national identities in East and West often represented the psychological exclusion of the other German part, which potentially bears grave consequences. Although the gap between East and West regarding hiring standards and wage levels continued to decrease, and although the conversion rate and rising wage levels allowed for an immediate participation in the consumer society, the persistence of widespread unemployment has imposed a considerable threat to the country's political stability. Although so far no major civil unrest had been reported, this does not guarantee that there will not be any in the near future. Employment not only offers the financial means to participate in the consumer society, but it affects one's self-respect and self-esteem. Political and economic authorities have to realize that the Western levels of prosperity and consumption were one of the decisive raisons d'être of the revolution. To reach the "promised land" of the West gave the *Wende* a different direction and called for the unification with the Federal Republic. These fundamental motivations ultimately have to be met by the unified Germany. Otherwise, perceptions of a two-class society, of Westerners exploiting Easterners, will continue to haunt inner unity.

Social safety and security go hand in hand with employment. With a secure job, stability and predictability could again re-emerge as patterns of life for East Germans. The dramatic demographic pressures in the East not only showed a remarkable adaptability to the sudden and abrupt changes that affected one's existence but also indicated a widespread feeling of insecurity of what the future might bring. To develop affirmative loyalties to unified Germany, people at least have to be given the prospect of re-establishing a sound balance in their lives. When looking at empirical evidence, the Easterners' inferior perception of a political takeover by the West was certainly justified. The feeling of misrepresentation and prevailing attitudes of the illegitimate nature of the transformation processes have to be addressed to avoid further disintegration which could possibly lead to separation. Although inexperience and involvement with the SED regime represented a severe obstacle in the recruitment of East Germans to public appointments, political parties, public administration, and private enterprises are well-advised to deliberately employ Easterners in particular in senior posts that carry responsibility and publicity. East and West have to realize that they share a common political destiny. In this respect, sharing a nation's destiny implies sharing responsibility. As a vital step in this direction, the impact of Easterners on the national public agenda—within the media, within political parties, within political and economic decision making processes—has to increase. Only then can East Germans come to the conclusion that they are contributing to the processes of shaping the nation's future.

Such developments would undermine the most important reason for voting for the neo-Communists. The PDS so far has not challenged the democratic political structures of the Federal Republic and it remains unlikely that the party will do so in the future. Instead, the PDS has represented a lively contribution to the existing party landscape as an alternative on the political left, as well as a vital agent of political representation in the new *Länder*. Nonetheless, the party constituted a reservoir for the anti-Western protest vote. The continuous support for the neo-Communists in the East and their almost complete lack of status in the West have symbolized the split between the Eastern and Western psyche. For East Germans, the PDS formed a vital excluding identity marker which raised the Eastern public's self-esteem as a defiant, special, and different community. The need to define the party and its voters on difference and exclusion resulted from the Eastern impression of a second-class and colonized Eastern citizenry. The above described integration processes, however, would significantly soften the motivation to vote for the PDS.

The legacy of the *Stasi* added further bricks to the "Wall in the mind." In rhetoric, the entire Eastern society was put on trial over the alleged collaboration with the totalitarian SED regime. Western accusations were complemented by Eastern suspicions as to whether one's friend or even family member had been a spy. In the East, repression and denial emerged that intended to close an unpleasant and tormenting chapter in one's personal history. Nonetheless, only a full address of the *Stasi* practicalities, of personal involvement and guilt is able to overcome denial and repression. This, however, should be undertaken without the condescending arrogance that divided the nation into Western prosecutors and Eastern criminals. The discourse should also include references to West Germany's failures in properly addressing the Third Reich in the immediate postwar era. *Stasi* informants might be the most recent immoral villains, but this collaboration with an unjust regime was certainly not unique to German history. From this perspective, Westerners have no right to judge Easterners on their moral deficiencies.

Despite the presence of the basic civic standards of participation and political interest, Easterners showed considerable deficiencies in the civic-political sphere. All too often the blame for economic or political shortcomings was simply directed against abstract elites, predominantly from the West. This tendency to look for scapegoats survived as a legacy of the GDR era. Communism and totalitarianism did not prepare the individual for competition in a democratic, pluralistic, and market-oriented environment. People longed for the former guardianship of the state that had organized their lives. The urge and necessity to make decisions and to accept responsibility for them, however, was perceived by many as a great burden. Not surprisingly, the crash course in citizenship left much to be desired. People found it difficult to redefine their relationship to the state when they consistently used to be against it. This "deficit of trust" (Stern 1993: 124) born out of repression and curtailed liberties during the GDR era represents a severe danger to democracy.

East Germans have to internalize citizenship virtues of democratic rights and democratic responsibilities. The structures of political parties, interest groups, or federal and *Länder* parliaments had been recognized and used as agents of individual demands. Nonetheless, democratic stability in the new *Länder* relied on the implementation of sound political Western structures and satisfactory levels of material prosperity. These have yet to be complemented by affirmative orientations. Democracy in the East needs to be filled with meaning. People obeyed democratic rules as organizing principles of society. However, East Germans have to internalize that democracy not only offers such givens as freedom and justice but furthermore offers opportunities to participate and to influence. As seen in West Germany, fostering civic virtues demands time. In the *Bonn* Republic it took some twenty years for a confident citizenry to emerge that expressed and pursued democratic rights and civic opportunities. This, however, should not prevent the agents of political education, such as political parties, the media, or schools from placing deliberate efforts on overcoming the existing gap in citizenship virtues.

Such affirmative and confident developments in the economic and civic spheres have the potential to encounter the resurgence of ethnic chauvinism and xenophobia in the new *Länder*. The overemphasis on ethnicity would lose its ultimate edge as the last bastion of self-esteem since other identity markers are able to compensate for it. Nonetheless, the establishment of such standards as multiculturalism and ethnic tolerance was complicated by confused ethnic standards in the old GDR. The official political culture propagated internationalism and Socialist brotherhood, yet ethnic chauvinism against Poles or Czechs was widespread, and strict travel restrictions hindered the appreciation of foreign cultures and customs. Additionally, the ethnic homogeneity and the political climate of the GDR did not foster tolerance or respect, while the SED never properly addressed the genocide and moral barbarism of the Third Reich. Civic values of tolerance and respect did not develop naturally but instead were delegated from above with the state as the regulator of moral codes. With unification, this watchdog function of the state disappeared and ethnic chauvinism was given the opportunity to freely develop. In the West, tolerance and civility were more advanced. Yet the xenophobic violence between 1991 and 1993 was not an exclusively Eastern phenomenon. The political system of the *Bonn* Republic was never forced to accommodate multiculturalism. Despite granting political asylum and immigration to ethnic Germans, and despite incoming guest workers, West Germany remained a largely homogenous society. Half a century after *Auschwitz*, ethnic identities are likely to appear more pronounced in the German public psyche. In the West, the third postwar generation does not so readily accept the collective shame and responsibility as their parents had done. In the East, the demise of the Communist bloc gives ethnic identities the chance to re-emerge after decades of officially propagated Socialist internationalism. The united Germany therefore faces the challenge of giving emerging ethnic identities a positive direction. Both West and East Germans still have to develop a proper balance in their ethnic identities—one which is proudly aware of the culture, customs, and traditions of the German nation combined with tolerance for and appreciation of cultural difference and diversity.

Nostalgia and the sentimental longing for a secure past provided an emotional anchor of orientation for many East Germans. Values and standards that were generated by forty years of Socialism and totalitarianism could not easily be left behind or replaced by orientations to the unified nation. Subsequently, Easterners started to place their past into a selective perspective. This longing for safety, stability, and familiarity indicated a fear of failing within the new societal, economic, and political systems. Nobody wanted the GDR back, but also nobody wanted it to be taken away from them. This virtual GDR-reality imposed a significant threat to inner unification. Germany's democratic stability could be in danger when people selectively and affectionately remember the totalitarian past and disproportionally criticize the present. Germany therefore ought to establish an environment that gives Eastern identities enough room to flourish. In the first years after unification, Easterners were streamlined into second-class Westerners. But given the short time span in which to adapt to a vastly different form of life, East Germans still possess emotional attachments and loyalties that are linked to the GDR past. After 1989, the transformation processes heavily condemned all former experiences and formative orientations. However, identities are not only embedded in the present but also in the past. The specific form of life under the SED regime will for some time feature as an identity marker in particular for those who found it difficult to succeed under the new political, economic, and societal rules. It therefore remains crucial to allow for the continued existence of a particular East German identity that gives reference to past experiences and orientations. Only then can alienating attitudes to the unified nation be avoided. Dual identities based on the vastly different Eastern experiences under totalitarian rule should develop alongside supportive orientations to the unified nation. The GDR era has to be integrated into the public psyche of both East and West. Education authorities, the media and the general public discourse ought to give marked attention to East German life prior to 1989—not the current selective nostalgic expression but instead the conscious address of all positive and negative aspects of it. Germans in East and West now share a common political destiny but as yet they do not share a common mental base on which to build the future. Furthering knowledge of, as well as fostering interest in, the respective other German part, however, could mark a vital step toward inner unity.

Bibliography

PUBLIC OPINION SURVEYS

Allensbacher Archiv. *IfD Umfrage*. Several monthly issues. Institut für Demoskopie. Allensbach, 1991–1992.

Allensbacher Berichte. Several monthly issues. Institut für Demoskopie. Allensbach, 1990–1995.

Emnid. *Informationen*. Several annual volumes. Bielefeld, 1983–1995.

Förster, Peter, and Günter Roski. *Die DDR zwischen Wende und Wahl*. Berlin: Linksdruck, 1990.

Gruner und Jahr. *Dialoge 4*. Hamburg: Stern Bibliothek, 1995.

Gruner und Jahr. *Dialoge 3*. Hamburg: Stern Bibliothek, 1990.

Institut für Demoskopie. *Demokratieverankerung in der Bundesrepublik Deutschland*. Allensbach: Verlag für Demoskopie, 1979.

Institut für Demoskopie. *Jahrbuch der öffentlichen Meinung*. Vol. VI. Allensbach: Verlag für Demoskopie, 1976.

Institut für Demoskopie. *Jahrbuch der öffentlichen Meinung*. Vol V. Allensbach: Verlag für Demoskopie, 1974.

Köhler, Anne. "Infratest Kommunikationsforschung. Marschierte der DDR-Bürger mit?" In Ute Gerhardt and Ekkehard Mochmann (eds.). *Gesellschaftlicher Umbruch 1945–1990*. München: Oldenbourg, 1992, 59–80.

Niemann, Heinz. *Meinungsforschung in der DDR. Die geheimen Berichte des Instituts für Meinungsforschung an das Politbüro der SED*. Berlin: Bund, 1993.

Noelle-Neumann, Elisabeth. *Demoskopische Geschichtsstunde*. Osnabrück: Fromm, 1991.

Noelle-Neumann, Elisabeth. *The Germans: Public Opinion Polls 1967–80*. Westport, Conn.: Greenwood, 1981.

Noelle-Neumann, Elisabeth, and Renate Köcher. *Allensbacher Jahrbuch der Demoskopie 1984–1992*. München: Saur, 1993.

Politbarometer. Several monthly issues. Forschungsgruppe Wahlen e.V. Institut für Wahlanalysen und Gesellschaftsbeobachtung. Mannheim, 1979–1995.

Roth, Dieter. "Die Volkskammerwahl in der DDR am 18. März 1990." In Ulrike Liebert and Wolfgang Merkel (eds.), *Die Politik zur deutschen Einheit*. Opladen: Leske und Budrich, 1991, 115–138.

POLITICAL PARTIES AND INTEREST GROUPS

Bund für Umwelt und Naturschutz Deutschland (BUND). Information according to Press Office. Bonn, 1996.

Bundesverband mittelständischer Wirtschaft, Regional Office Potsdam. Information according to Press Office. Potsdam, 1994.

Bündnis 90/die Grünen. Information according to Press Office. Bonn, 1996.

Christlich Demokratische Union (CDU). Information according to Press Office. Bonn, 1996.

Christlich Soziale Union (CSU). Information according to Press Office. München, 1996.

Deutscher Gewerkschaftsbund (DGB). Information according to Bundesvorstand, Press Office. Düsseldorf, 1996.

Deutscher Reisebüro-Verband. Information according to Press Office. Frankfurt/Main, 1996.

Freie Demokratische Partei (FDP). Information according to Press Office. Bonn, 1996.

Greenpeace, Information according to Press Office. Hamburg, 1996.

Naturschutzbund. Information according to Press Office. Bonn, 1996.

Partei des Demokratischen Sozialismus (PDS). Information according to Press Office. Berlin, 1996.

Sozialdemokratische Partei Deutschland (SPD). Information according to Press Office. Bonn, 1996.

NEWSPAPERS, MAGAZINES, AND OTHERS

Bundesanstalt für Arbeit. Information according to Press Office, Nürnberg, 1996.

Bundesministerium des Inneren. *Verfassungsschutzbericht.* Dortmund: Busche, 1995.

Bundesministerium des Inneren. *Verfassungsschutzbericht.* Dortmund: Busche, 1994.

Bundesministerium des Inneren. *Verfassungsschutzbericht.* Dortmund: Busche, 1993.

Bundesministerium des Inneren. *Verfassungsschutzbericht.* Dortmund: Busche, 1992.

Der Spiegel. Several weekly issues. Hamburg, 1990–1996.

Deutsche Bundesbank. Information according to Press Office. Frankfurt/Main, 1995.

Die Zeit. Several weekly issues. Hamburg, 1994.

Frankfurter Allgemeine Zeitung. Several daily issues. Frankfurt/Main, 1995.

Ministerium für Arbeit, Soziales und Gesundheit des Landes Sachsen-Anhalt. Information according to Press Office. Magdeburg, 1995.

Organisation for Economic Cooperation and Development. *Social Expenditure 1960–1990,* Paris, 1985.

Philip Morris. Information according to Press Office. München, 1997.

Philip Morris. Information according to Press Office. München, 1995.

Pohl, Klaus. *Waiting Room Germany.* [Play based on numerous interviews with East Germans during 1994]. First performed at the Royal Court Theatre. London, November 9, 1995.

Statistical Yearbook of the Federal Republic. Several annual volumes. Wiesbaden: Metzler und Poeschel.

Statistical Yearbook of the German Democratic Republic. Several annual volumes. Berlin (Ost): Staatsverlag.

SECONDARY SOURCES

Almond, Gabriel, and Sidney Verba. *The Civic Culture Revisited.* Newbury Park, Calif.: Sage, 1989.

Almond, Gabriel and Sidney Verba. *The Civic Culture: Political Attitudes and Democracy in Five Nations.* Princeton, N.J.: Princeton University Press, 1963.

Ammer, Thomas. "Die Parteien in der DDR." In Alf Mintzel and Heinrich Oberreuter (eds.), *Parteien in der Bundesrepublik Deutschland.* Opladen: Leske und Budrich, 1992, 421–484.

Ammer, Thomas. "Stichwort: Flucht aus der DDR." *Deutschland Archiv* 22, 11 (1989): 1206–1208.

Anderson, Benedict. *Imagined Communities: Reflections on the Origin and Spread of Nationalism.* London: Verso, 1983.

Asche, Klaus. "Zur wirtschaftlichen Lage in den östlichen Bundesländern." *Deutschland Archiv* 27, 3 (1994): 232–237.

Ash, Timothy Garton. "Germany's Choice." *Foreign Affairs* 73, 4 (1994): 65–81.

Baldauf, Monika, and Walter Klingler. "Hörfunk: Stablie Nutzung bei wachsendem Angebot." *Mediaperspektiven* 8 (1994): 409–418.

Bark, Dennis L., and David R. Gress. *A History West Germany.* Cambridge: Blackwell, 1993.

Barry, Brian. *Sociologists, Economists and Democracy.* London: Collier-Macmillan, 1970.

Barth, Fredrik. *Ethnic Groups and Boundaries: The Social Organization of Culture Difference.* London: Allen & Unwin, 1969.

Bauer, Petra, and Oskar Niedermayer. "Extrem rechtes Potential in den Ländern der Europäischen Gemeinschaft." *Aus Politik und Zeitgeschichte* 11 (1990): 15–26.

Beetham, David. *The Legitimation of Power.* London: Macmillan, 1991.

Bell, Daniel. *The Radical Right.* Garden City, N.Y.: Doubleday, 1964.

Belwe, Katharina. "Arbeitskultur und Arbeitskollektiv." In Hans-Georg Wehling (ed.), *Politische Kultur in der DDR.* Stuttgart: Kohlhammer, 1989, 94–109.

Beyme, Klaus von. *Das Politische System der Bundesrepublik Deutschland nach der Vereinigung.* München: Piper, 1991.

Boll, Bernhard. "Interest Organisation and Intermediation in the New Länder." *German Politics* 3, 1 (1994): 114–128.

Bortfeldt, Heinrich. "Die Ostdeutschen und die PDS." *Deutschland Archiv* 27, 12 (1994): 1283–1287.

Braunthal, Gerard. "Civil Liberties: The Issue of Migrants." In Peter H. Merkl (ed.), *The Federal Republic of Germany at Forty-Five.* New York: New York University Press, 1995, 206–218.

Chandler, William M. "Immigration Politics and Citizenship in Germany." In Peter H. Merkl (ed.), *The Federal Republic of Germany at Forty-Five.* New York: New York University Press, 1995, 344–356.

Clemens, Clay. "Disquiet on the Eastern Front: The Christian Democratic Union in Germany's New Länder." *German Politics* 2, 2 (1993): 200–223.

Connor, Walker. "A Nation Is a Nation, Is a State, Is an Ethnic Group, Is a . . ." *Ethnic and Racial Studies* 1, 4 (1978): 377–388.

Conradt, David P. "Changing German Political Culture." In Gabriel A. Almond and Sidney Verba (eds.), *The Civic Culture Revisited.* Newbury Park, Calif.: Sage, 1989, 212–272.

Cordell, Karl. "The Role of the Evangelical Church in the GDR." *Government and Opposition* 25, 1 (1990): 48–59.

Crow, Kimberly, and Mariana Hennig. "Wohnen and soziale Infrastruktur von Familien in den neuen Budesländern." In Hans Bertram (ed.), *Ostdeutschland in Wandel.* Opladen: Leske und Budrich, 1995, 99–123.

Dalton, Russel L. *Politics in Germany.* New York: HarperCollins, 1993.

Darschin, Wolfgang, and Bernward Frank. "Tendenzen im Zuschauerverhalten." *Mediaperspektiven* 3 (1994): 98–110.

Darschin, Wolfgang, and Bernward Frank. "Tendenzen im Zuschauerverhalten." *Mediaperspektiven* 4 (1995): 154–165.

Degenhart, Christoph. *Staatsrecht I.* Heidelberg: Müller, 1988.

Diesener, Gerald, and Rainer Gries. "Nachkriegsgeschichte als Kommunikationsgeschichte." *Deutschland Archive* 26, 1 (1993): 21–30.

Durkheim, Emile. *The Division of Labour in Society.* Toronto: Macmillan, 1933.

Easton, David. *A Systems Analysis of Political Life.* Chicago: University of Chicago Press, 1965.

Eckart, Karl. "Der wirtschaftliche Umbau in den neuen Bundesländern." *Deutschland Archiv* 28, 6 (1995): 578–588.

Eisel, Stephan. "The Politics of a United Germany." *Daedalus* 123, 1 (1994): 149–171.

Eisenhammer, John. "Germans Pay a Price for Freedom Fire." *Independent on Sunday*, January 8, 1995, 7.

Ellwein, Thomas, Ekkehard Lippert, and Ralf Zoll. *Politische Beteiligung in der Bundesrepublik.* Göttingen: Otto Schwarz, 1975.

Fagen, Richard. *The Transformation of Political Cultures in Cuba.* Stanford, Calif.: Stanford University Press, 1965.

Fijalkowski, Jürgen. "Aggressive Nationalism, Immigration Pressure and Asylum Policy Disputes in Contemporary Germany." *International Migration Review* 27, 4 (1993): 850–869.

Frei, Norbert. "Hörfunk und Fernsehen." In Wolfgang Benz (ed.), *Die Geschichte der Bundesrepublik Deutschland,* Vol. 4. Frankfurt/Main: Fischer, 1989, 417–463.

Fuchs, Dieter, Jürgen Gerhards, and Edeltraut Roller. "Wir und die anderen. Ethnozentrismus in den zwölf Ländern der Europäischen Gemeinschaft." *Kölner Zeitschrift für Soziologie und Sozialpsychologie* 45, 2 (1993): 238–253.

Fulbrook, Mary. "Aspects of Society and Identity in the New Germany." *Daedalus* 123, 1 (1994): 211–234.

Gabriel, Oscar W. "Politscher Protest und politische Unterstützung in den neuen Bundesländern." In Hans Bertram (ed.), *Ostdeutschland im Wandel: Lebensverhältnisse und politische Einstellungen.* Opladen: Leske und Budrich, 1995, 173–205.

Geertz, Clifford. *The Interpretation of Cultures.* New York: Basic Books, 1983.

Gensicke, Thomas. "Die Stimmung ist besser als die Lage." *Deutschland Archiv* 27, 8 (1994): 802–815.

Gibbins, John R. *Contemporary Political Culture*. London: Sage, 1989.

Glaeβner, Gert-Joachim. *Die andere deutsche Republik*. Opladen: Westdeutscher Verlag, 1989.

Gloannec, Anne Marie Le. "On German Identity." *Daedalus* 123, 1 (1994): 129–148.

Golz, Hans-Georg. "Wir müssen lernen, mit Fremden zu leben." *Deutschland Archiv* 28, 1 (1995): 4–8.

Golz, Hans-Georg. "Seriöse Zahlen zum IM-Bestand." *Deutschland Archiv* 27, 4 (1994): 343–344.

Golz, Hans-Georg. "Einwanderungsland Bundesrepublik." *Deutschland Archiv* 27, 6 (1994a): 564–657.

Golz, Hans-Georg. "Halbzeit im Superwahljahr." *Deutschland Archiv* 27, 7 (1994b): 675–679.

Golz, Hans-Georg. "PDS von innen." *Deutschland Archiv* 27, 9 (1994c): 903–904.

Gries, Rainer. "Der Geschmack der Heimat." *Deutschland Archive* 27, 10 (1994): 1041–1057.

Grundmann, Siegfried. "Zur Akzeptanz und Integration von Beamten aus den alten in den neuen Bundesländern." *Deutschland Archiv* 27, 1 (1994): 31–42.

Grunenberg, Antonia. "Zwei Deutschlands—zwei Identitäten? Über deutsche Identität in der Bundesrepublik Deutschland und der DDR." In Gert-Joachim Glaeβner (ed.), *Die DDR in der Arä Honecker*. Opladen: Westdeutscher Verlag, 1988, 94–110.

Habermas, Jürgen. *Die nachholende Revolution. Kleine politische Schriften VII*. Frankfurt am Main: Suhrkamp, 1990.

Haendcke-Hoppe-Arndt, Maria. "Wer wuβte was? Der ökonomische Niedergang der DDR." *Deutschland Archiv* 28, 6 (1995): 588–602.

Haese, Ute. "Katholische Kirche in der DDR und MfS." *Deutschland Archiv* 27, 2 (1994): 130–140.

Hansch, Winfried. "Wanderungen aus den alten Bundesländern in die Region Brandenburg/Berlin." *Deutschland Archiv* 26, 3 (1993): 286–296.

Haungs, Peter. "Die CDU: Prototyp einer Volkspartei." In Alf Mintzel and Heinrich Oberreuter (eds.), *Parteien in der Bundesrepublik Deutschland*. Opladen: Leske und Budrich, 1992, 172–216.

Heater, Derek. *Citizenship*. London: Longman, 1990.

Helwig, Gisela. "Auf Dauer arbeitslos." *Deutschland Archiv* 28, 4 (1995): 342–343.

Hertle, Hans-Hermann. "Der Weg in den Bankrott der DDR-Wirtschaft." *Deutschland Archiv* 25, 2 (1992): 127–145.

Hesse, Joachim Jens, and Thomas Ellwein. *Das Regierungssystem der Bundesrepublik*. Opladen: Westdeutscher Verlag, 1992.

Hesse, Kurt R. *Westmedien in der DDR*. Köln: Wissenschaft und Politik, 1988.

Hirschmann, Albert O. *A Propensity of Self-Subversion*. Cambridge, Mass.: Harvard University Press, 1995.

Inglehart, Ronald. *The Silent Revolution*. Princeton, N.J.: Princeton University Press, 1977.

Insider-Komitee. "Das politische Wirken der Kirchen in der DDR und die Reaktionen des MfS." *Deutschland Archiv* 27, 4 (1994): 374–407.

Iwand, Wolf Michael. *Paradigma Politische Kultur*. Opladen: Leske und Budrich, 1985.

Janowitz, Morris. *The Reconstruction of Patriotism*. Chicago: University of Chicago Press, 1983.

Kleβmann, Christoph. "The Burden of the Past in the Two German States." In Margy Gerber and Roger Woods (eds.), *The End of the GDR and the Problems of Integration*. New York: New York University Press, 1993, 195–210.

Klinger, Fred. "Soziale Konflikte und offene Gewalt." *Deutschland Archiv* 26, 2 (1994): 147–161.

Kocka, Jürgen. "The Crisis of Unification." *Daedalus* 123, 1 (1994): 173–192.

Kommers, Donald P. "The Basic Law and Reunification." In Peter H. Merkl (ed.), *The Federal Republic at Forty-Five*. New York: New York University Press, 1995, 187–205.

Krisch, Henry. "Der Wandel der politischen Kultur und politische Stabilität in der DDR." In Gert-Joachim Glaeβner (ed.), *Die DDR in der Arä Honecker*. Opladen: Westdeutscher Verlag, 1988, 151–166.

Krisch, Henry. *The German Democratic Republic: The Search for Identity*. Boulder, Colo.: Westview, Press 1985.

Kühnel, Steffen, and Michael Terwey. "Gestörtes Verhältnis? Die Einstellung der Deutschen zu Ausländern in der Bundesrepublik." In Michael Braun and Peter Ph. Mohler (eds.), *Blickpunkt Gesellschaft. Band 3*. Opladen: Westdeutscher Verlag, 1994, 71–105.

Lease, Gary. "Religion, the Churches and the German 'Revolution' of November 1989." *German Politics* 1, 2 (1992): 264–273.

Leenen, Wolf Rainer. "Ausländerfeindlichkeit, fremdenfeindliche Gewalt und politische Öffentlichkeit." *Deutschland Archiv* 28, 6 (1995): 603–624.

Leenen, Wolf Rainer. "Ausländerfeindlichkeit in Deutschland." *Deutschland Archiv* 25, 10 (1992): 1039–1054.

Lemke, Christiane. "Eine politische Doppelkultur." In Hans-Georg Wehling (ed.), *Politische Kultur in der DDR*. Stuttgart: Kohlhammer, 1989, 81–93.

Lijphart, Arend. "The Structure of Inference." In Gabriel Almond and Sidney Verba (eds.), *The Civic Culture Revisited*. Newbury Park, Calif.: Sage, 1989, 37–56.

Lipset, Seymour Martin. "Some Social Requisites of Democracy." *American Political Science Review* 53, 1 (1958): 69–105.

Löwenhaupt, Stefan. "Bürger und Verwaltung in den fünf neuen Bundesländern." In Hans Bertram (ed.), *Ostdeutschland im Wandel: Lebensverhältnisse und politische Einstellungen*. Opladen: Leske und Budrich, 1995, 155–171.

Marshall, Barbara. "German Migration Policies." In Gordon Smith et al., *Developments in German Politics*. London: Macmillan, 1992, 247–263.

Merkl, Peter H. "Are the Old Nazis Coming Back?" In Peter H. Merkl (ed.), *The Federal Republic of Germany at Forty-Five*. New York: New York University Press, 1995, 427–484.

Mertes, Michael. "Germany's Social and Political Culture: Change Through Consensus." *Daedalus* 123, 1 (1994): 1–32.

Meuschel, Sigrid. *Legitimation und Parteiherrschaft in der DDR*. Frankfurt/Main: Suhrkamp, 1992.

Meyer, Gerd. "Der versorgte Mensch." In Hans-Georg Wehling (ed.), *Politische Kultur in der DDR*. Stuttgart: Kohlhammer, 1989, 29–53.

Meyer-Seitz, Christian. "SED-Einfluß auf die Justiz in der Ära Honecker." *Deutschland Archiv* 28, 1 (1995): 32–43.

Muller, Steven. "Democracy in Germany." *Daedalus* 123, 1 (1994): 33–56.

Müller-Rommel, Ferdinand, and Thomas Poguntke. "Die Grünen." In Alf Mintzel and Heinrich Oberreuter (eds.), *Parteien in der Bundesrepublik Deutschland.* Opladen: Leske und Budrich, 1992, 319–361.

Olivier, Kurt. "ADN–Spitze der Informationskette." *Deutschland Archiv* 28, 3 (1995): 244–255.

Oppenheim, A. N. *Civic Education and Participation in Democracy.* London: Sage, 1977.

Parsons, Talcott, and Edward Shils. *Towards a General Theory of Action.* Cambridge, Mass.: Harvard University Press, 1951.

Pateman, Carole. "The Civic Culture: A Philosophique Critique." In Gabriel Almond and Sidney Verba (eds.), *The Civic Culture Revisited.* Newbury Park, Calif.: Sage, 1989, 57–102.

Patrick, Glenda. "Political Culture." In Giovanni Satori (ed.), *Social Science Concepts: A Systemic Analysis.* London: Sage, 1984, 265–314.

Pfahl-Traughber, Armin. "Wandlung zur Demokratie?" *Deutschland Archiv.* 28, 4 (1995): 359–369.

Pittmann, Margit. "Women's Equality in the German Democratic Republic." *Political Affairs* 66, 3 (1987): 14–18.

Poguntke, Thomas, and Rüdiger Schmitt-Beck. "Still the Same with a New Name? Bündnis 90/Die Grünen after the Fusion." *German Politics* 3, 1 (1994): 91–113.

Rattinger, Hans. "Parteineigungen in Ostdeutschland vor und nach der Wende." In Hans Bertram (ed.), *Ostdeutschland im Wandel: Lebensverhältnisse und politische Einstellungen.* Opladen: Leske und Budrich, 1995, 231–253.

Rudzio, Wolfgang. *Das politische System der Bundesrepublik Deutschland.* Opladen: Leske und Budrich, 1991.

Rytlewski, Ralf. "Ein neues Deutschland?" In Hans-Georg Wehling (ed.), *Politische Kultur in der DDR.* Stuttgart: Kohlhammer, 1989, 11–28.

Sailer, Sybille. "Das Arbeitskollektiv als soziales Subjekt technisch-ökonomischer Leistungsfähigkeit." *Zeitschrift für Philosophie* 37, 2 (1989): 148–149.

Sakowsky, Dagmar. "Arbeitslosigkeit im vereinten Deutschland." *Deutschland Archiv* 27, 2 (1994): 118–129.

Schatz, Heribert, Christofer Habig, and Nikolous Immer. "Medienpolitik." In Klaus von Beyme and Manfred G. Schmidt (eds.), *Politik in der Bundesrepublik Deutschland.* Opladen: Westdeutscher, 1990, 331–359.

Scherer, Klaus-Jürgen. "Gab es eine DDR-Identität?" In Rolf Reißig and Gert-Joachim Glaeßner (eds.), *Das Ende eines Experiments.* Berlin: Dietz, 1991, 296–316.

Schmid, Günther. "Beschäftigungs-und Arbeitsmarktpolitik." In Klaus von Beyme and Manfred G. Schmidt (eds.), *Politik in der Bundesrepublik Deutschland.* Opladen: Westdeutscher, 1990, 228–254.

Schmid, Josef. "Die CDU in Ostdeutschland." *Deutschland Archiv* 27, 8 (1994): 793–801.

Schmidt, Hans-Walter. "Schaufenster des Ostens." *Deutschland Archive* 27, 4 (1994): 364–372.

Schmidt, Manfred G. "Sozialpolitik." In Klaus von Beyme and Manfred G. Schmidt (eds.), *Politik in der Bundesrepublik Deutschland.* Opladen: Westdeutscher, 1990, 126–149.

Schmitt, Hermann. "So dicht war die Mauer nicht! Über Parteibindungen und Cleavages im Osten Deutschlands." In Peter Eisenmann (ed.), *Die Entwicklung der Volksparteien im vereinten Deutschland.* München: Saur, 1992a, 229–252.

Schmitt, Hermann. "Die Sozialdemokratische Partei Deutschlands." In Alf Mintzel and Heinrich Oberreuter (eds.), *Parteien in der Bundesrepublik Deutschland.* Opladen: Leske und Budrich, 1992b, 133–171.

Schneider, Peter. *The Wall Jumper.* New York: Pantheon, 1983.

Schöpflin, George. "Nationalism and Ethnicity in Europe, East and West." In Charles A. Kupchan, (ed.), *Nationalism and Nationalities in the New Europe.* Ithaca, N.Y.: Cornell University Press, 1995, 37–66.

Schulz, Wilfred. "Die PDS und der SED/DDR Antifaschismus." *Deutschland Archiv* 27, 4 (1994): 408–413.

Schumpeter, Joseph A. *Capitalism, Society and Democracy.* London: Routledge, 1992.

Sinus Institut. *5 Millionen Deutsche: "Wir sollten wieder einen Führer haben."* Hamburg: Reinbek, 1981.

Smith, Anthony D. *National Identity.* London: Penguin, 1991.

Smith, Anthony D. *The Ethnic Origins of Nations.* Oxford: Basil Blackwell, 1986.

Smith, Gordon. *Democracy in Western Germany: Parties and Politics in the Federal Republic.* London: Heinemann, 1982.

Sontheimer, Kurt. *Deutschlands politische Kultur.* München: Piper, 1990.

Spittmann, Else. "PDS—Anwalt der Ostdeutschen?" *Deutschland Archiv* 27, 7 (1994): 673– 674.

Stern, Fritz. "Freedom and Its Discontents." *Foreign Policy* 72, 4 (1993): 108–125.

Sternberger, Dolf. *Verfassungspatriotismus.* Frankfurt am Main: Insel, 1979.

Stiller, Gabriele. "Pädagogismus versus Unterhaltung." In Hans-Georg Wehling (ed.), *Politische Kultur in der DDR.* Stuttgart: Kohlhammer, 1989, 147–157.

Street, John. "Political Culture—from Civic Culture to Mass Culture." *British Journal of Political Science* 24, 1 (1993): 95–114.

Strotmann, Michael. "Die Last der Vergangenheit." *Deutschland Archiv* 28, 8 (1995): 806–822.

Tiemann, Heinrich. "Gewerkschaften in Ostdeutschland." *Deutschland Archiv* 27, 2 (1994): 155–163.

Tucker, Robert C. "Culture, Political Culture and Communist Society." *Political Science Quarterly* 88, 2 (1973): 173–190.

Verba, Sidney. "Comparative Political Culture." In Lucian W. Pye and Sidney Verba (eds.), *Political Culture and Political Development.* Princeton, N.J.: Princeton University Press, 1965, 512–560.

Wagner, Gert. "Zur Entwicklung der Marktwirtschaft in den neuen Bundesländern." In Ute Gerhardt and Ekkehard Mochmann (eds.), *Gesellschaftlicher Umbruch 1945–1990.* München: Oldenbourg, 1992, 81–92.

Warnecke, Peter. "Der Gebrauch der elektonischen Massenmedien im Alltag der Werktätigen in der DDR." *Rundfunkjournalismus in Theorie und Praxis* 24, 1 (1989): 7–97.

Weber, Hermann. *Die DDR 1945–1990*. München: Oldenbourg, 1993.
Weber, Max. *Economy and Society*. New York: Bedminster, 1968.
Weber, Max. *Gesammelte Schriften*. Tübingen: J.C.B. Mohr, 1958.
Weber, Max. *Wirtschaft und Gesellschaft*. Tübingen: J.C.B. Mohr, 1953.
Welch, Stephen. *The Concept of Political Culture*. Basingstoke: Macmillan, 1993.
Westle, Bettina. "Nationale Identität der Deutschen nach der Vereinigung." In Hans Rattinger, Oscar W. Gabriel, and Wolfgang Jogodzinski (eds.), *Wahlen und politische Einstellungen im vereinten Deutschland*. Frankfurt am Main: Peter Lang, 1994, 453–499.
Wilenga, Frieso. "Schatten der deutschen Geschichte." *Deutschland Archiv* 27, 10 (1994): 1058–1073.
Wilke, Jürgen. "Medien DDR." In Elisabeth Noelle-Neumann, Winfried Schulz and Jürgen Wilk (eds.), *Publizistik Massen-Koomunikation, Das Fischer Lexikon*. Frankfurt am Main: Fischer, 1989, 156–168.
Woods, Roger. "Civil Society, Critical Intellectuals." In Margy Gerber and Roger Woods (eds.), *The End of the GDR and the Problems of Integration*. New York: Univeristy Press of America, 1993, 53–70.
Wuthe, Gerhard. "Probleme der nationalen Identität." *Politische Vierteljahresschrift*, Sonderband 23 (1987): 197–204.
Zimmermann, Hartmut. "Machtverteilung und Partizipationschancen. Zu einigen Aspekten des politisch-sozialen Systems in der DDR." In Gert-Joachim Glaeßner (ed.), *Die DDR in der Arä Honecker*. Opladen: Westdeutscher Verlag, 1988, 214–283.
Zwahr, Helmut. *Ende einer Selbstzerstörung*. Göttingen: Vandenhoeck und Ruprecht, 1993.

Index

About the Author

ANDREAS STAAB is Academic Development Officer, European Institute, London School of Economics and Political Science. He lectures on European and German politics and has published articles on German identity and German public administration.

ISBN 0-275-96177-X

9 0 0 0 0 >

EAN

9 780275 961770

HARDCOVER BAR CODE